THE SEVEN DEADLY SINS

nakaba suzuki presents

24

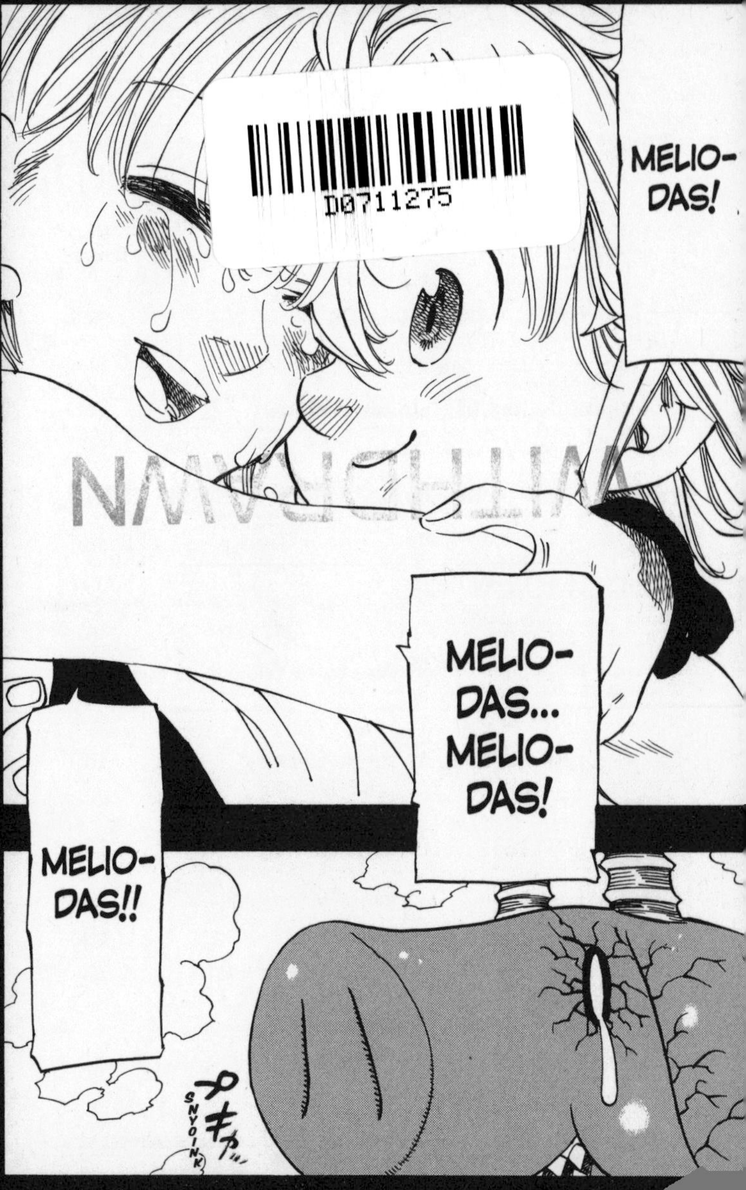
MELIO-DAS!
MELIO-DAS... MELIO-DAS!
MELIO-DAS!!
SNYOINK

CONTENTS

BOAR HAT
The Seven Deadly Sins

Chapter 189 - The Hero Rises!!

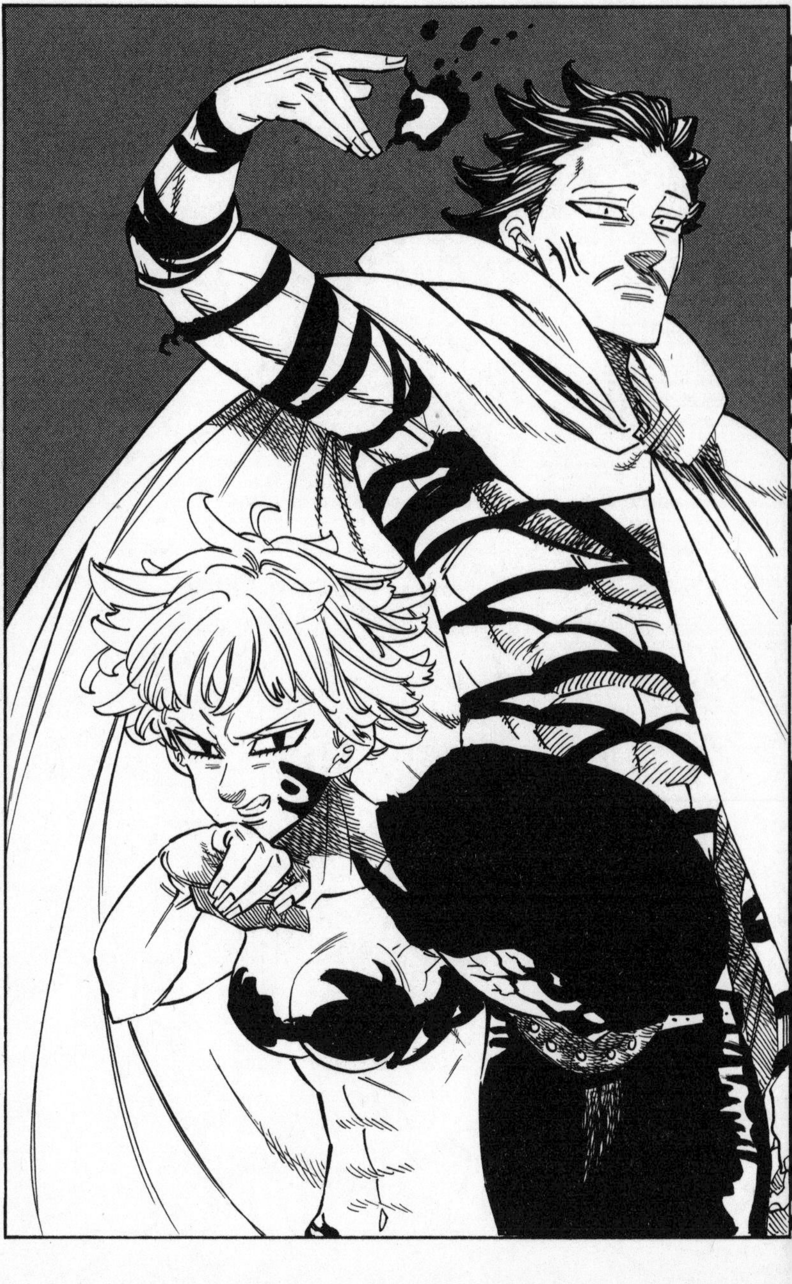

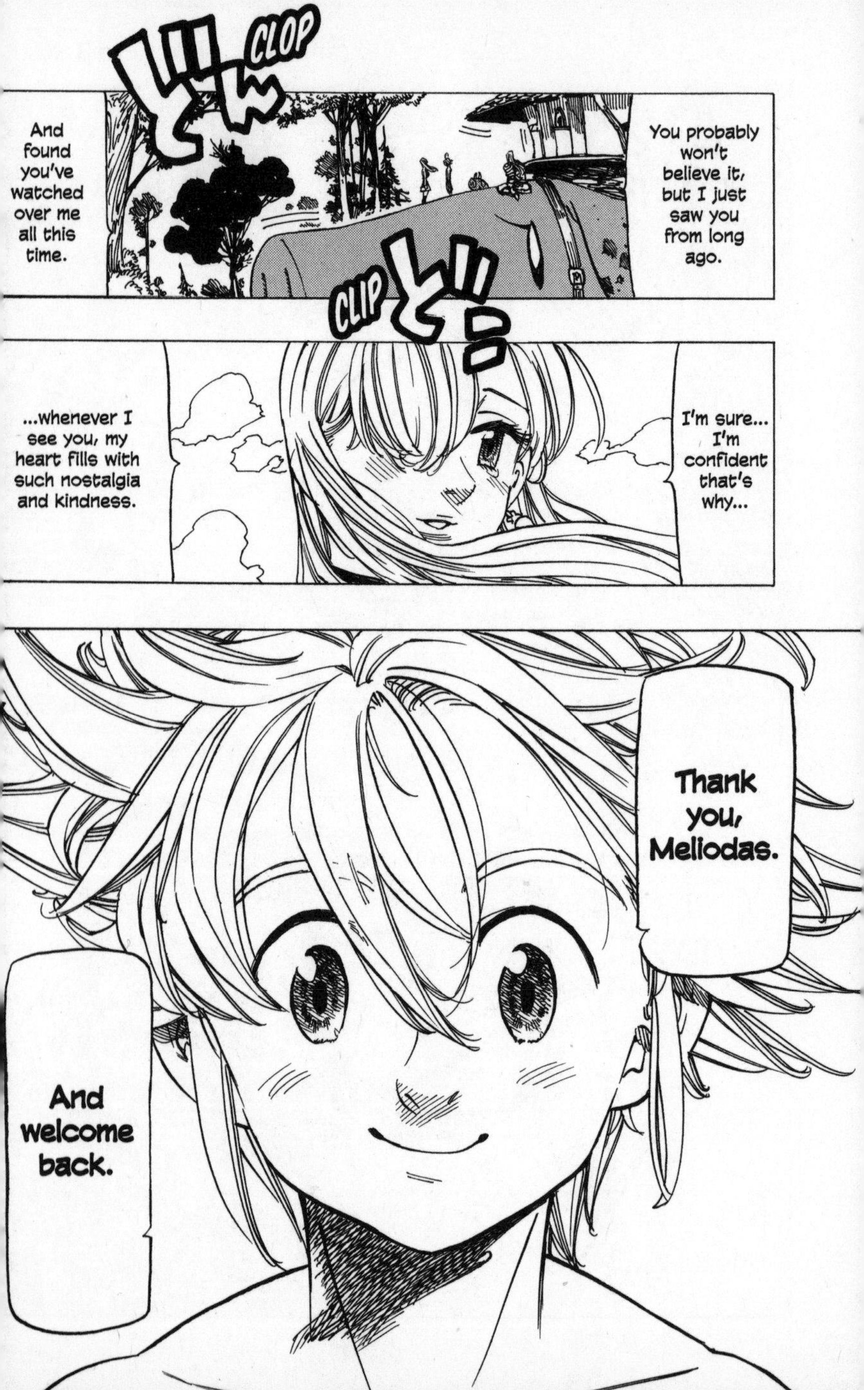
You probably won't believe it, but I just saw you from long ago.
CLOP
CLIP
And found you've watched over me all this time.
I'm sure... I'm confident that's why...
...whenever I see you, my heart fills with such nostalgia and kindness.
Thank you, Meliodas.
And welcome back.

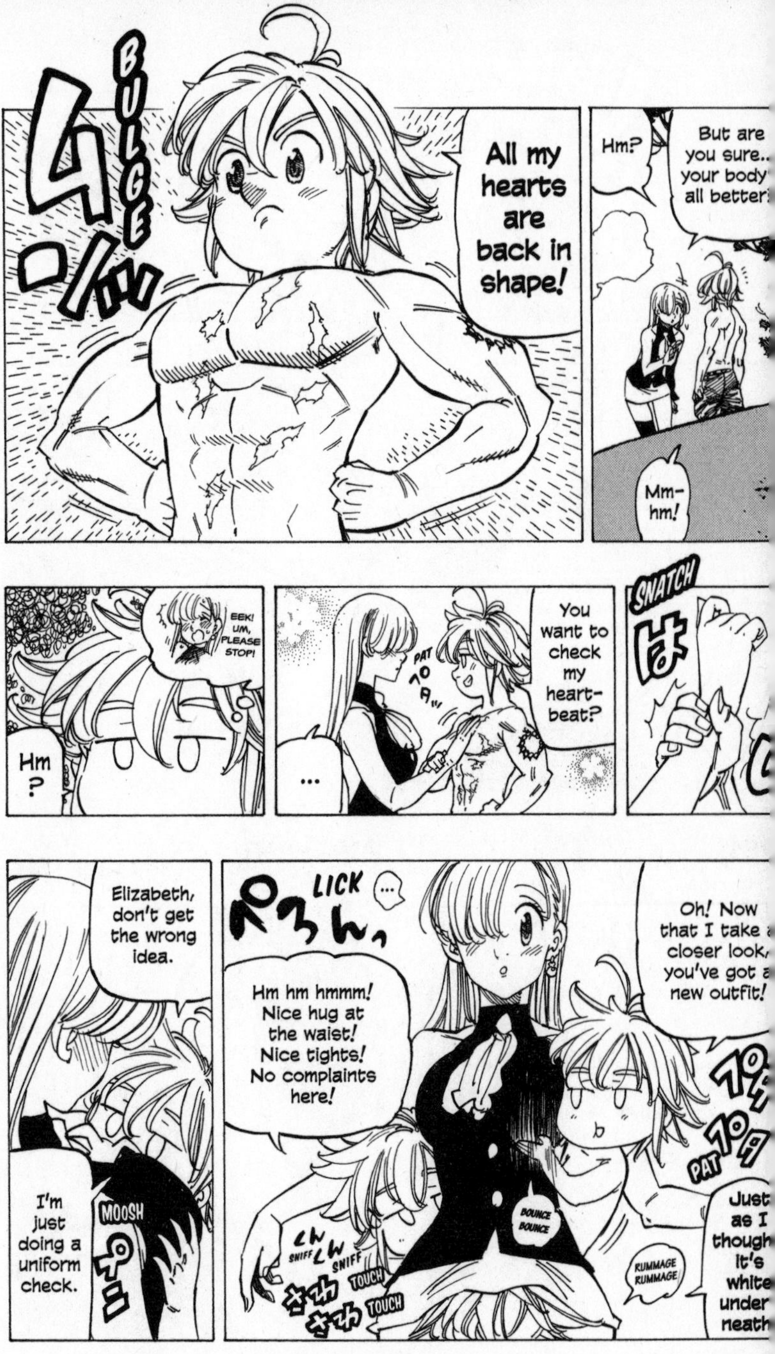
But are you sure.. your body all better
Hm?
Mm-hm!
All my hearts are back in shape!
BULGE
SNATCH
You want to check my heart-beat?
PAT
...
EEK! UM, PLEASE STOP!
Hm?
Oh! Now that I take a closer look, you've got a new outfit!
PAT
Just as I though it's white under neath
LICK
...
Hm hm hmmm! Nice hug at the waist! Nice tights! No complaints here!
BOUNCE BOUNCE
RUMMAGE RUMMAGE
SNIFF SNIFF
TOUCH TOUCH
Elizabeth, don't get the wrong idea.
MOOSH
I'm just doing a uniform check.

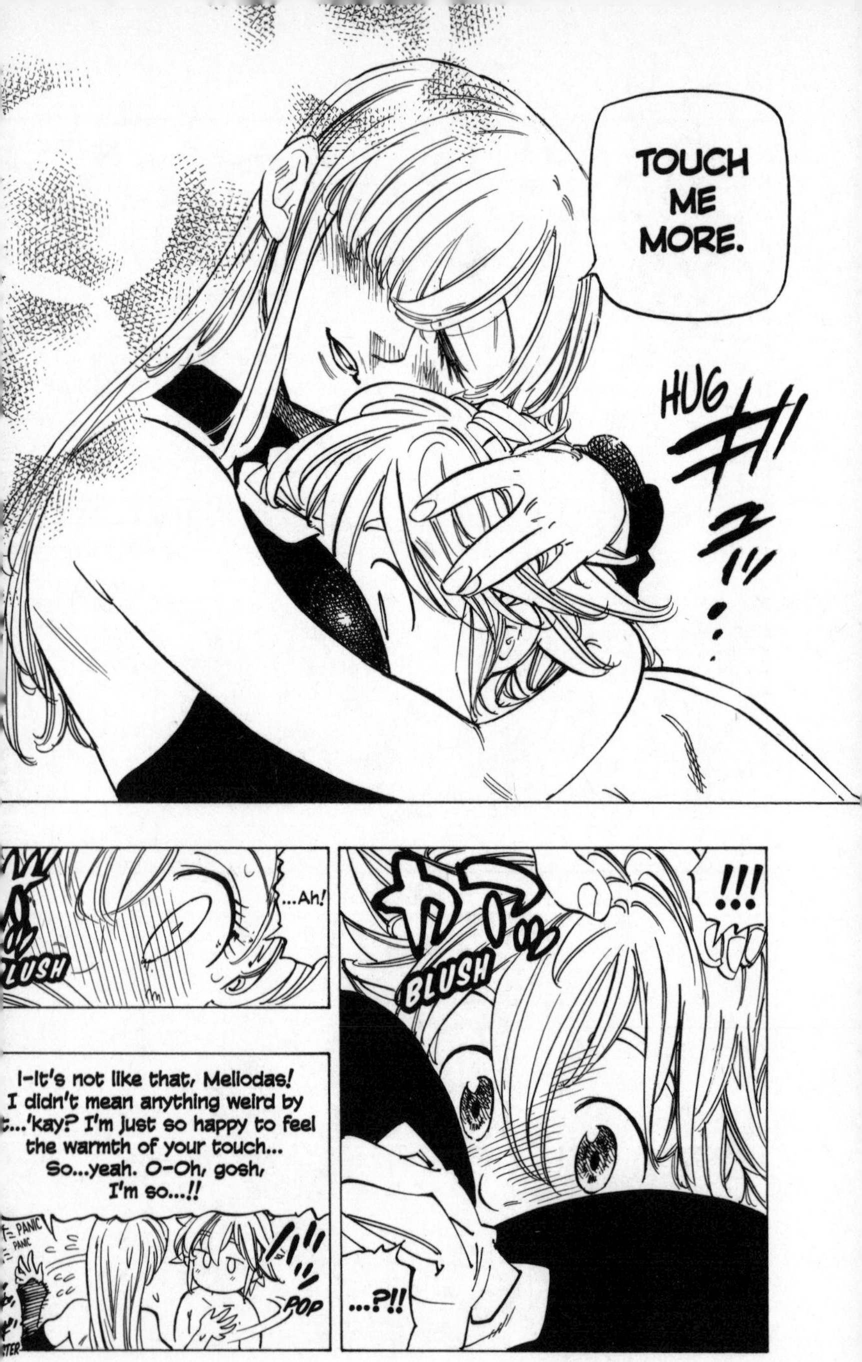
TOUCH ME MORE.
HUG
!!!
BLUSH
...?!!
...Ah!
LUSH
I-It's not like that, Meliodas! I didn't mean anything weird by t...'kay? I'm just so happy to feel the warmth of your touch... So...yeah. O-Oh, gosh, I'm so...!!
PANIC
PANIC
POP

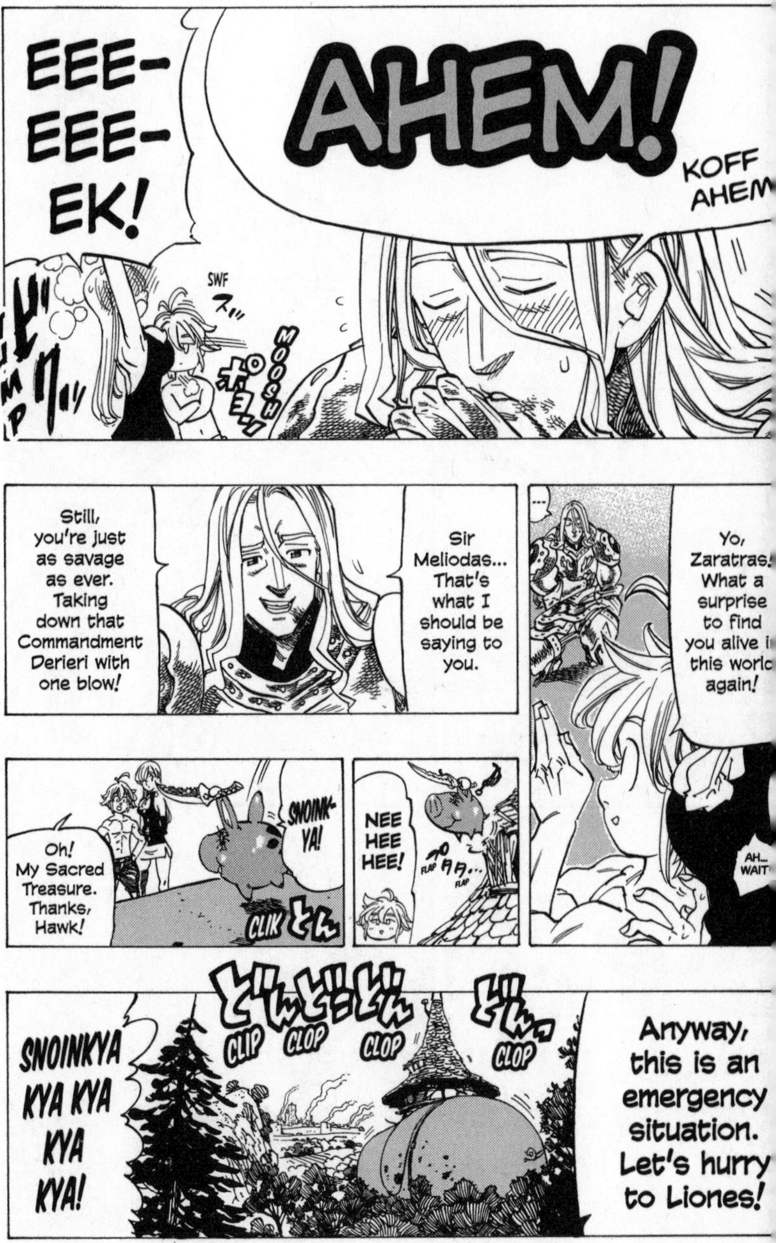

KOFF AHEM
AHEM!
EEE-EEE-EK!
SWF
MOOSH
JUMP
Yo, Zaratras! What a surprise to find you alive i this worl again!
...
AH... WAIT
Sir Meliodas... That's what I should be saying to you.
Still, you're just as savage as ever. Taking down that Commandment Derieri with one blow!
NEE HEE HEE!
FLAP FLAP
SNOINK-YA!
CLIK
Oh! My Sacred Treasure. Thanks, Hawk!
Anyway, this is an emergency situation. Let's hurry to Liones!
CLOP
CLOP
CLOP
CLIP
SNOINKYA KYA KYA KYA KYA!

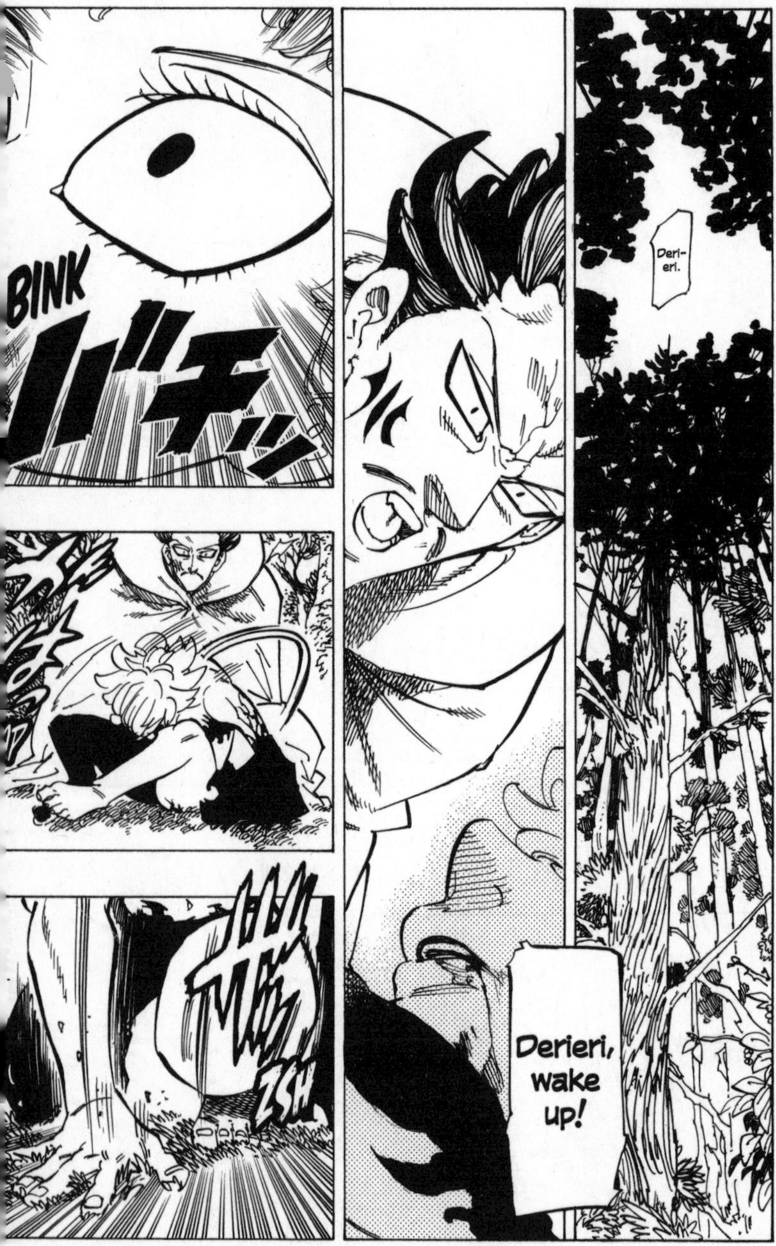
Deri-
eri.
Derieri, wake up!
BINK
ZSH

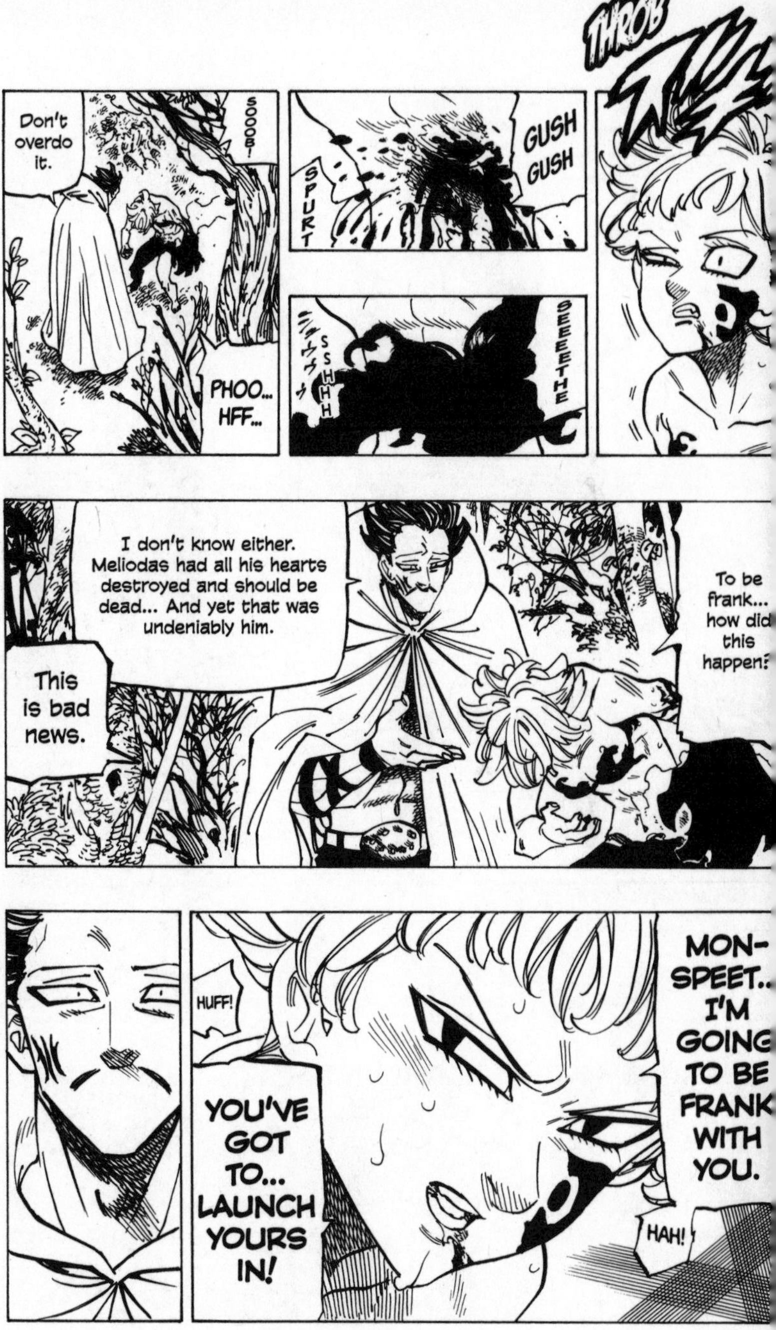
THROB
GUSH GUSH
SPURT
SEEEETHE
SSHHH
SOOOB!
Don't overdo it.
SSHH
PHOO... HFF...
To be frank... how did this happen?
I don't know either. Meliodas had all his hearts destroyed and should be dead... And yet that was undeniably him.
This is bad news.
MON-SPEET... I'M GOING TO BE FRANK WITH YOU.
HAH!
HUFF!
YOU'VE GOT TO... LAUNCH YOURS IN!

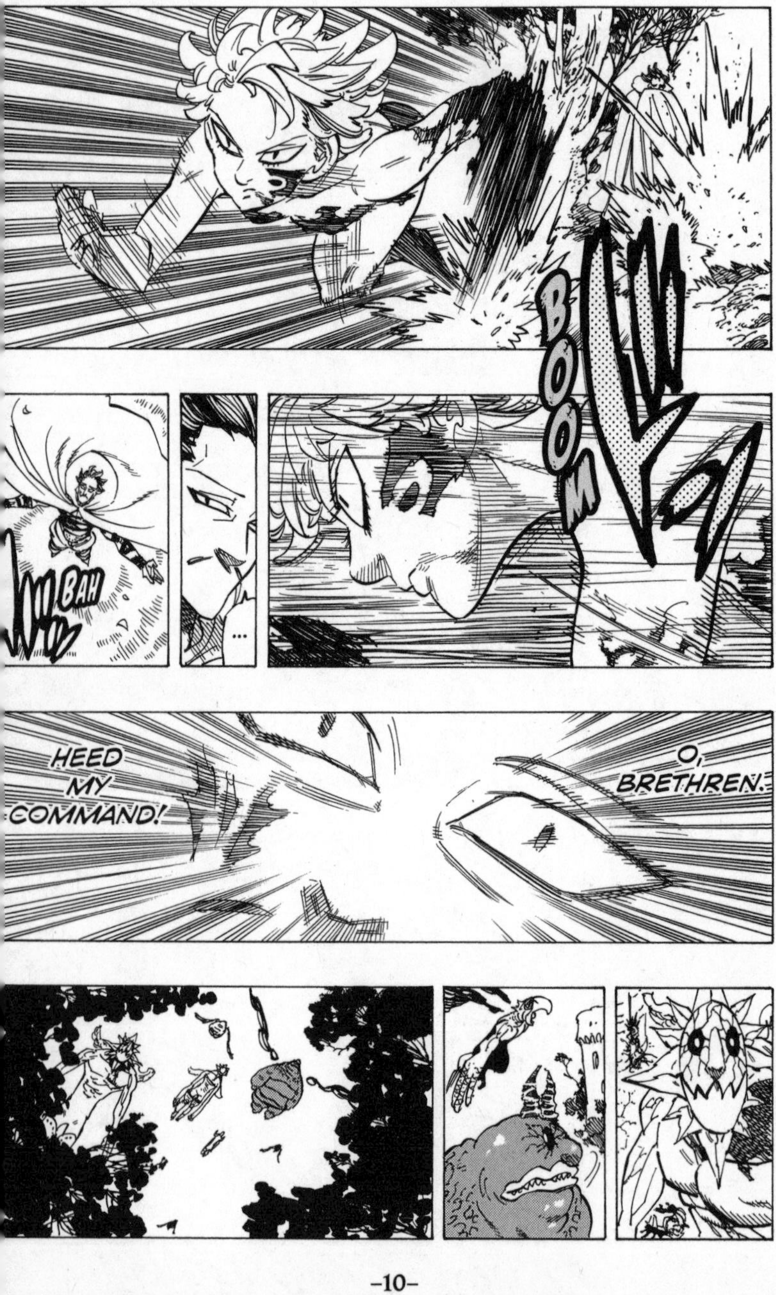
BOOM
...
BAH
O, BRETHREN.
HEED MY COMMAND!

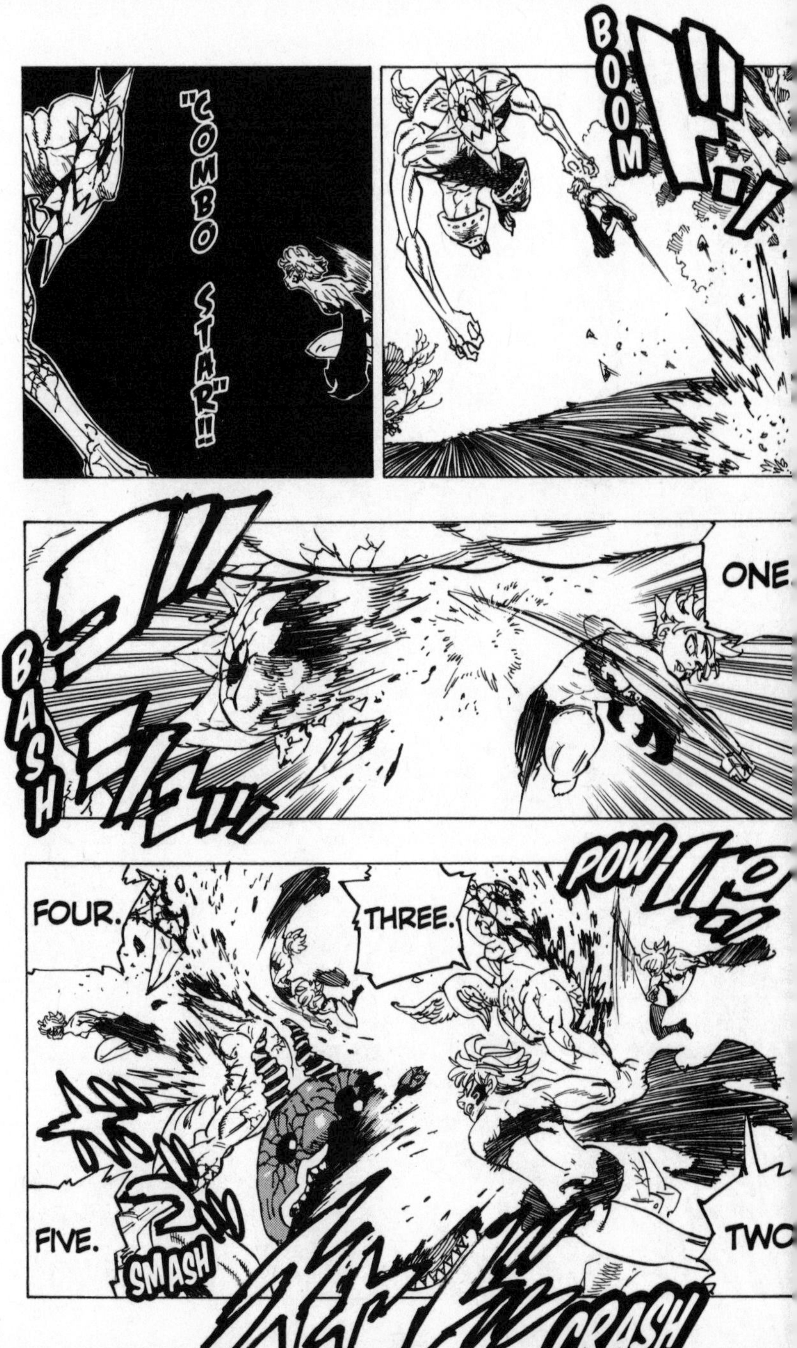
BOOM
"COMBO STAR"!!
ONE.
BASH
POW
TWO
CRASH
THREE.
FOUR.
FIVE.
SMASH

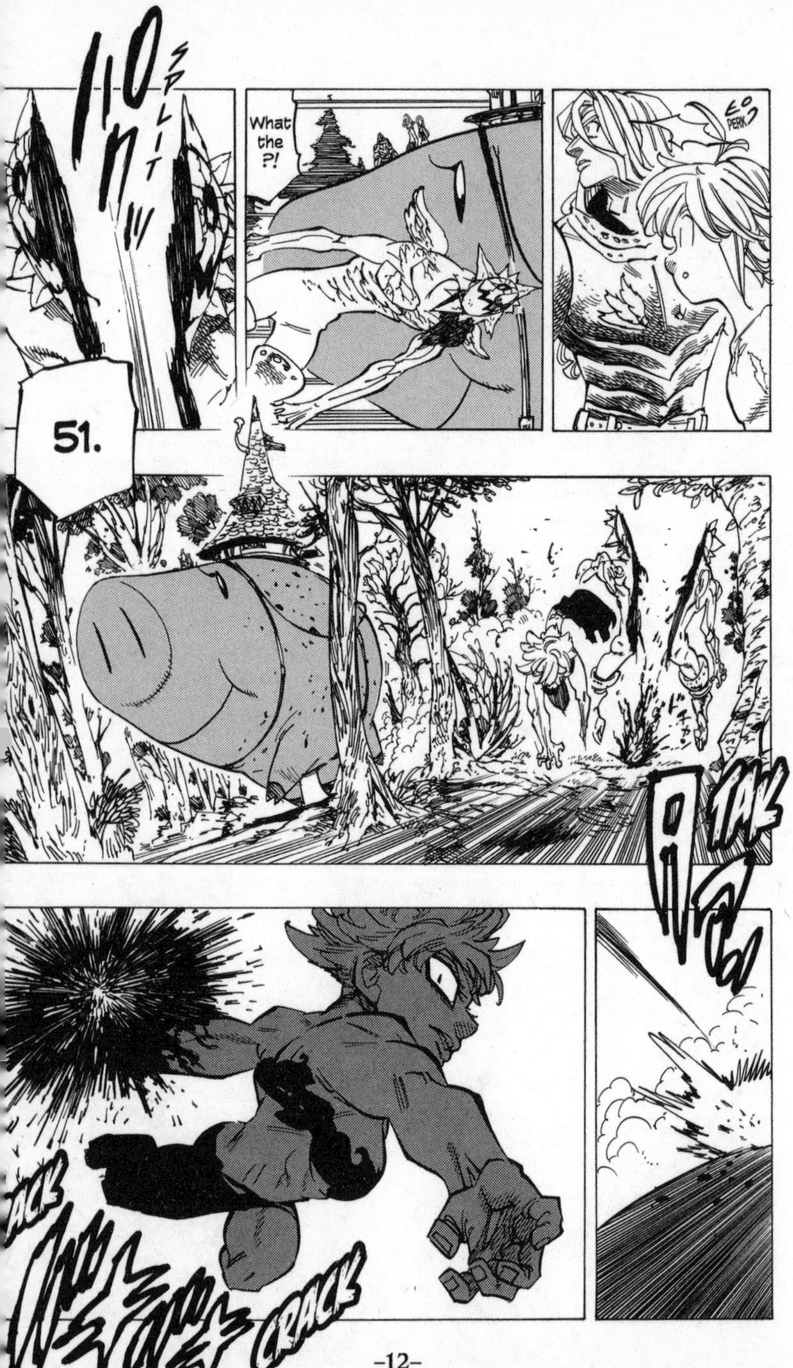
PERK
What the ?!
SPLIT
51.
TAK
CRACK
CRACK

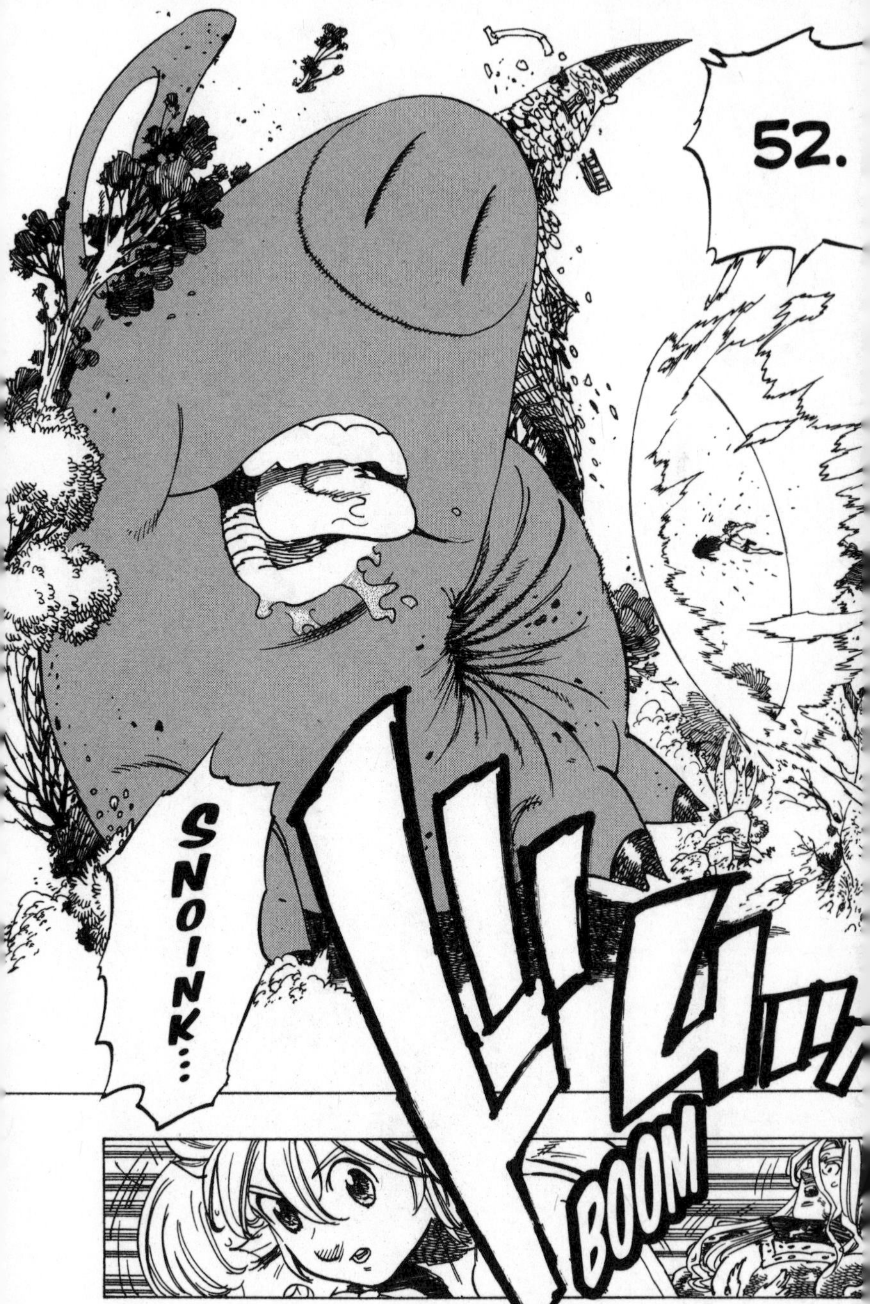
52.
SNOINK...
BOOM

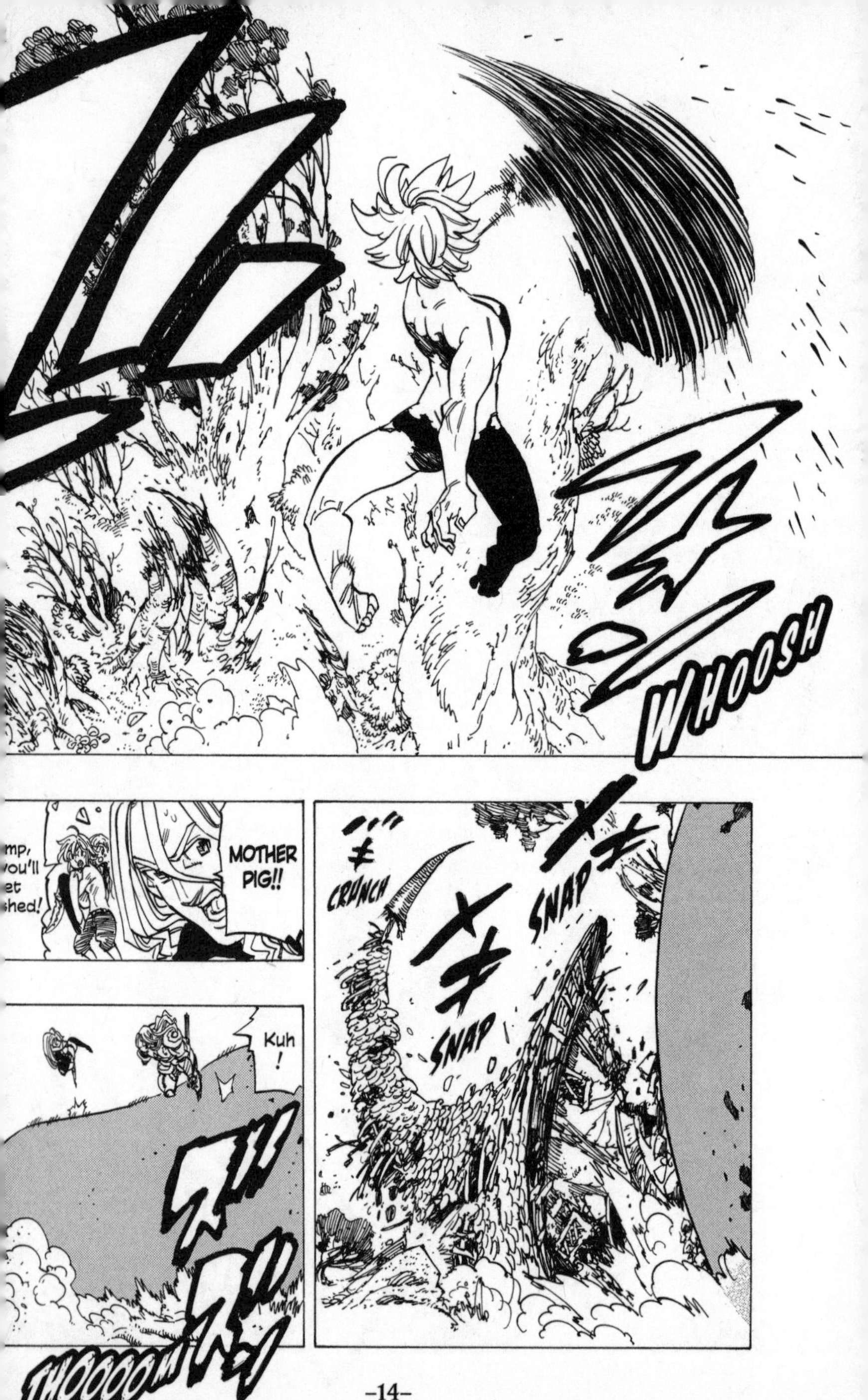
WHOOSH
CRUNCH
SNAP
SNAP
MOTHER PIG!!
Kuh!
THOOOOM

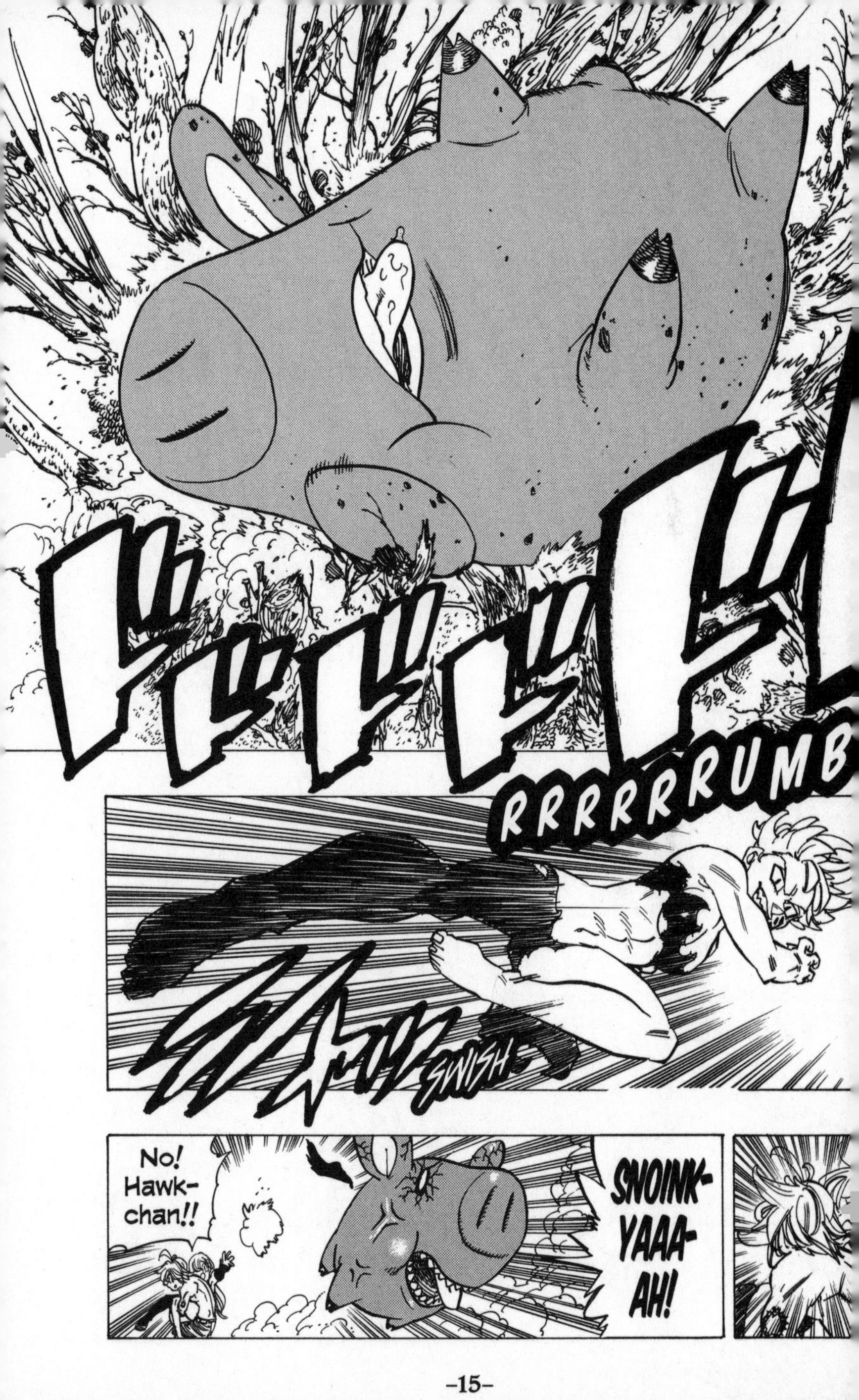
RRRRRRUMB
SWISH
SNOINK-YAAAAH!
No! Hawk-chan!!

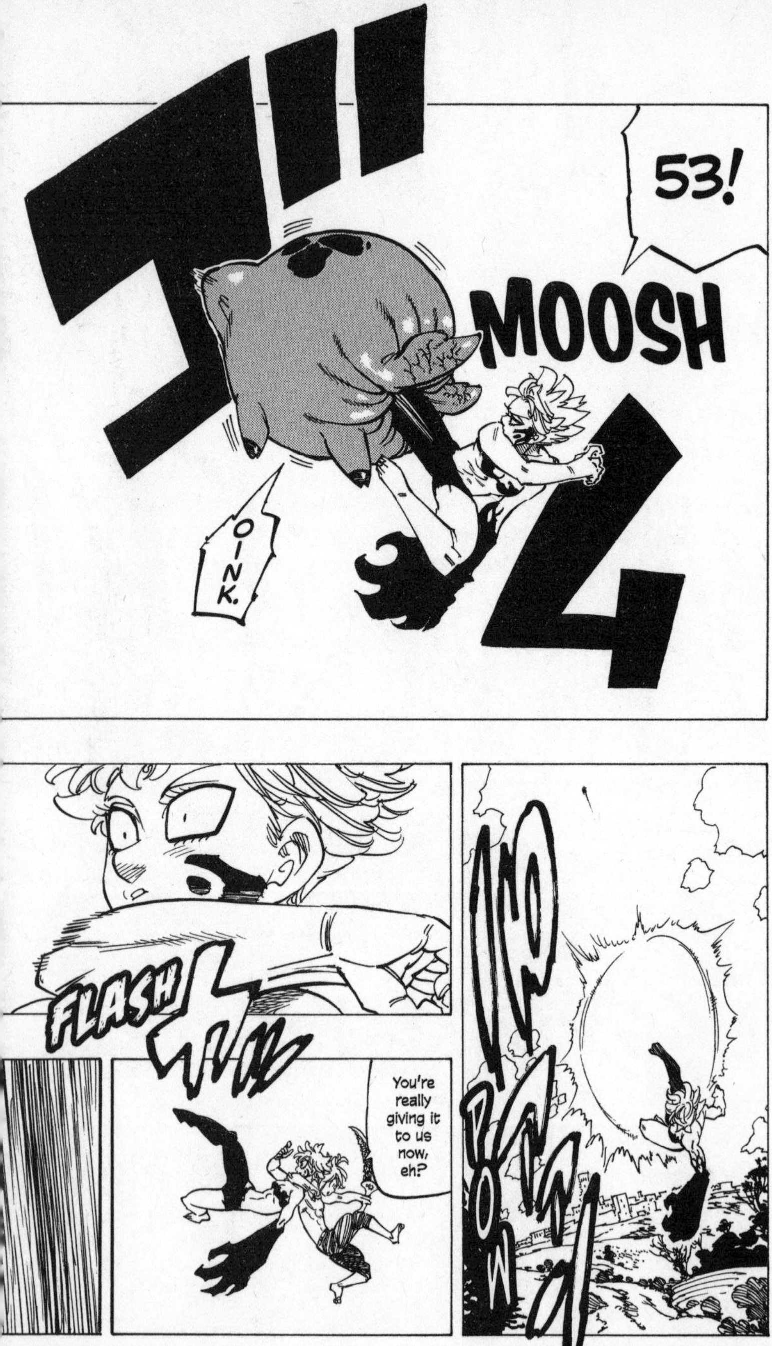
53!
MOOSH
OINK.
POW
FLASH
You're really giving it to us now, eh?

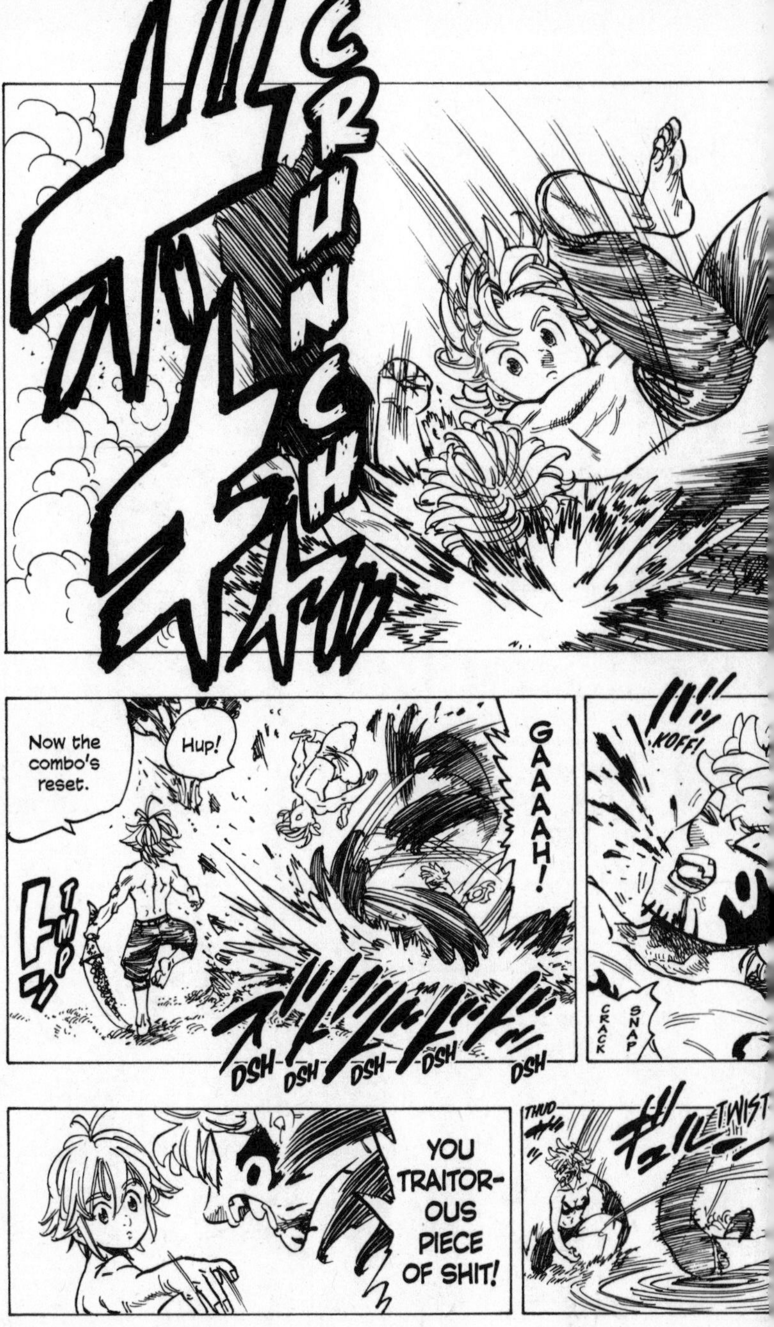
CRUNCH
KOFF!
CRACK
SNAP
GAAAAH!
Hup!
Now the combo's reset.
TMP
DSH DSH DSH DSH DSH
THUD
TWIST
YOU TRAITOROUS PIECE OF SHIT!

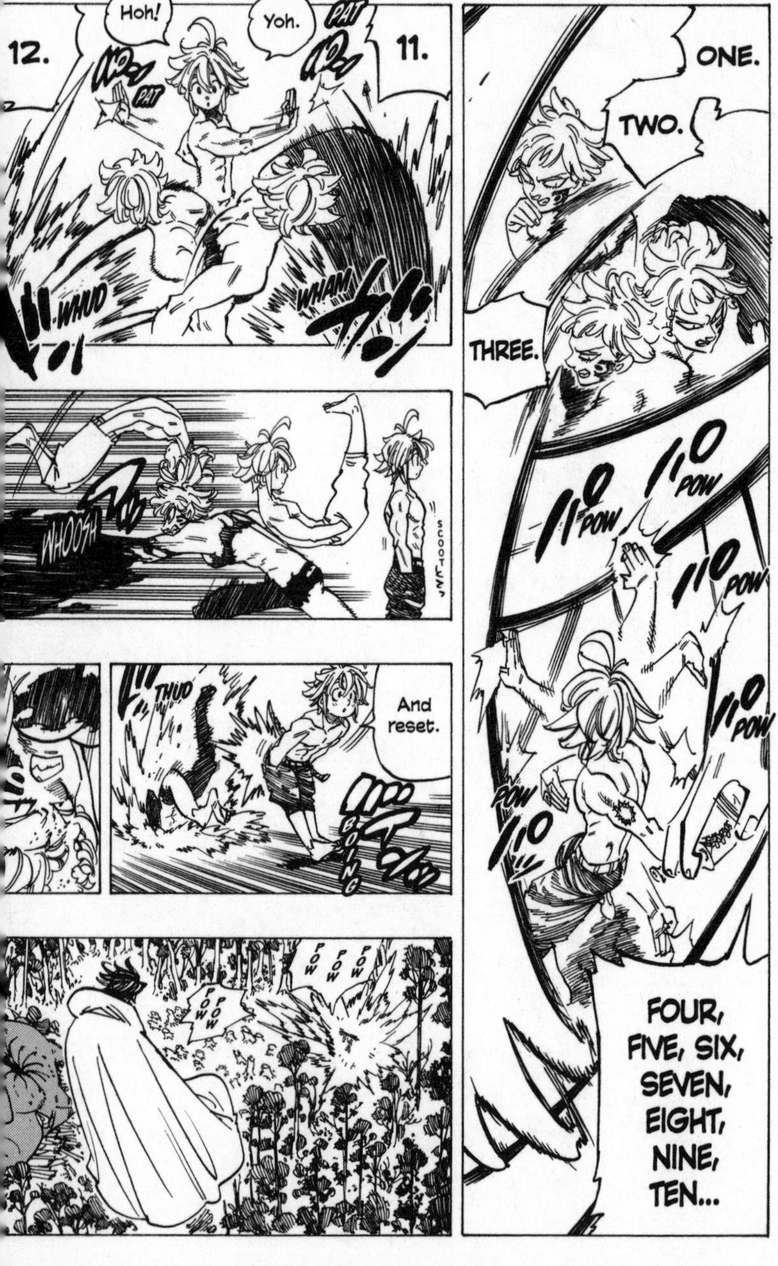

ONE.
TWO.
THREE.
POW
POW
POW
POW
POW
FOUR, FIVE, SIX, SEVEN, EIGHT, NINE, TEN...
PAT
Yoh.
11.
Hoh!
PAT
12.
WHAM
WHUD
SCOOT
WHOOSH
And reset.
BOING
THUD
POW POW POW
POW POW

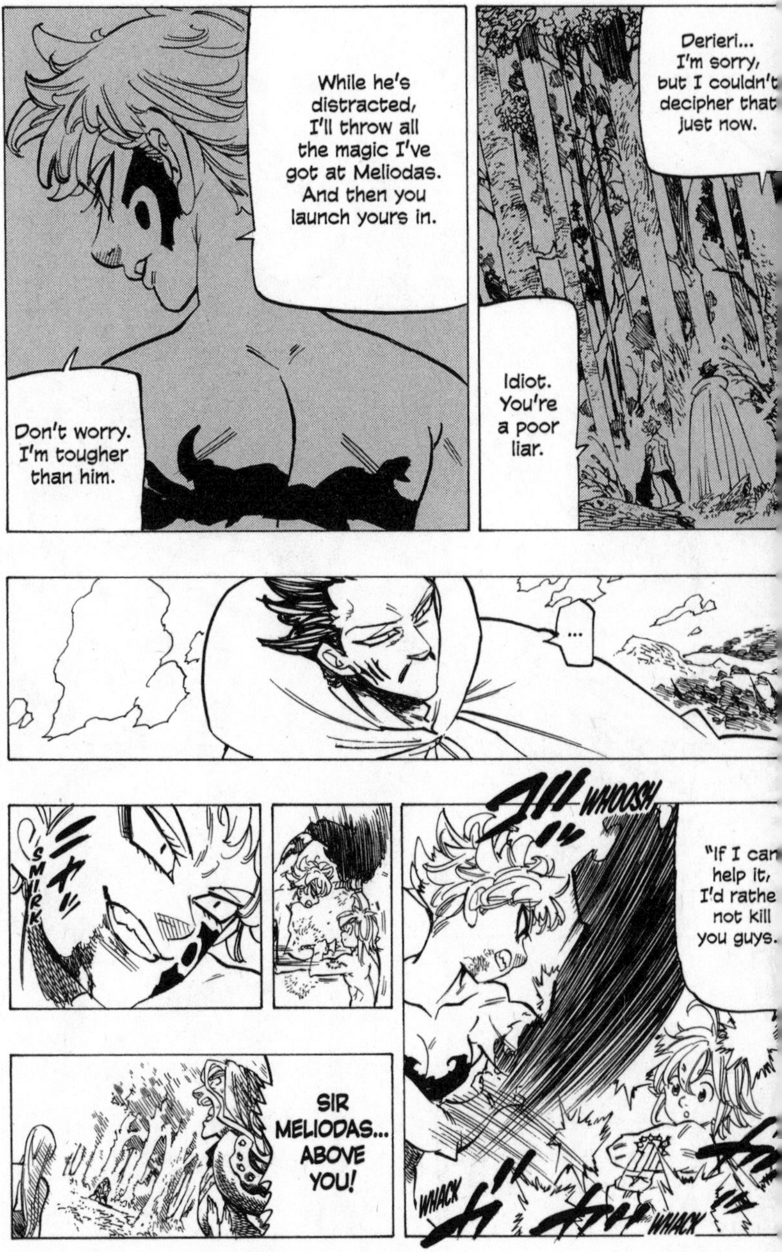
Derieri... I'm sorry, but I couldn't decipher that just now.
Idiot. You're a poor liar.
While he's distracted, I'll throw all the magic I've got at Meliodas. And then you launch yours in.
Don't worry. I'm tougher than him.
...
WHOOSH
"If I can help it, I'd rathe not kill you guys.
WHACK
WHACK
SMIRK
SIR MELIODAS... ABOVE YOU!

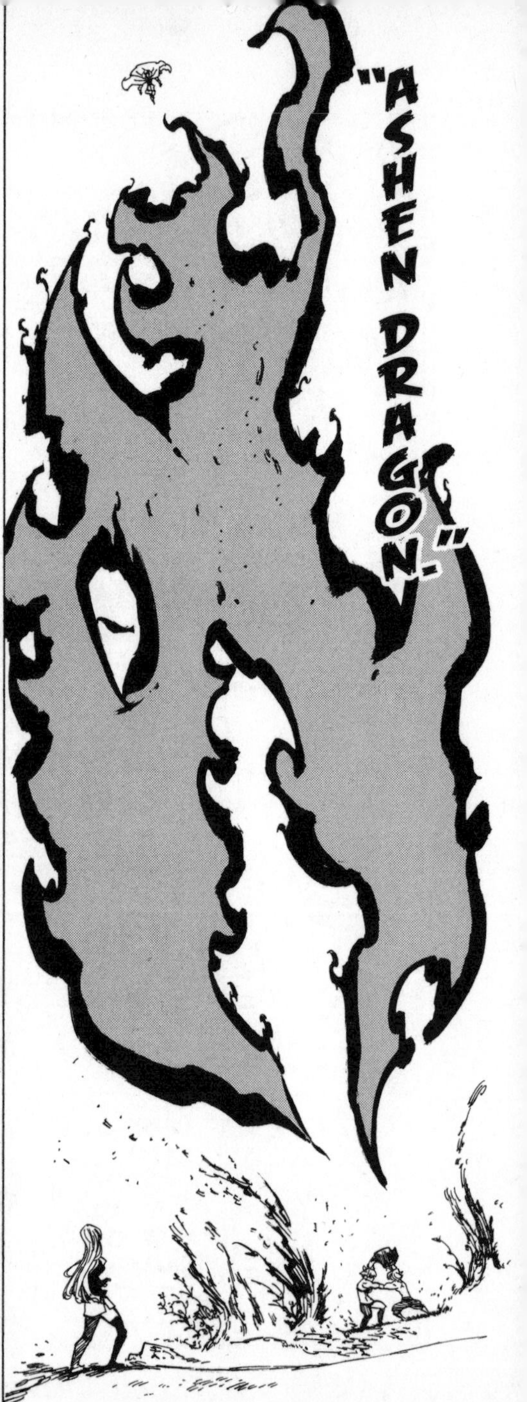
"ASHEN DRAGON."

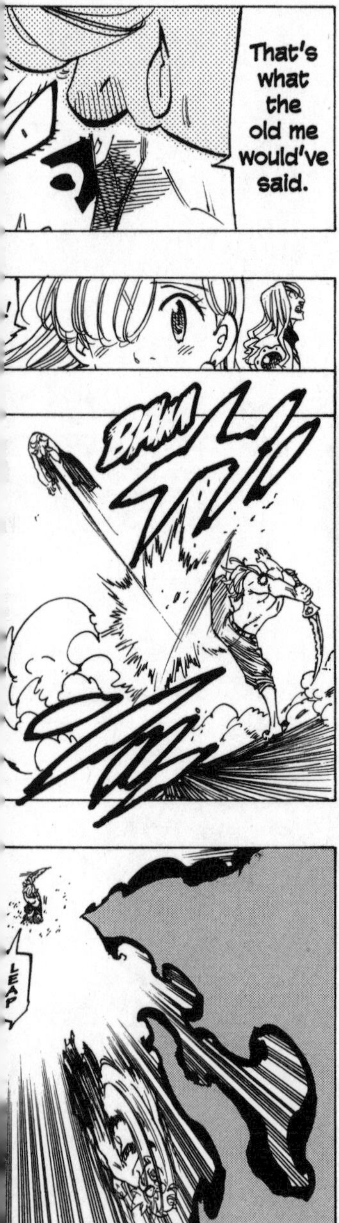
That's what the old me would've said.
!
BAM
LEAP

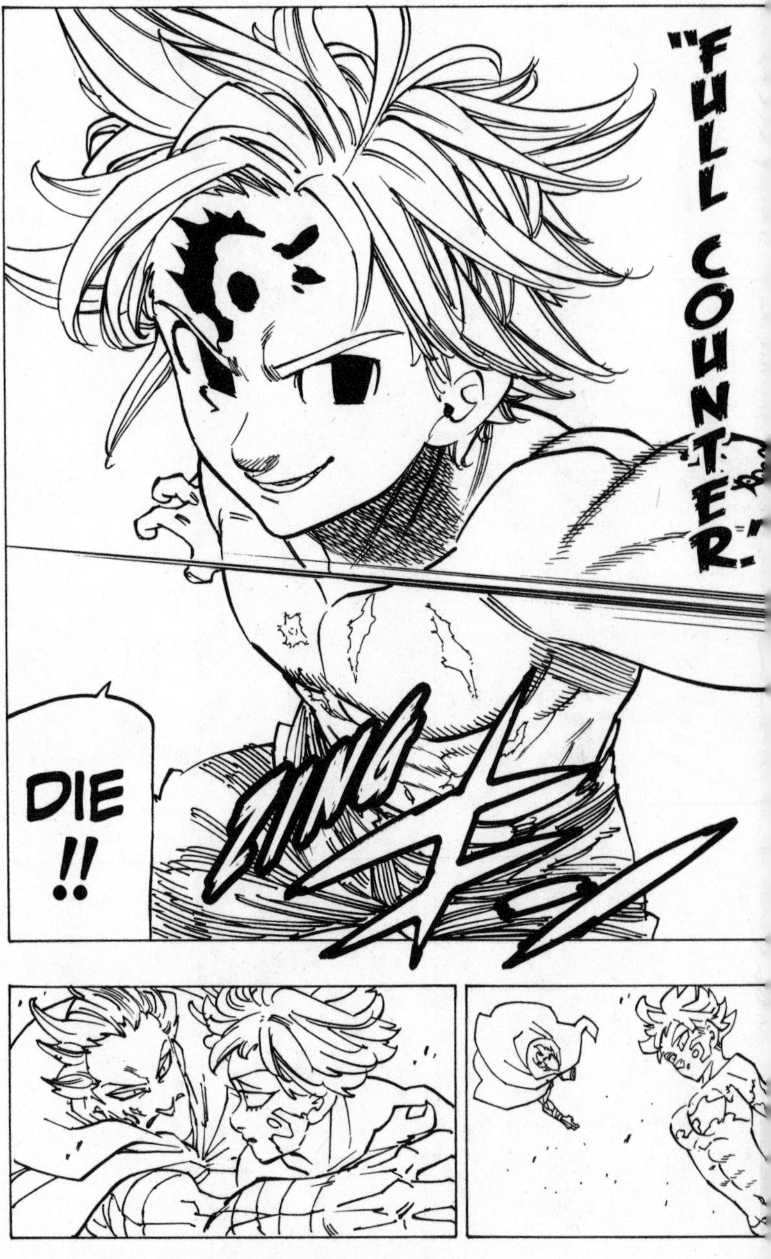
"FULL COUNTER."
DIE !!

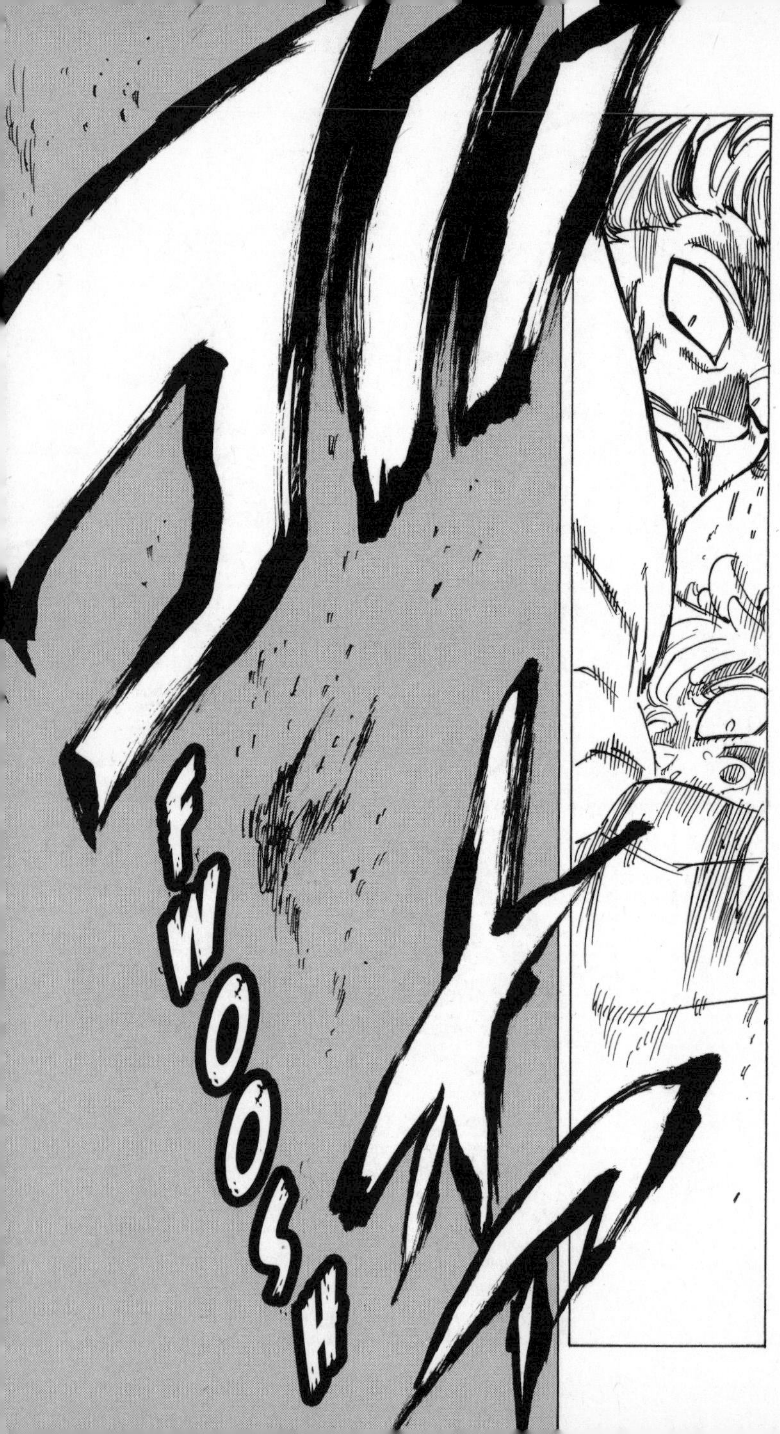
FWOOSH

Chapter 190 - Demon Part

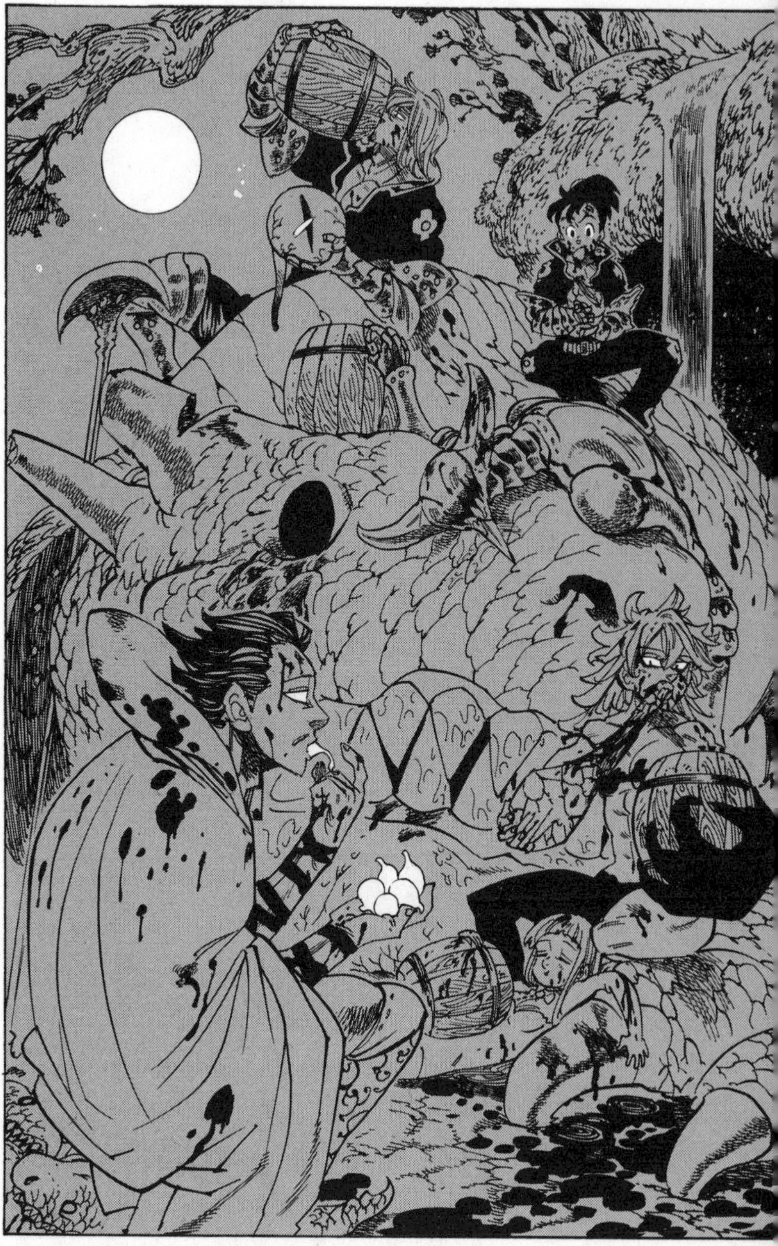

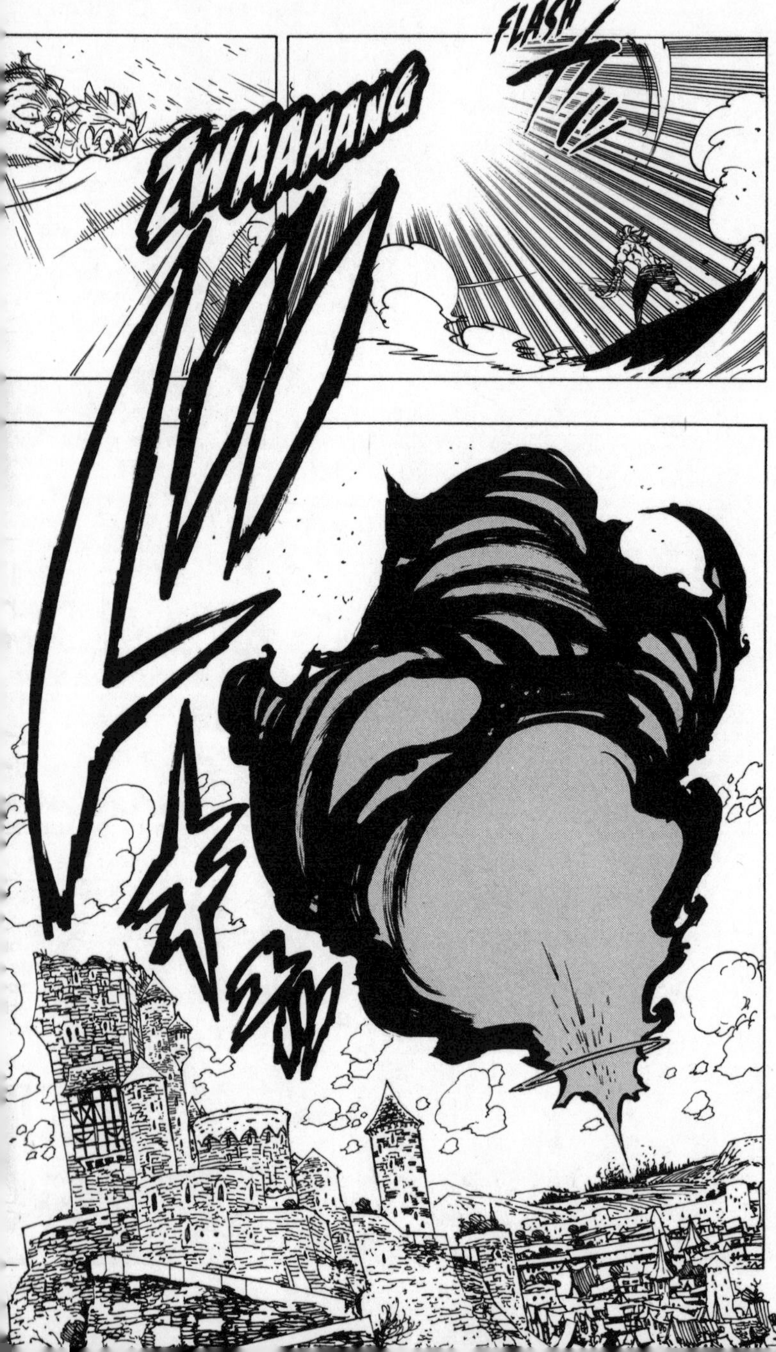
FLASH
ZWAAAAANG

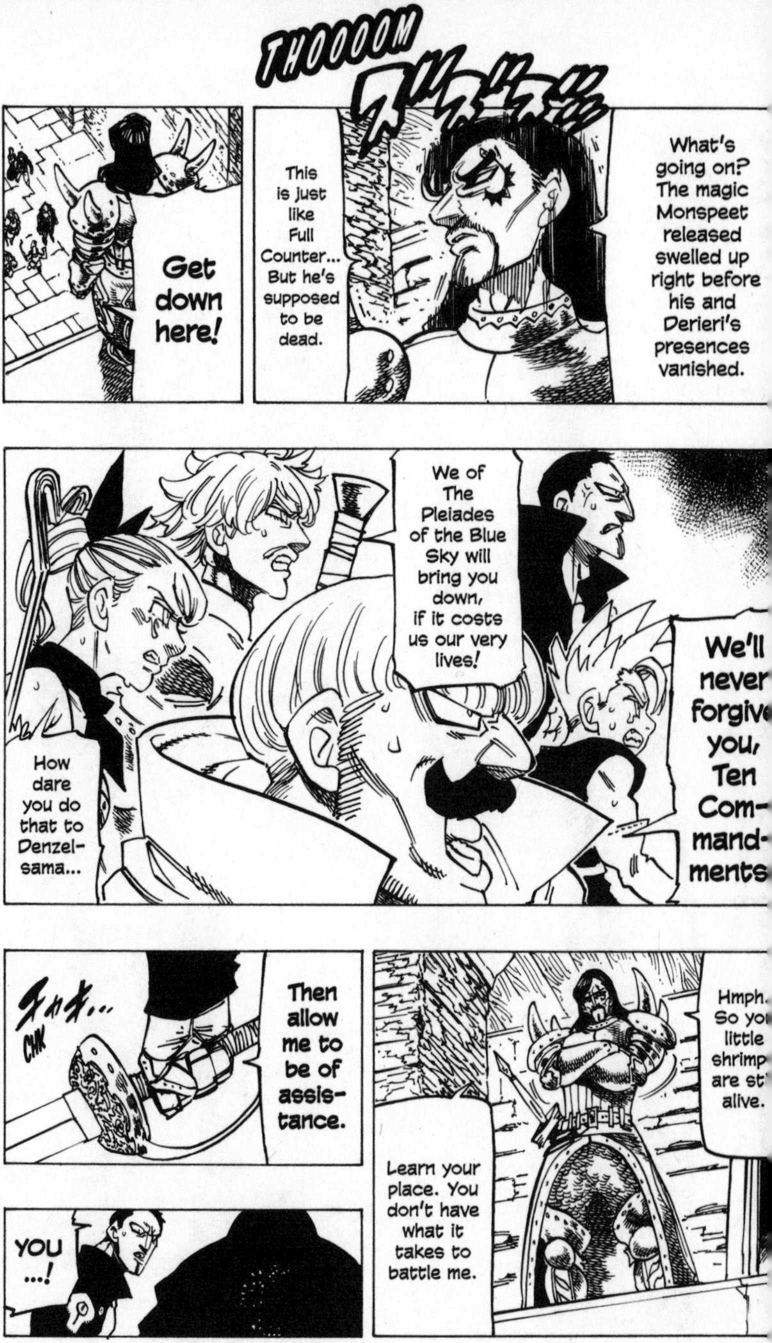
THOOOOM
What's going on? The magic Monspeet released swelled up right before his and Derieri's presences vanished.
This is just like Full Counter... But he's supposed to be dead.
Get down here!
We'll never forgiv you, Ten Com- mand- ments
We of The Pleiades of the Blue Sky will bring you down, if it costs us our very lives!
How dare you do that to Denzel-sama...
Hmph. So yo little shrimp are st alive.
Learn your place. You don't have what it takes to battle me.
Then allow me to be of assis- tance.
CHK
YOU ...!

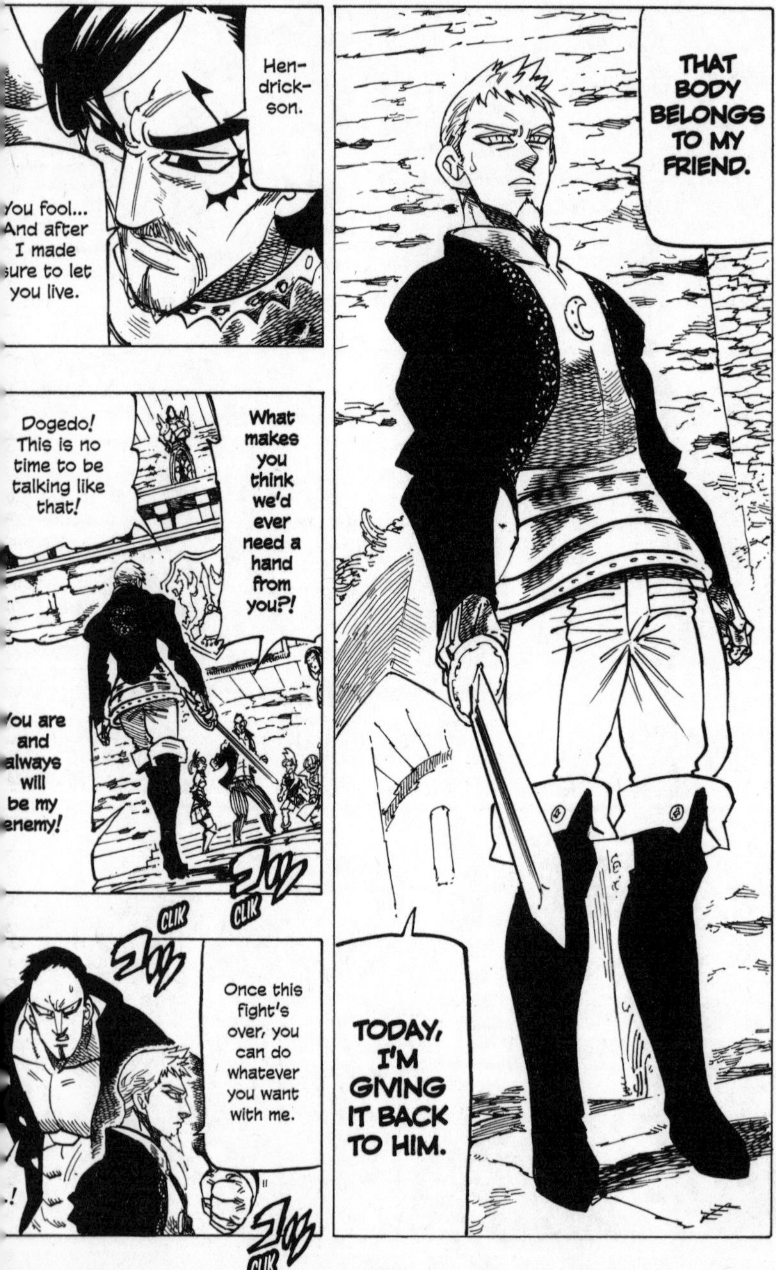
THAT BODY BELONGS TO MY FRIEND.
TODAY, I'M GIVING IT BACK TO HIM.
Hen-drick-son.
You fool... And after I made sure to let you live.
What makes you think we'd ever need a hand from you?!
Dogedo! This is no time to be talking like that!
You are and always will be my enemy!
CLIK
CLIK
Once this fight's over, you can do whatever you want with me.
CLIK

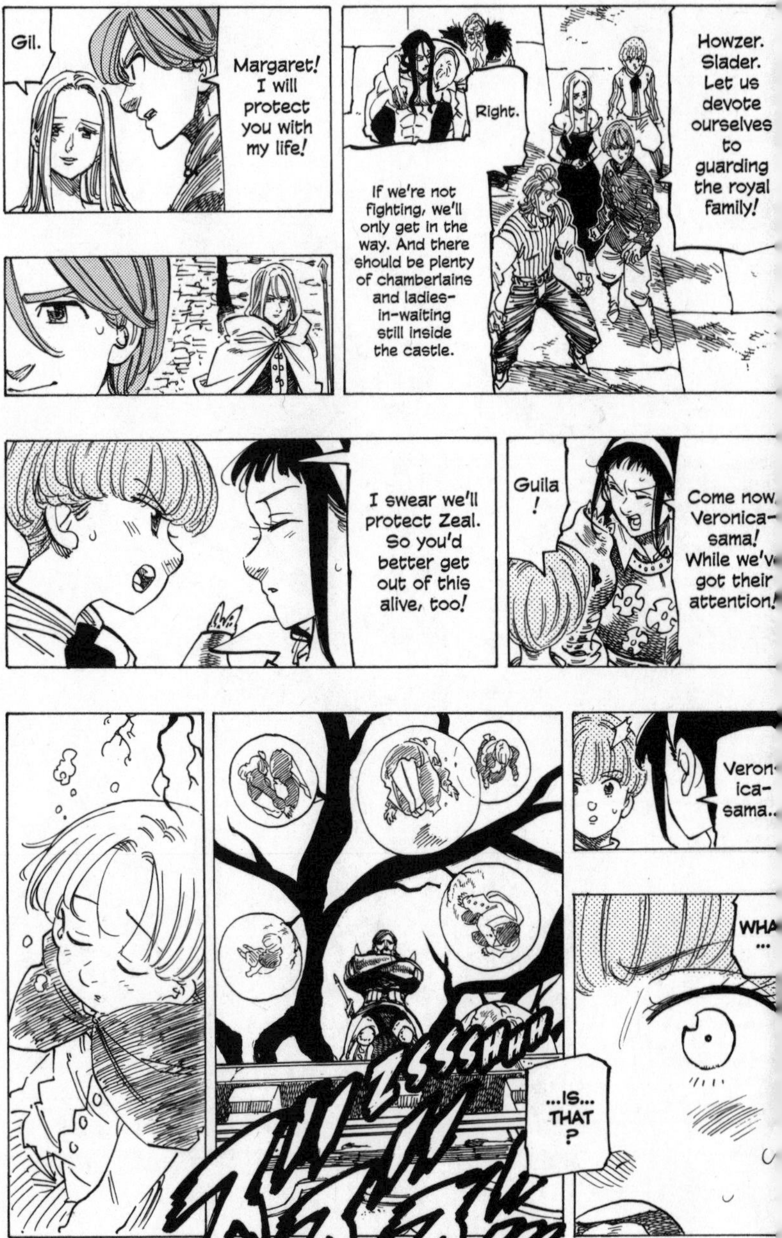
Howzer. Slader. Let us devote ourselves to guarding the royal family!
Right.
If we're not fighting, we'll only get in the way. And there should be plenty of chamberlains and ladies-in-waiting still inside the castle.
Gil.
Margaret! I will protect you with my life!
Come now Veronica-sama! While we'v got their attention!
Guila!
I swear we'll protect Zeal. So you'd better get out of this alive, too!
Veronica-sama...
WHA...
...IS... THAT?
ZSSSHHH

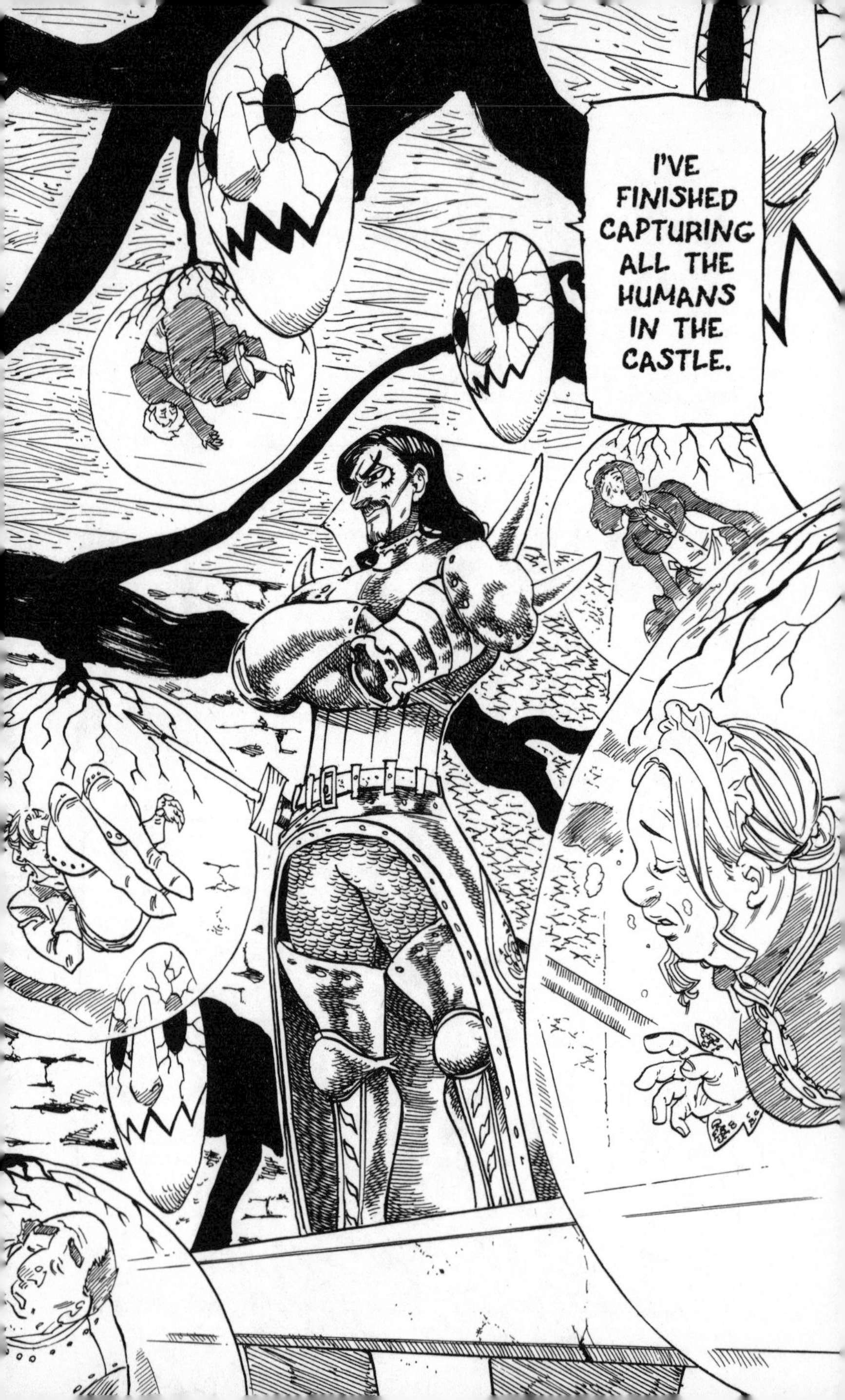
I'VE FINISHED CAPTURING ALL THE HUMANS IN THE CASTLE.

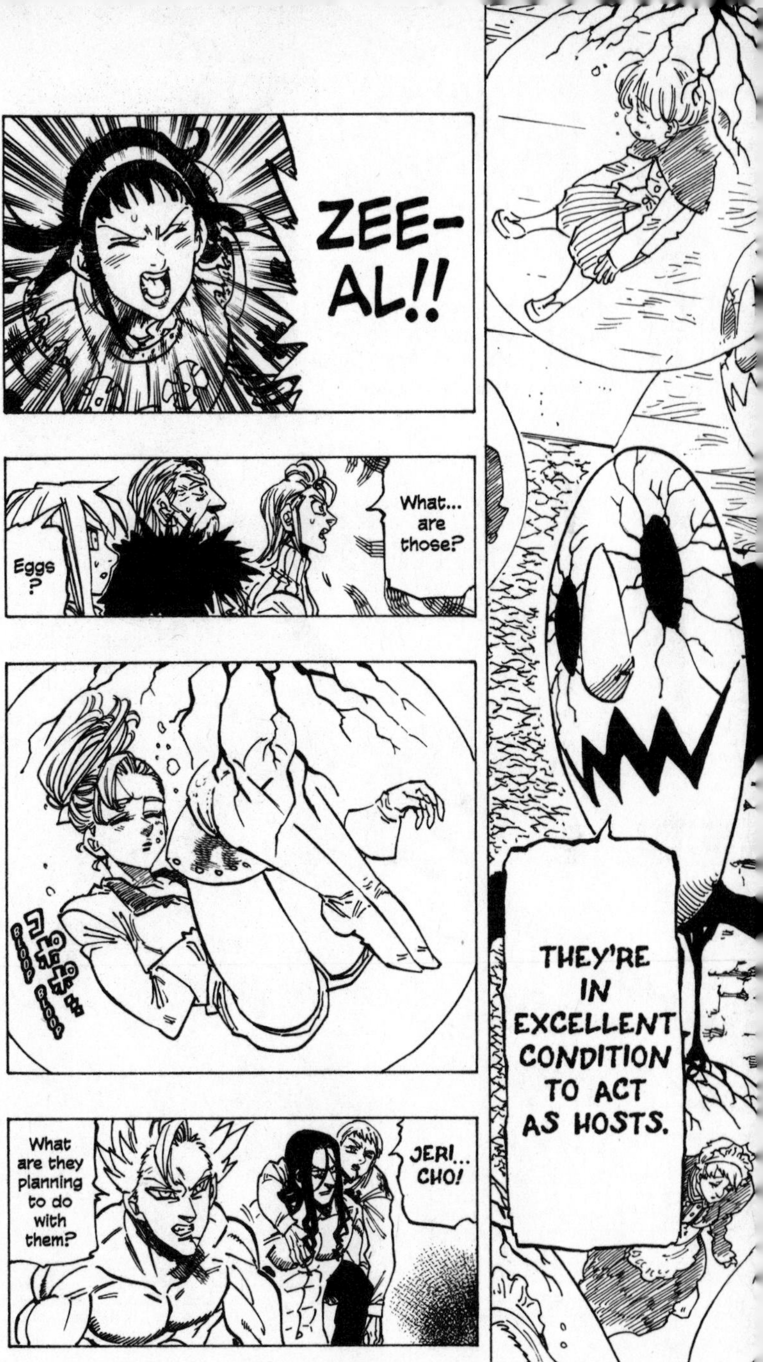
THEY'RE IN EXCELLENT CONDITION TO ACT AS HOSTS.
ZEE-AL!!
What... are those?
Eggs?
BLOOP BLOOP
JERI... CHO!
What are they planning to do with them?

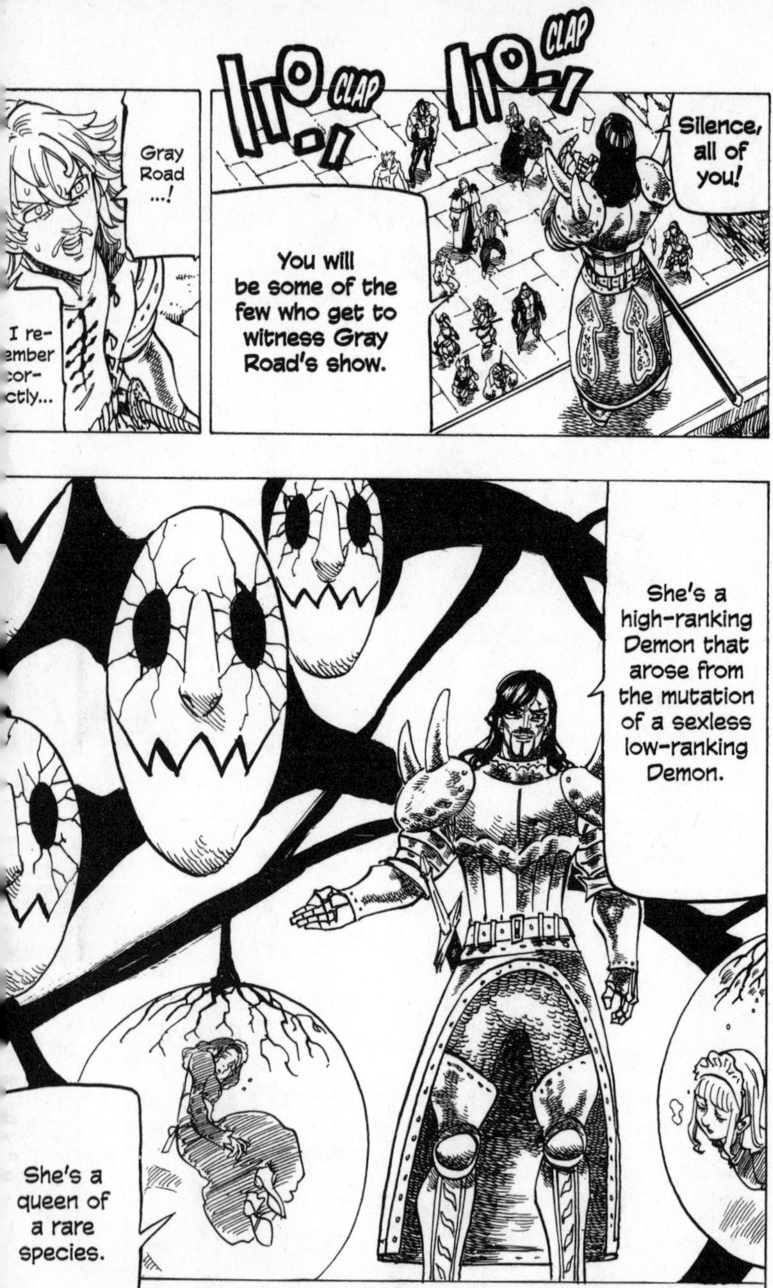
CLAP
Silence, all of you!
CLAP
You will be some of the few who get to witness Gray Road's show.
Gray Road ...!
I re- ember cor- ctly...
She's a high-ranking Demon that arose from the mutation of a sexless low-ranking Demon.
She's a queen of a rare species.

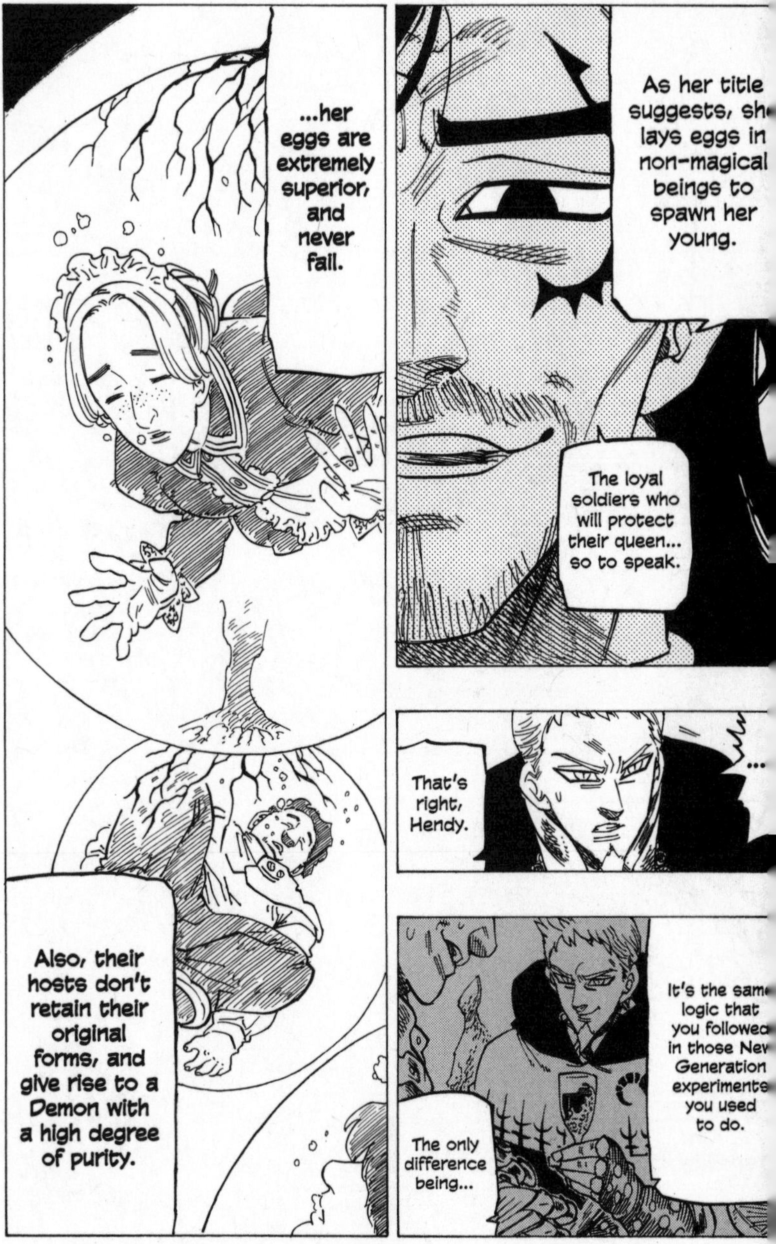
As her title suggests, sh lays eggs in non-magical beings to spawn her young.
The loyal soldiers who will protect their queen... so to speak.
...
That's right, Hendy.
It's the sam logic that you followe in those Ne Generation experiment you used to do.
The only difference being...
...her eggs are extremely superior, and never fail.
Also, their hosts don't retain their original forms, and give rise to a Demon with a high degree of purity.

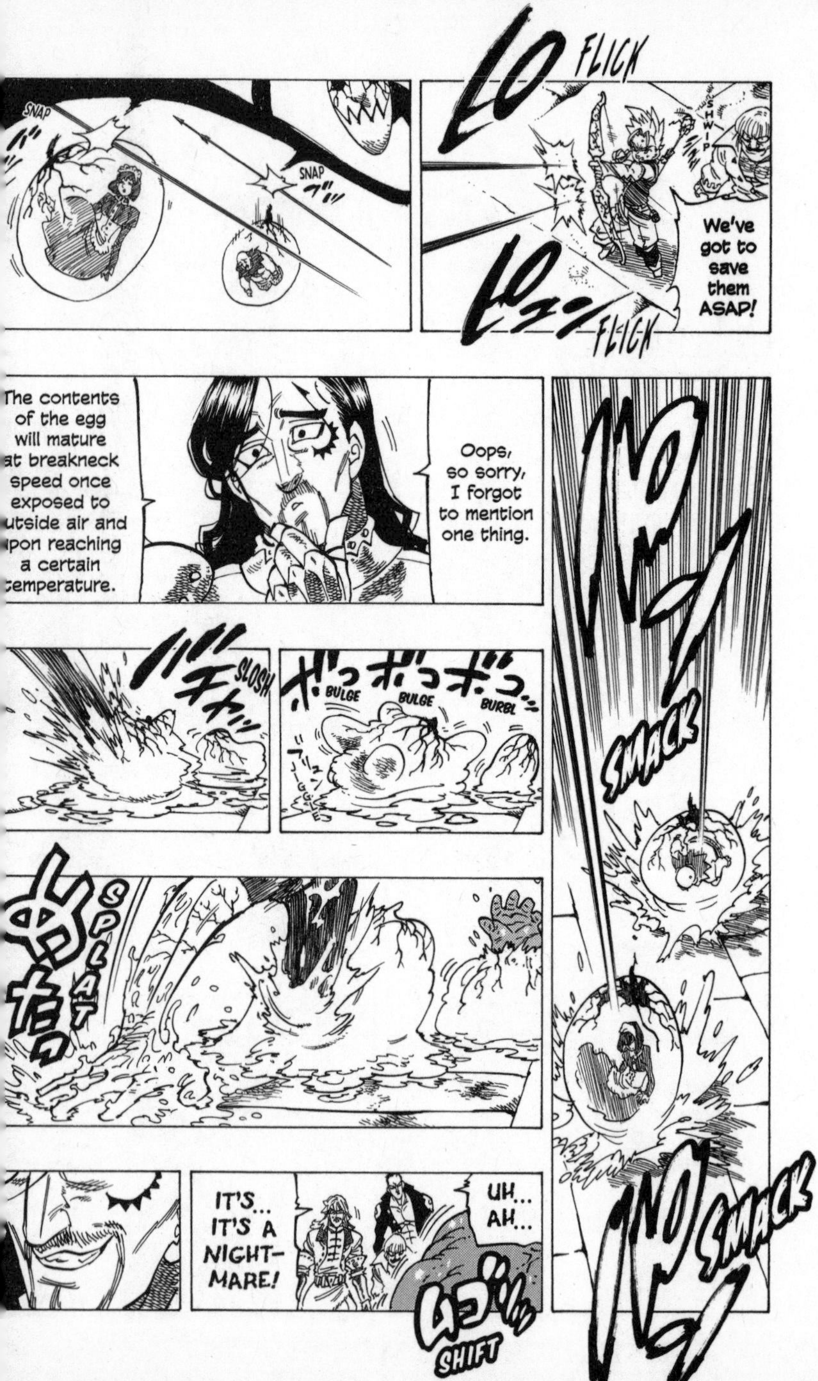
FLICK
SHWIP
We've got to save them ASAP!
FLICK
SNAP
SNAP
SMACK
SMACK
Oops, so sorry, I forgot to mention one thing.
The contents of the egg will mature at breakneck speed once exposed to utside air and pon reaching a certain emperature.
BULGE BULGE BURBL
JIGGLE
SLOSH
SPLAT
UH... AH...
SHIFT
IT'S... IT'S A NIGHTMARE!

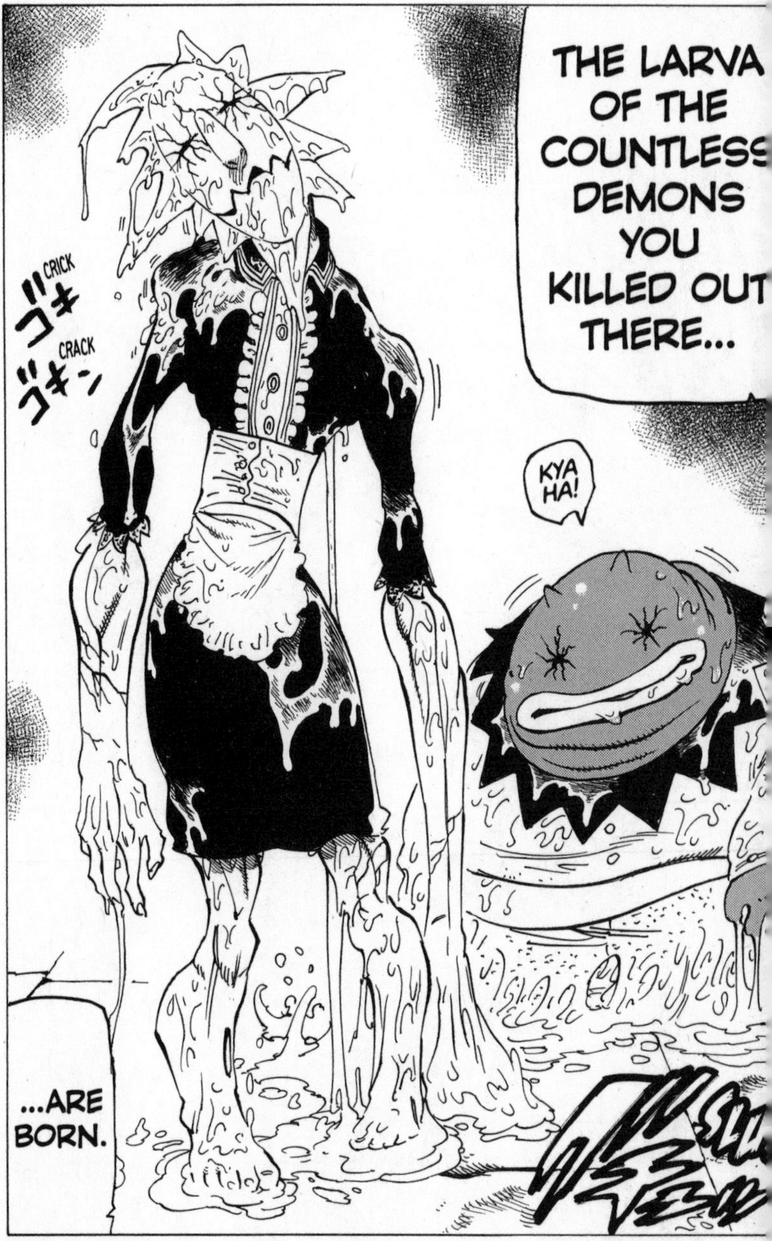
THE LARVA OF THE COUNTLESS DEMONS YOU KILLED OUT THERE...
KYA HA!
ゴキ CRICK
ゴキン CRACK
...ARE BORN.

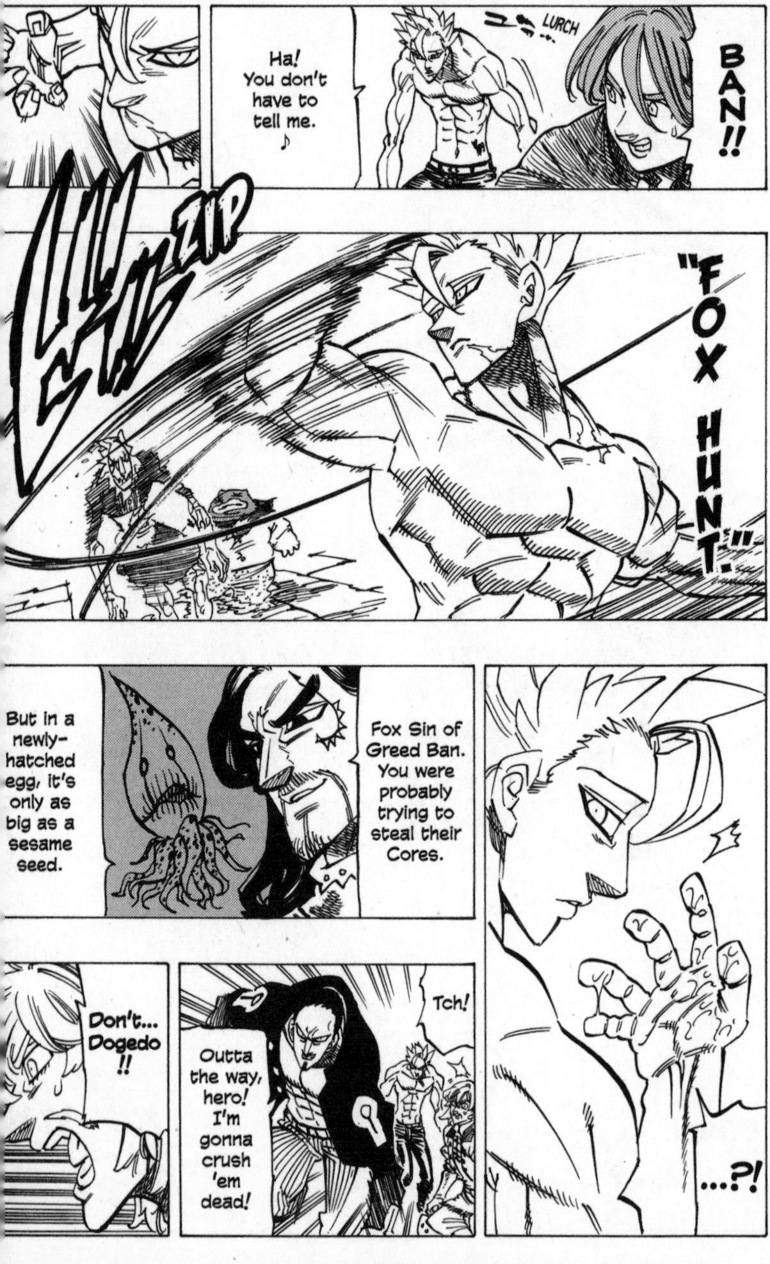
BAN!!
LURCH
Ha! You don't have to tell me. ♪
"FOX HUNT."
ZIP
...?!
Fox Sin of Greed Ban. You were probably trying to steal their Cores.
But in a newly-hatched egg, it's only as big as a sesame seed.
Tch!
Outta the way, hero! I'm gonna crush 'em dead!
Don't... Dogedo!!

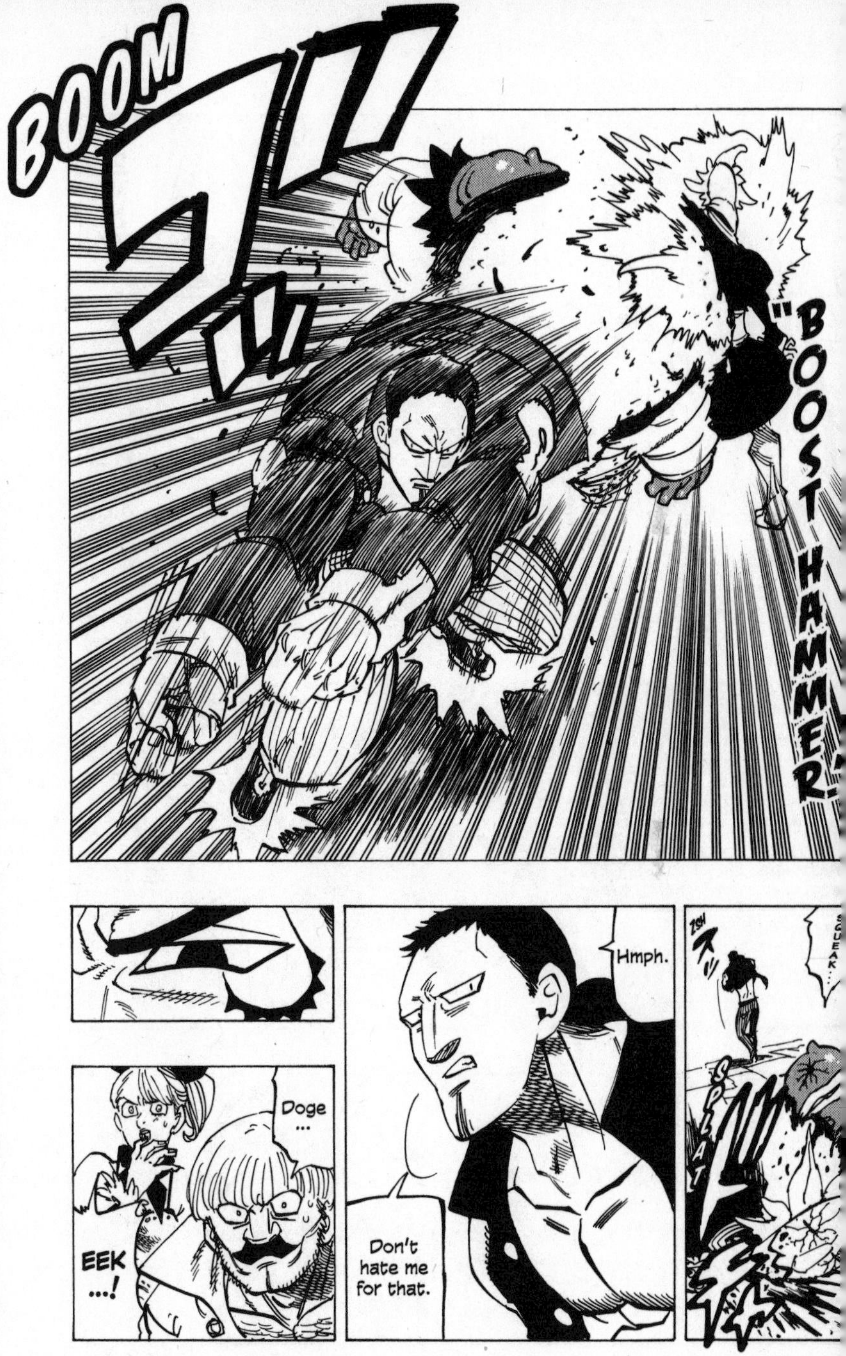
"BOOST HAMMER!!"
BOOM
ZSH
SQUEAK...
SPLAT
Hmph.
Don't hate me for that.
Doge ...
EEK ...!

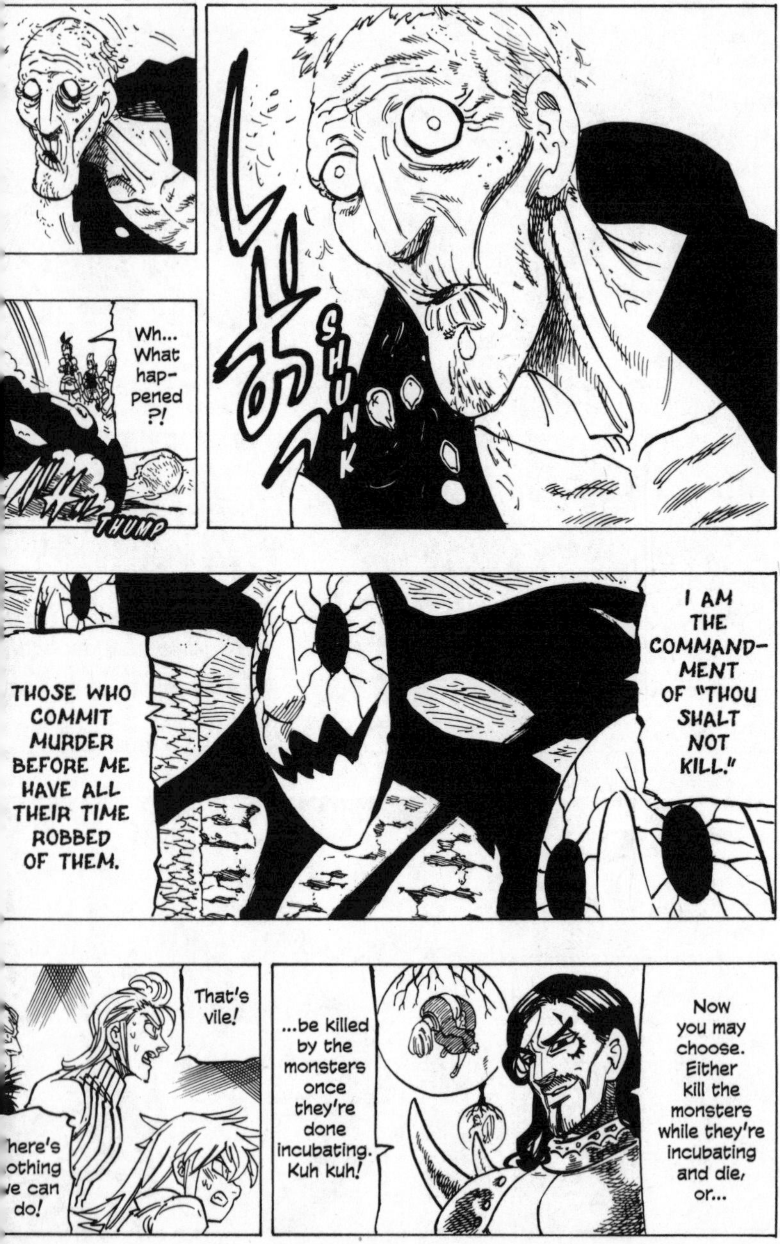
SHUNK
Wh... What hap-pened ?!
THUMP
I AM THE COMMAND-MENT OF "THOU SHALT NOT KILL."
THOSE WHO COMMIT MURDER BEFORE ME HAVE ALL THEIR TIME ROBBED OF THEM.
Now you may choose. Either kill the monsters while they're incubating and die, or...
...be killed by the monsters once they're done incubating. Kuh kuh!
That's vile!
here's othing e can do!

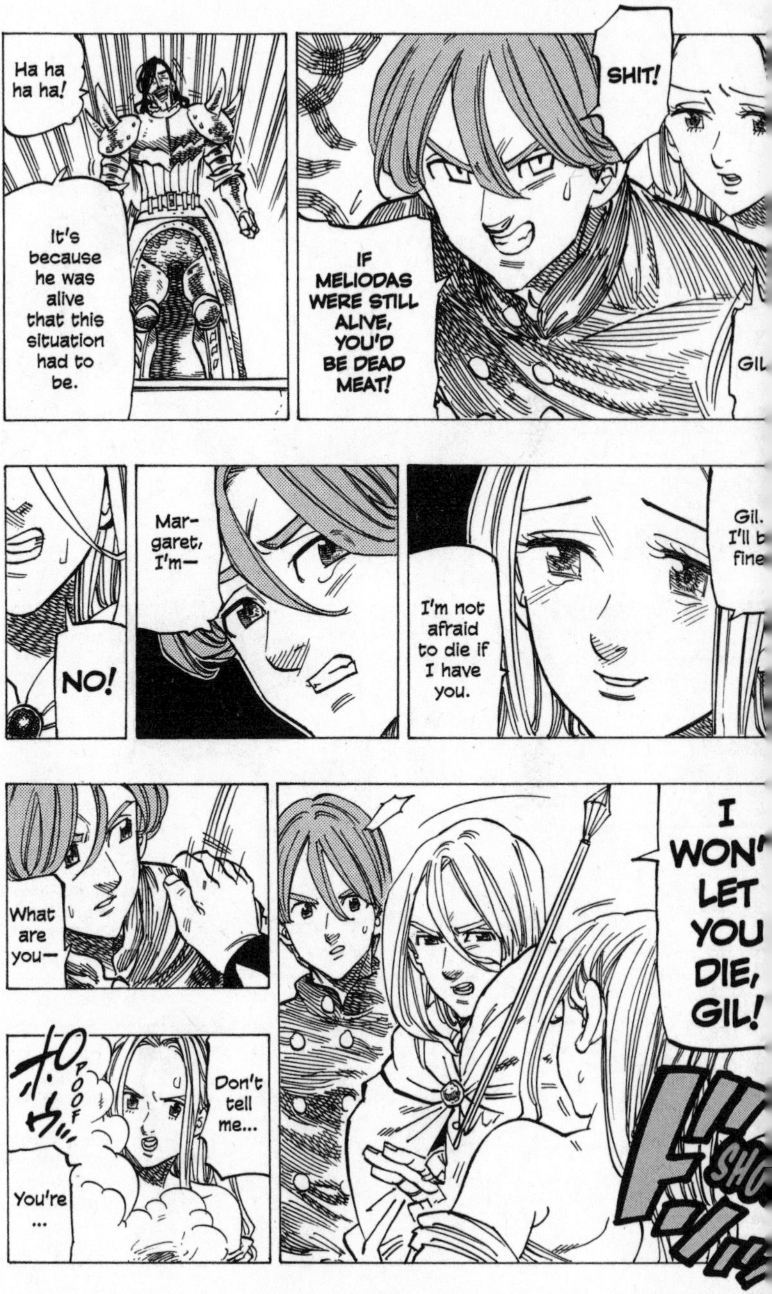
SHIT!
GIL
IF MELIODAS WERE STILL ALIVE, YOU'D BE DEAD MEAT!
Ha ha ha ha!
It's because he was alive that this situation had to be.
Gil. I'll b fine
I'm not afraid to die if I have you.
Margaret, I'm—
NO!
I WON' LET YOU DIE, GIL!
What are you—
Don't tell me...
POOF
You're ...

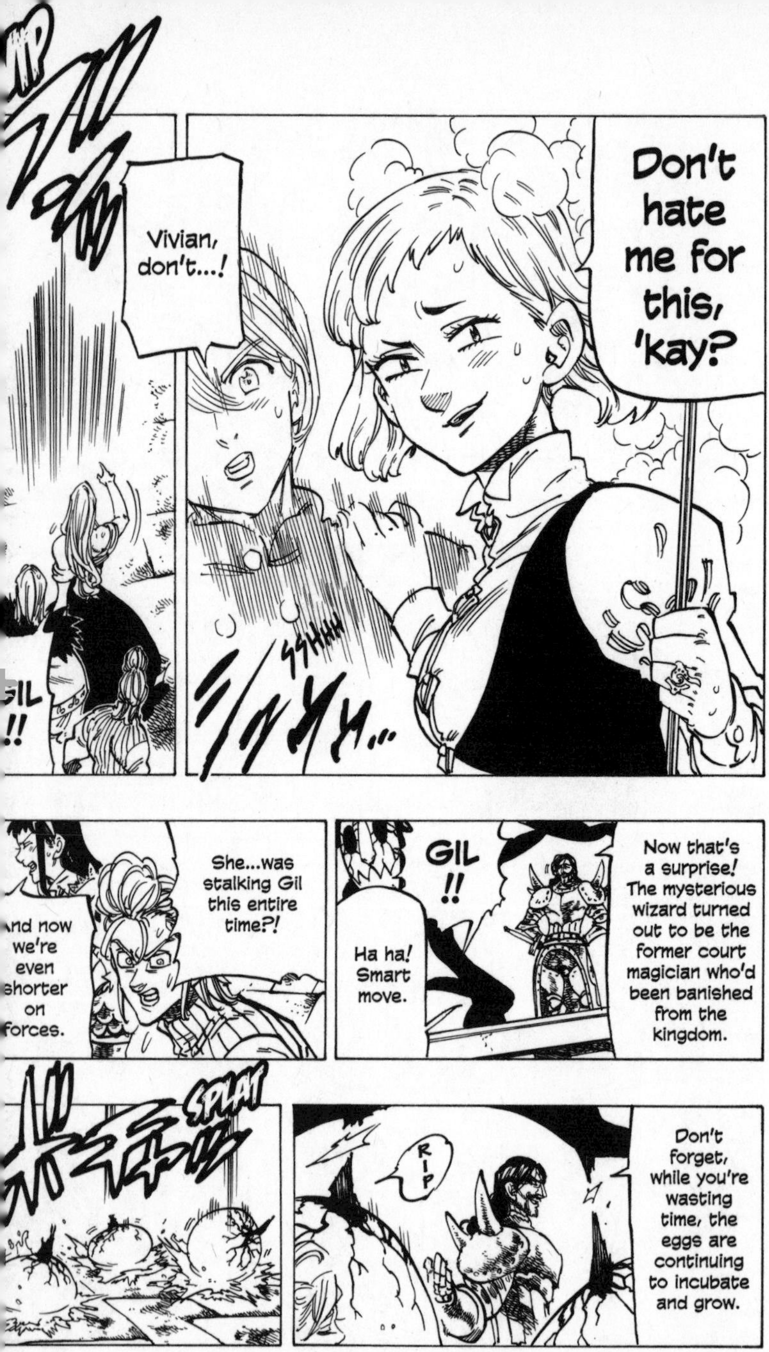
Don't hate me for this, 'kay?
Vivian, don't...!
SSHHH
WHIP
GIL!!
Now that's a surprise! The mysterious wizard turned out to be the former court magician who'd been banished from the kingdom.
GIL!!
Ha ha! Smart move.
She...was stalking Gil this entire time?!
nd now we're even shorter on forces.
Don't forget, while you're wasting time, the eggs are continuing to incubate and grow.
RIP
SPLAT

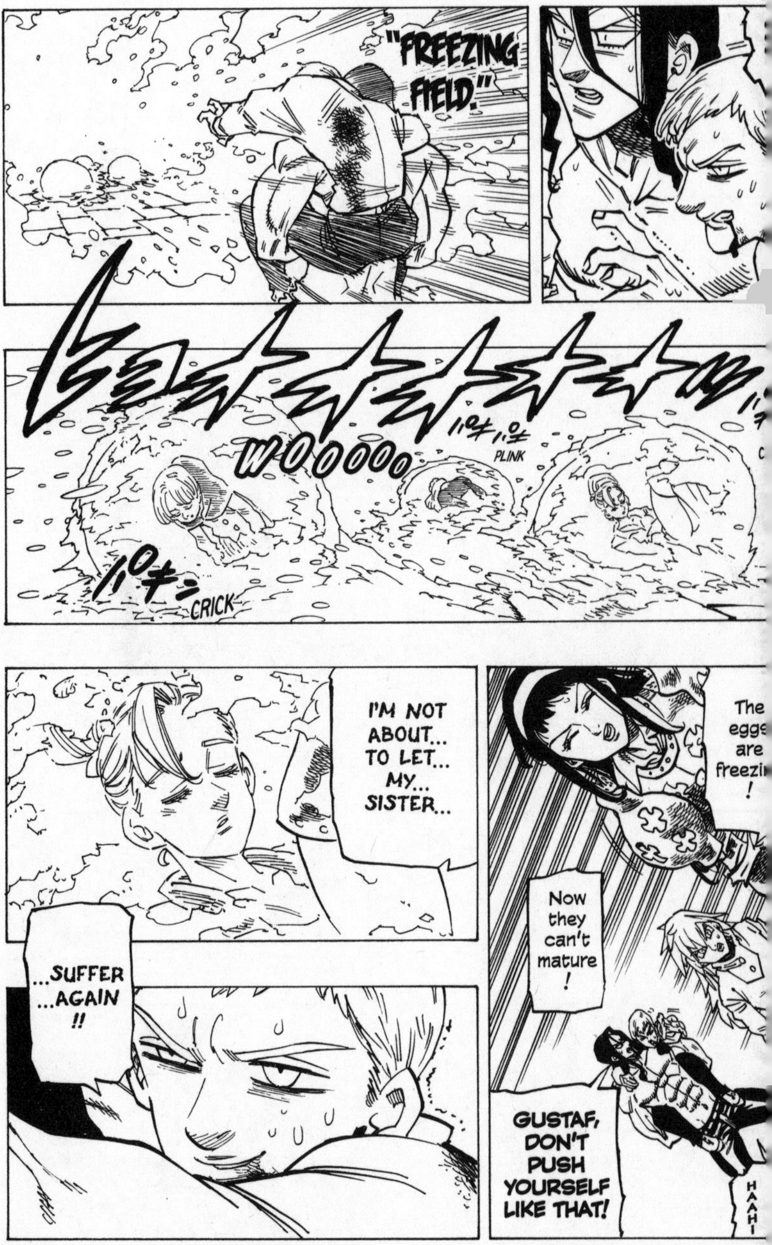
"FREEZING FIELD."
WOOOOO
PLINK
CRICK
The eggs are freezi !
Now they can't mature!
GUSTAF, DON'T PUSH YOURSELF LIKE THAT!
HAAHI
I'M NOT ABOUT... TO LET... MY... SISTER...
...SUFFER ...AGAIN!!

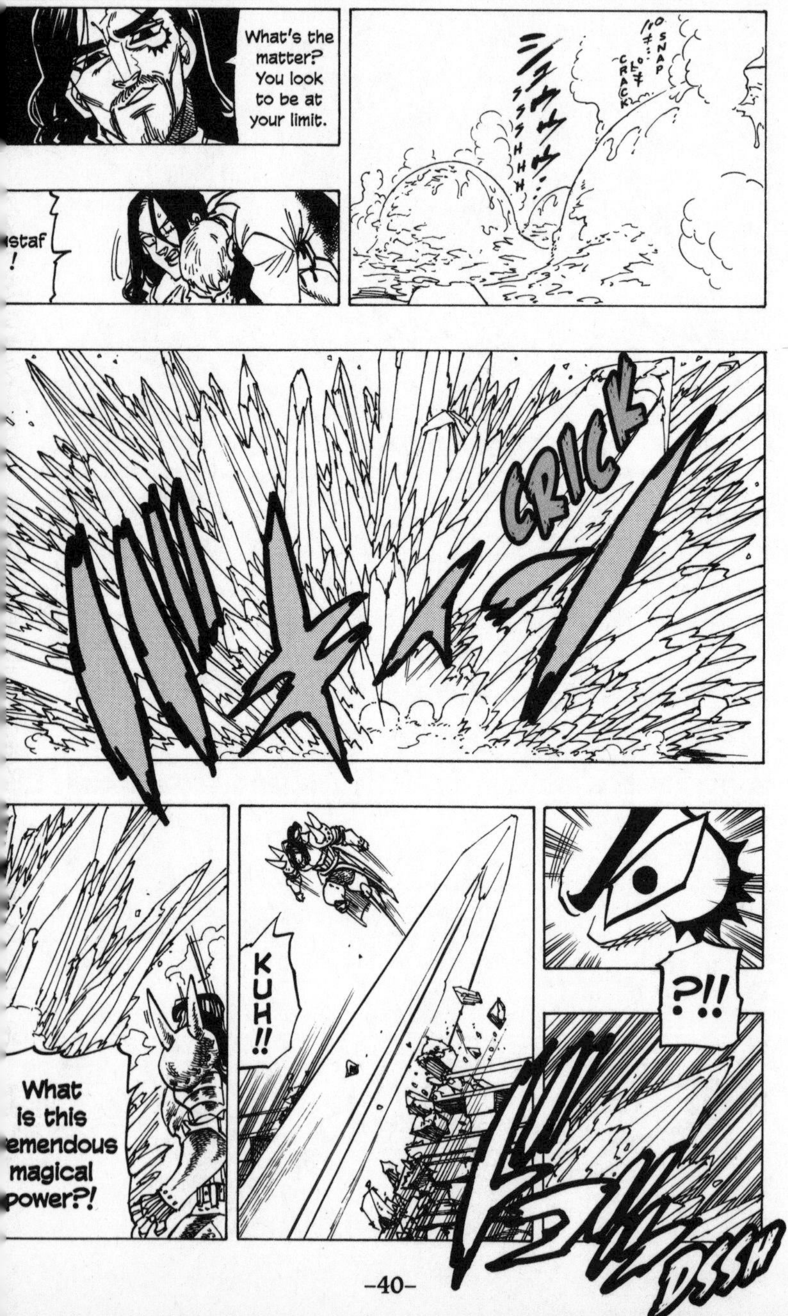
SNAP
CRACK
SSSSHHH
What's the matter? You look to be at your limit.
staf!
CRICK
?!!
KUH!!
What is this emendous magical power?!
DSSH

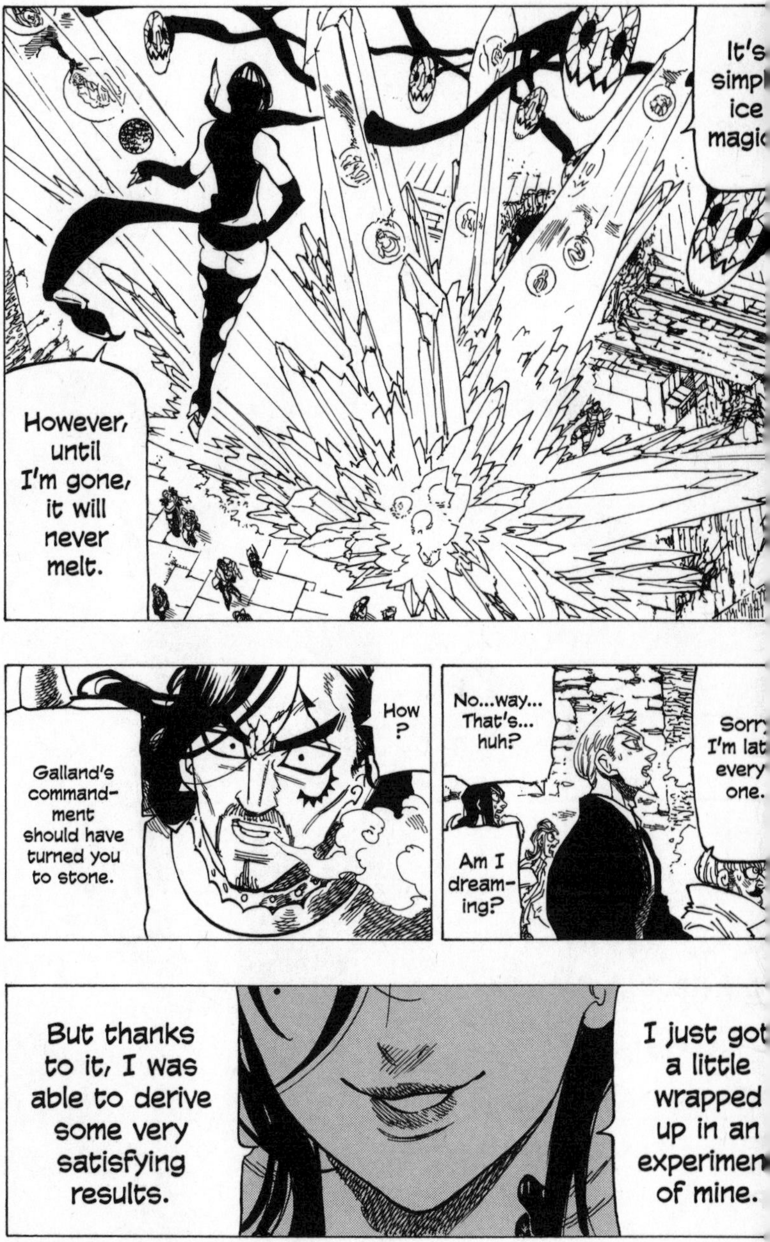
It's simp ice magi
However, until I'm gone, it will never melt.
Sor I'm la every one.
No...way... That's... huh?
Am I dream-ing?
How?
Galland's command-ment should have turned you to stone.
I just got a little wrapped up in an experimen of mine.
But thanks to it, I was able to derive some very satisfying results.

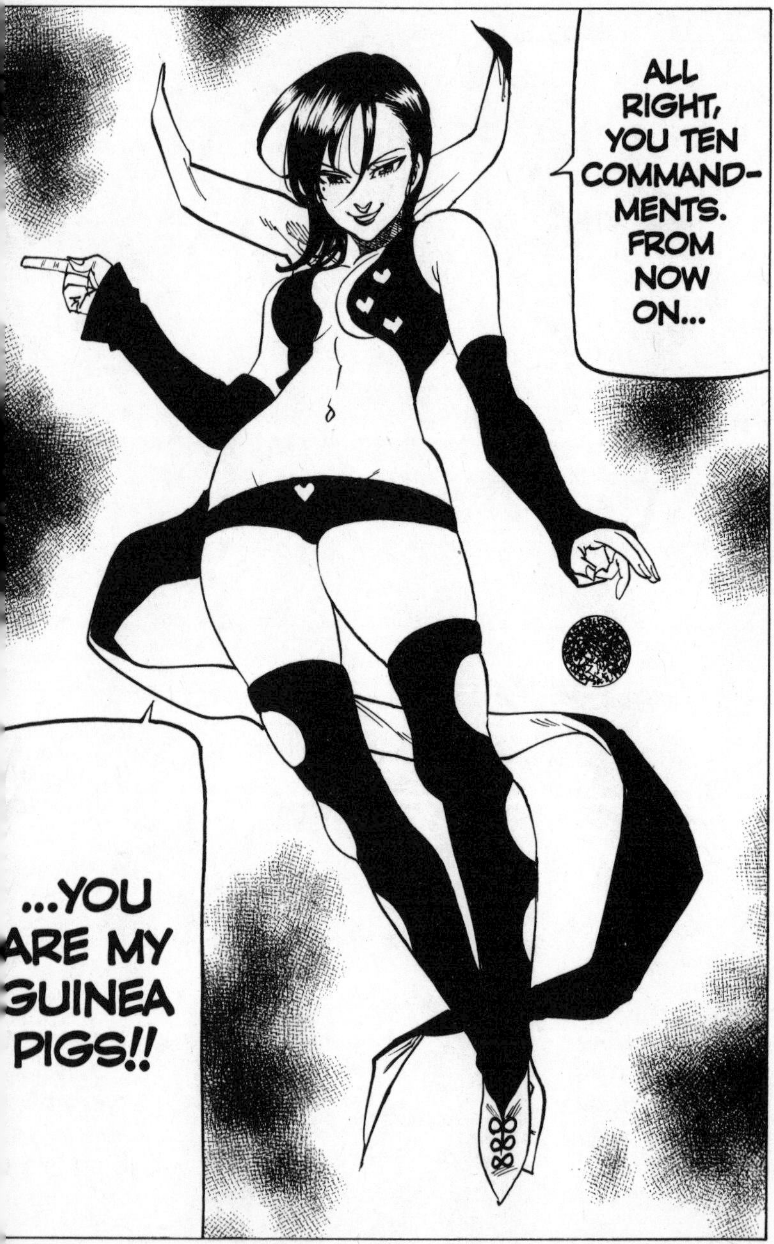
ALL RIGHT, YOU TEN COMMANDMENTS. FROM NOW ON...
...YOU ARE MY GUINEA PIGS!!

Chapter 191 - Insatiable Woman

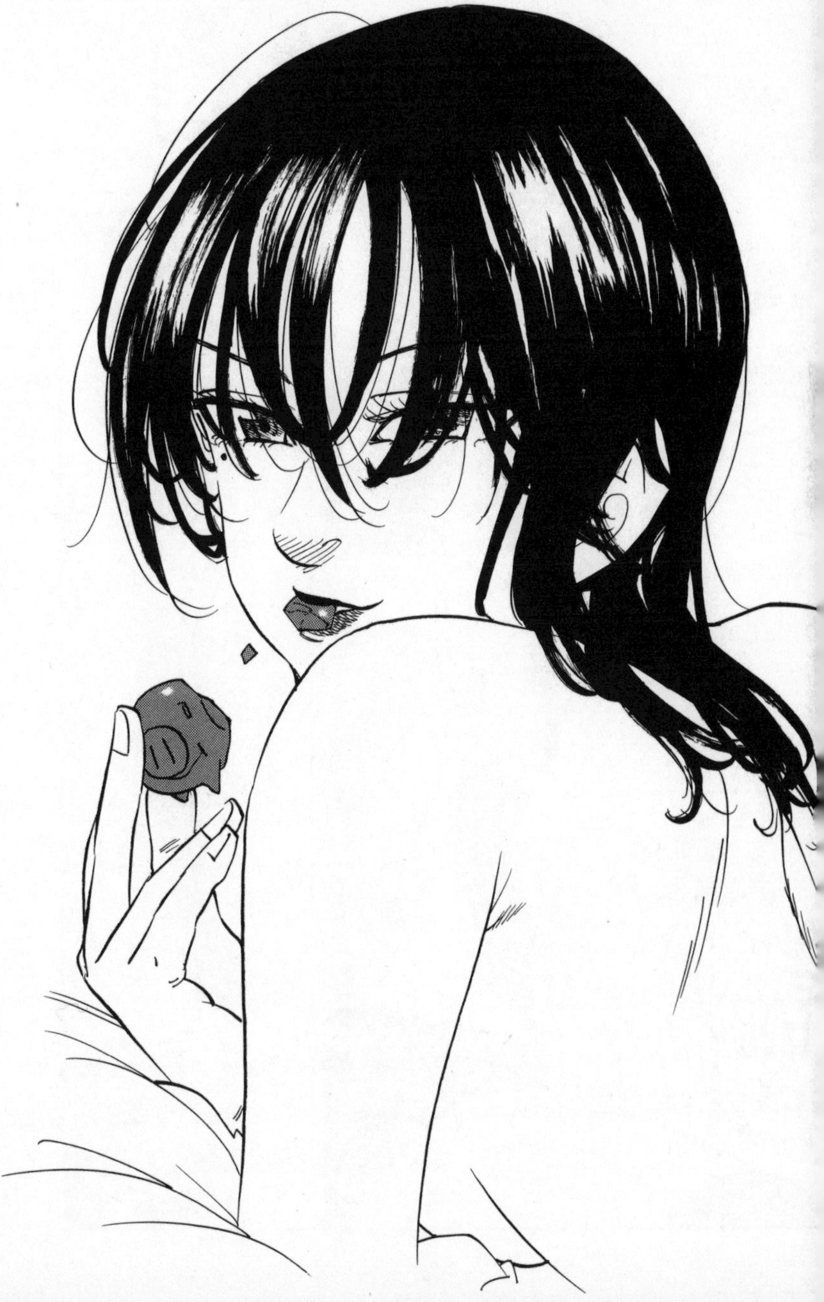

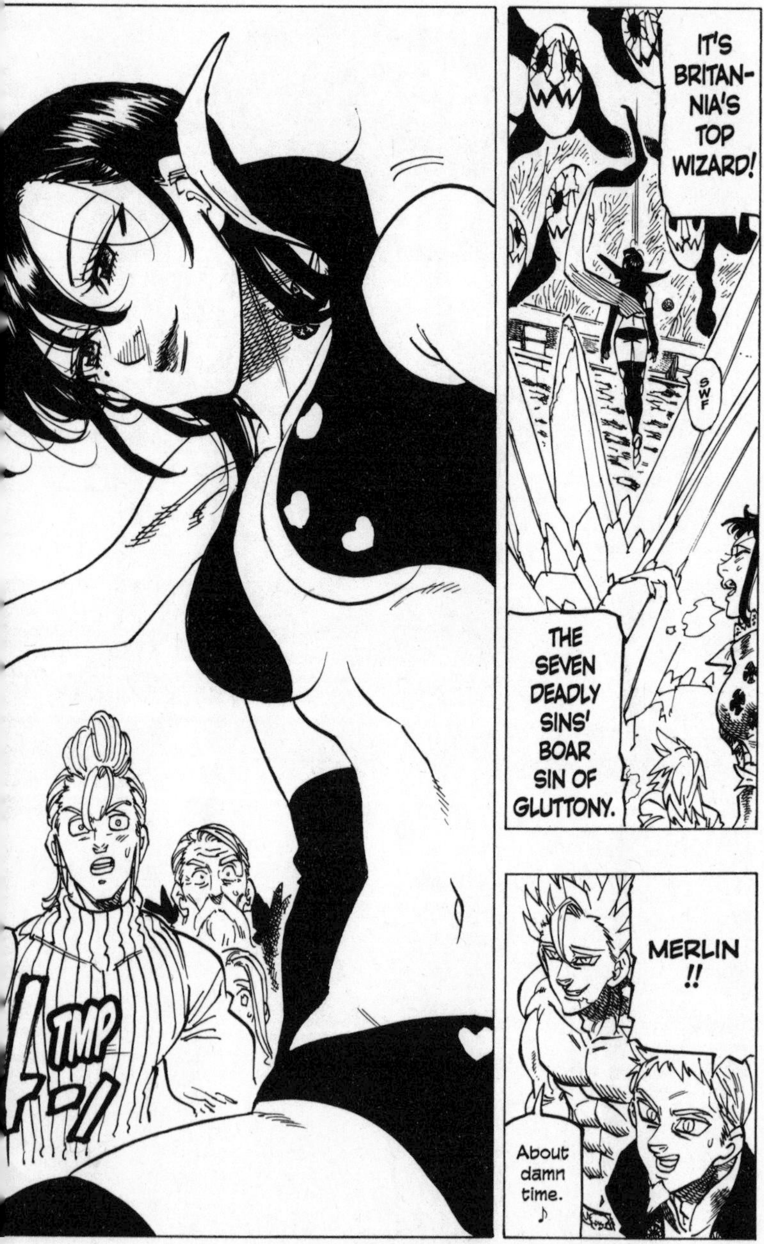
IT'S BRITANNIA'S TOP WIZARD!
SWF
THE SEVEN DEADLY SINS' BOAR SIN OF GLUTTONY.
MERLIN !!
About damn time. ♪
TMP

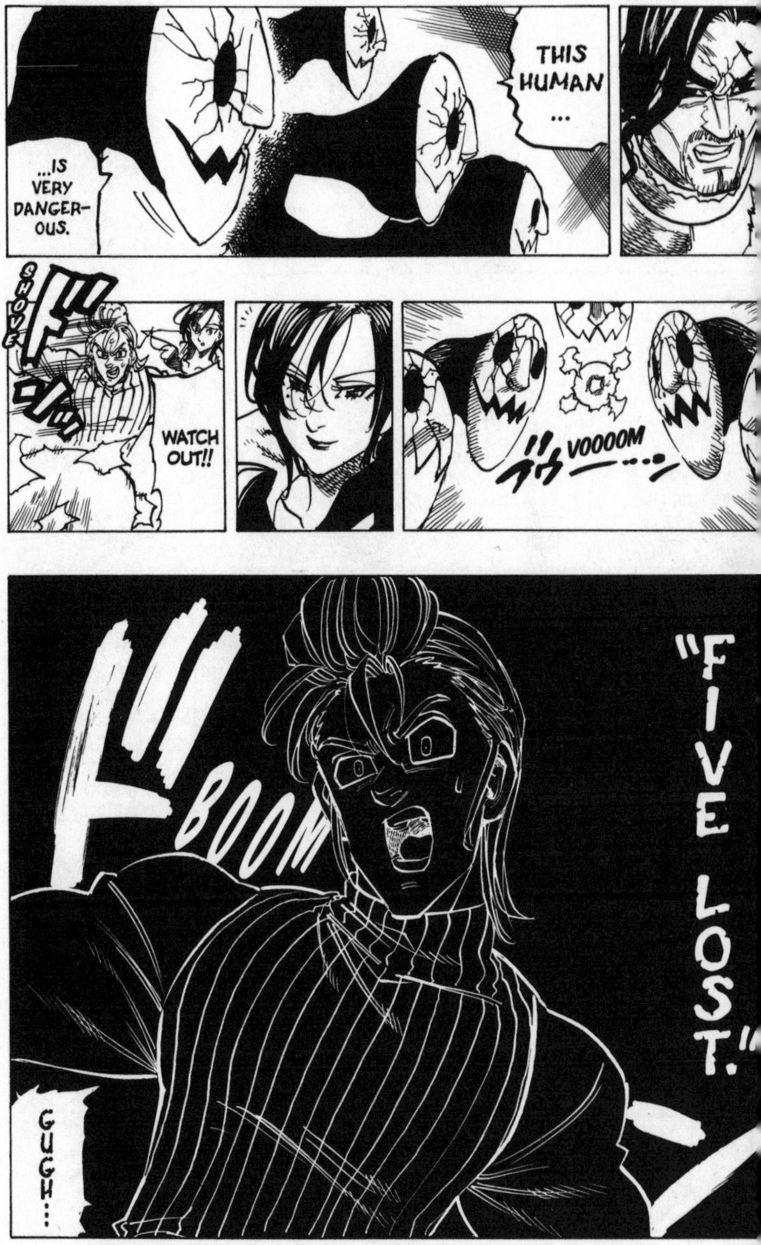
THIS HUMAN ...
...IS VERY DANGER-OUS.
VOOOOM
SHOVE
WATCH OUT!!
"FIVE LOST."
BOOM
GUGH...

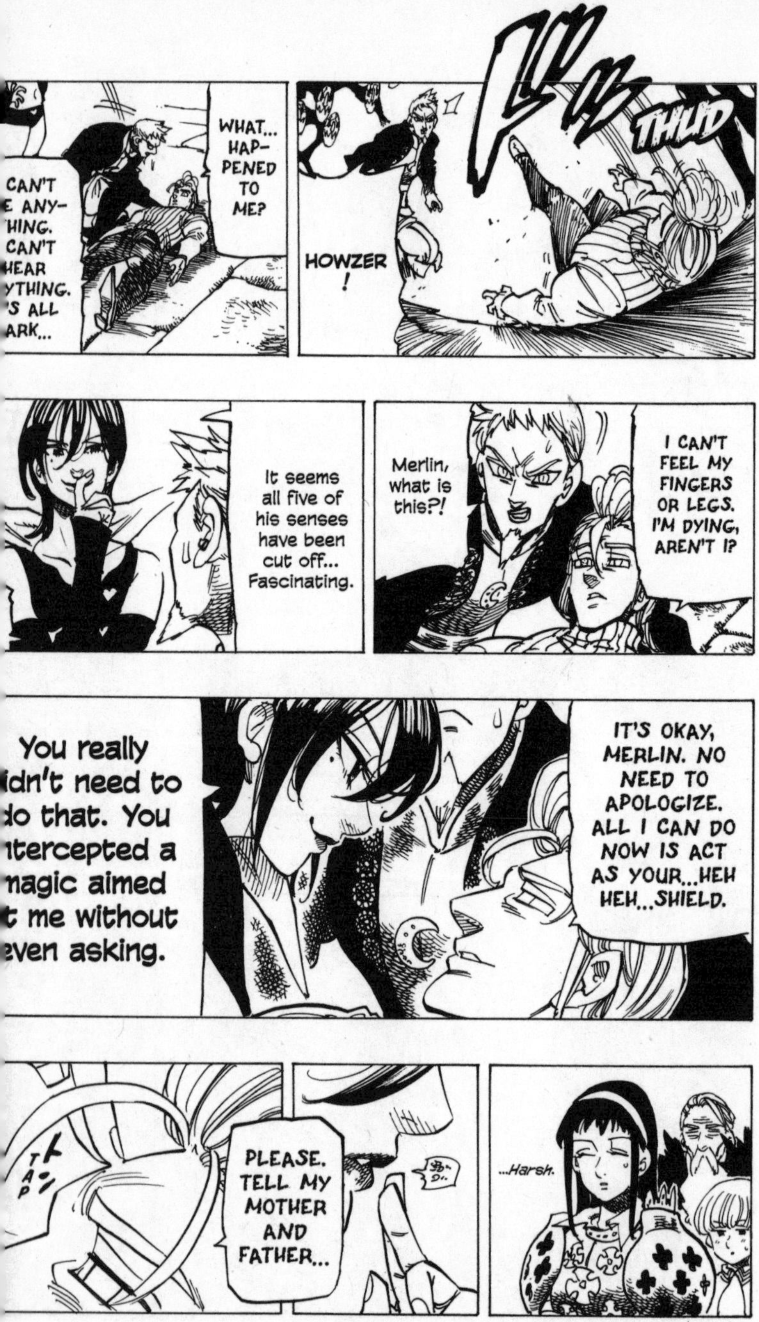
THUD
HOWZER!
WHAT... HAPPENED TO ME?
CAN'T E ANY-HING. CAN'T HEAR YTHING. 'S ALL ARK...
I CAN'T FEEL MY FINGERS OR LEGS. I'M DYING, AREN'T I?
Merlin, what is this?!
It seems all five of his senses have been cut off... Fascinating.
IT'S OKAY, MERLIN. NO NEED TO APOLOGIZE. ALL I CAN DO NOW IS ACT AS YOUR...HEH HEH...SHIELD.
You really idn't need to do that. You ntercepted a nagic aimed t me without even asking.
...Harsh.
PLEASE. TELL MY MOTHER AND FATHER...
TAP

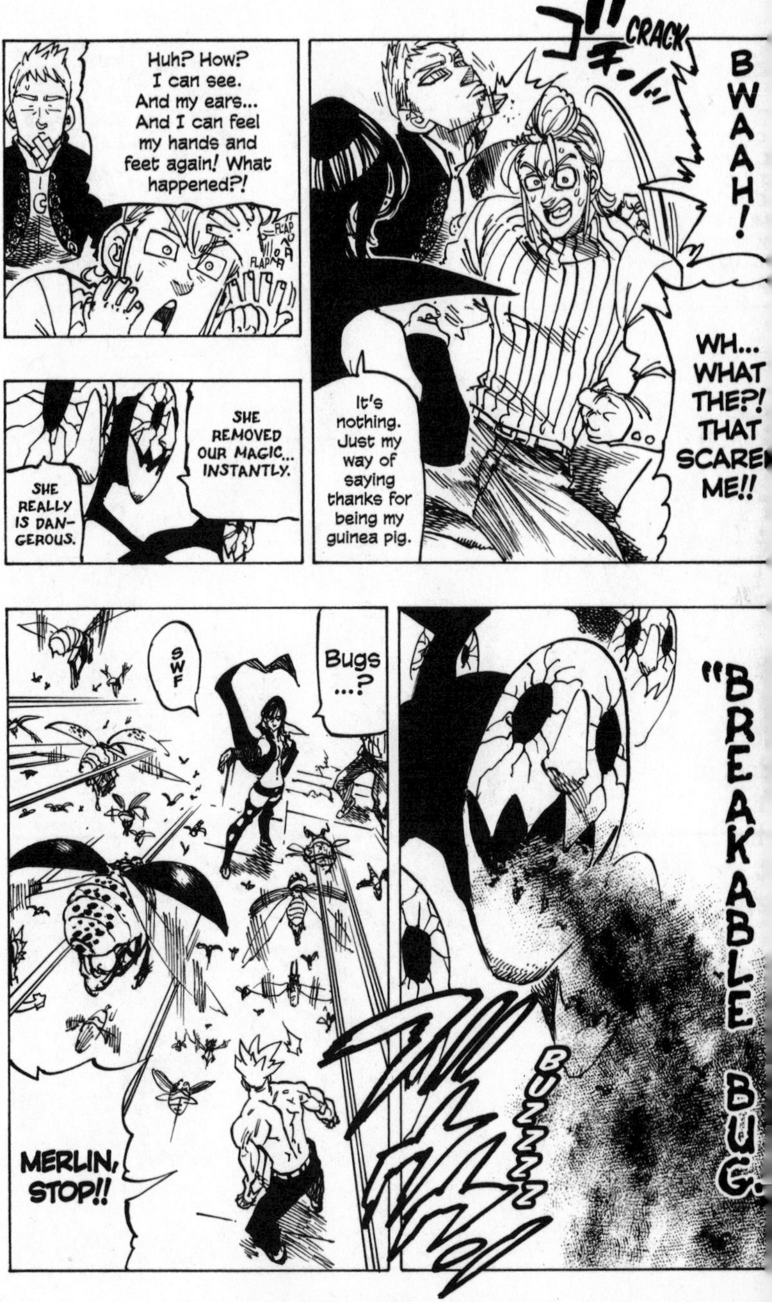
CRACK
BWAAH!
WH... WHAT THE?! THAT SCARE ME!!
It's nothing. Just my way of saying thanks for being my guinea pig.
Huh? How? I can see. And my ears... And I can feel my hands and feet again! What happened?!
FLAP
FLAP
SHE REMOVED OUR MAGIC... INSTANTLY.
SHE REALLY IS DANGEROUS.
"BREAKABLE BUG."
BUZZZZ
Bugs ...?
SWF
MERLIN, STOP!!

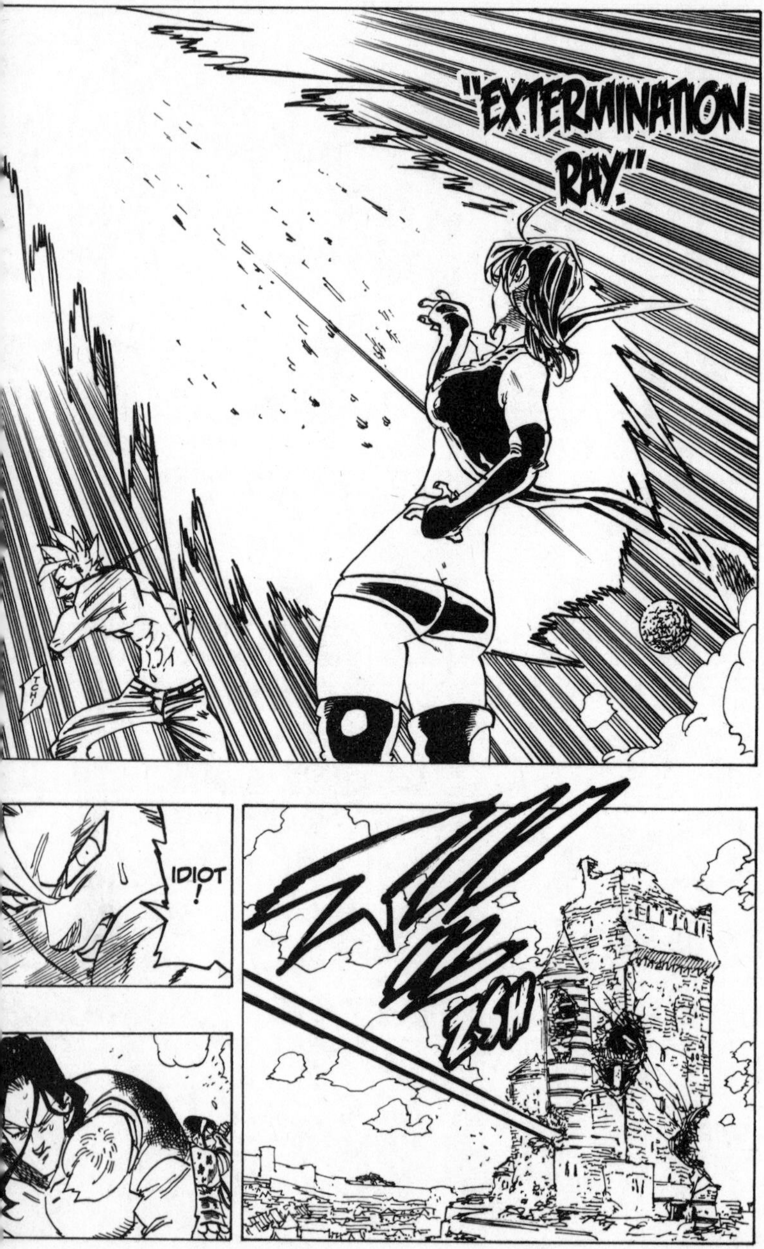
"EXTERMINATION RAY."
TCH!
ZSH
IDIOT!

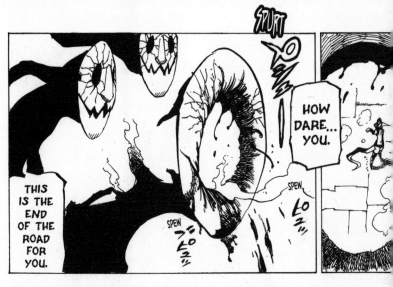

STURT

HOW DARE... YOU.

THIS IS THE END OF THE ROAD FOR YOU.

SPEW

SPEW

MERLIN !!

...WILL HAVE ALL THEIR TIME ROBBED OF THEM AND DECAY!

THOSE WHO DISOBEY OUR COMMANDMENT OF "THOU SHALL NOT KILL"...

CRICK

CRMBL

It... can't... be.

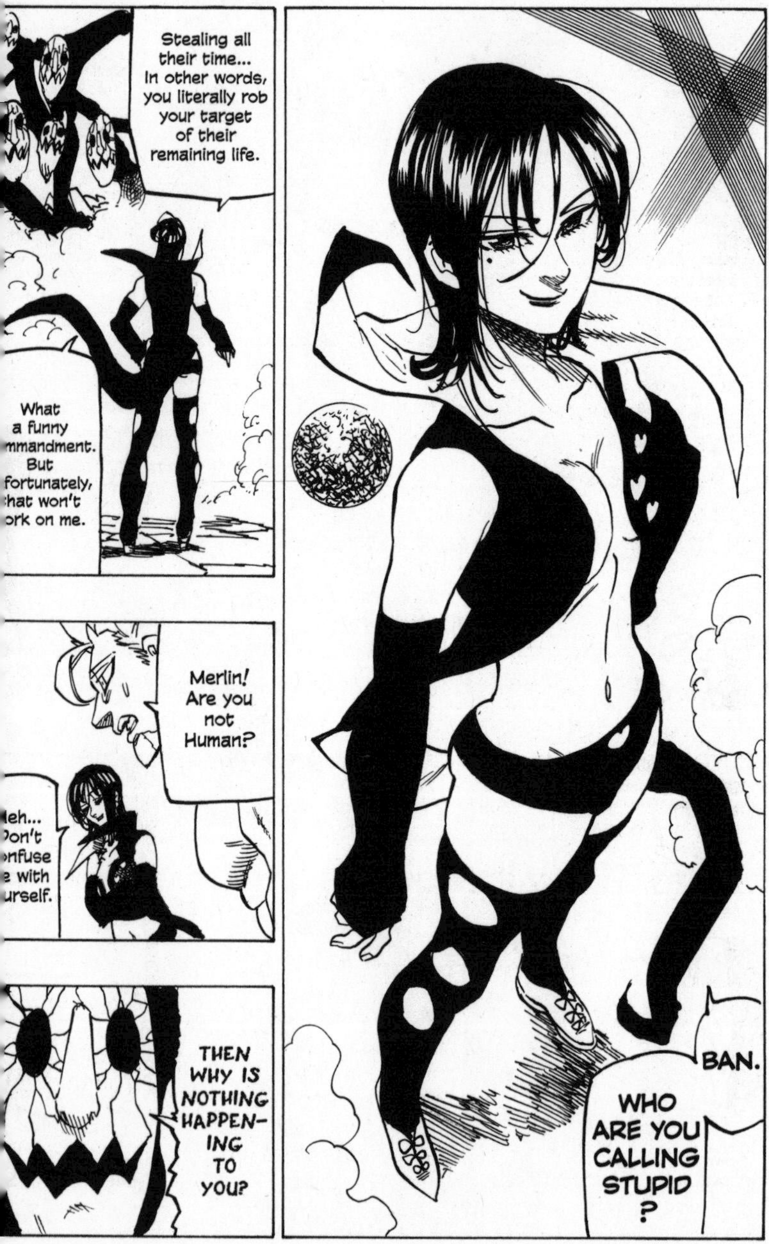

Stealing all their time... In other words, you literally rob your target of their remaining life.
What a funny mmandment. But fortunately, hat won't ork on me.
Merlin! Are you not Human?
leh... Don't nfuse e with urself.
THEN WHY IS NOTHING HAPPEN-ING TO YOU?
WHO ARE YOU CALLING STUPID ?
BAN.

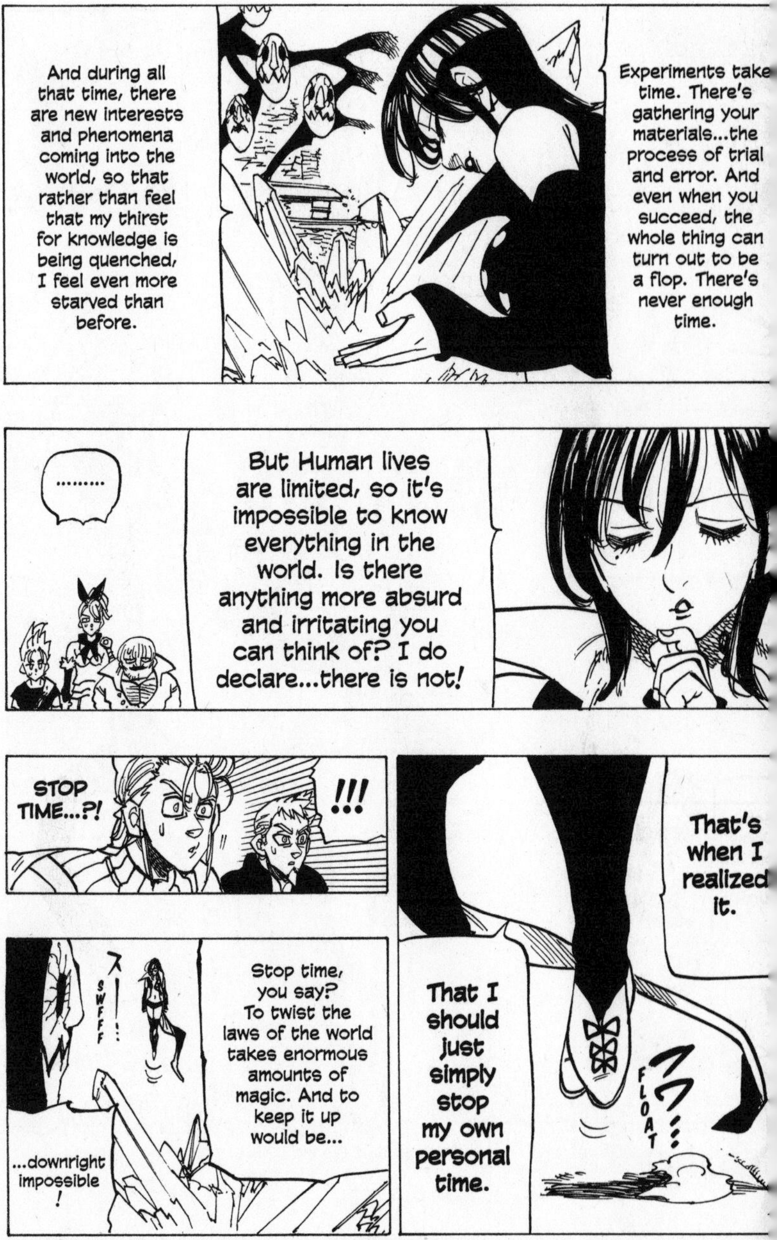
Experiments take time. There's gathering your materials...the process of trial and error. And even when you succeed, the whole thing can turn out to be a flop. There's never enough time.
And during all that time, there are new interests and phenomena coming into the world, so that rather than feel that my thirst for knowledge is being quenched, I feel even more starved than before.
But Human lives are limited, so it's impossible to know everything in the world. Is there anything more absurd and irritating you can think of? I do declare...there is not!
....
That's when I realized it.
That I should just simply stop my own personal time.
FLOAT
!!!
STOP TIME...?!
Stop time, you say? To twist the laws of the world takes enormous amounts of magic. And to keep it up would be...
SWFFF
...downright impossible!

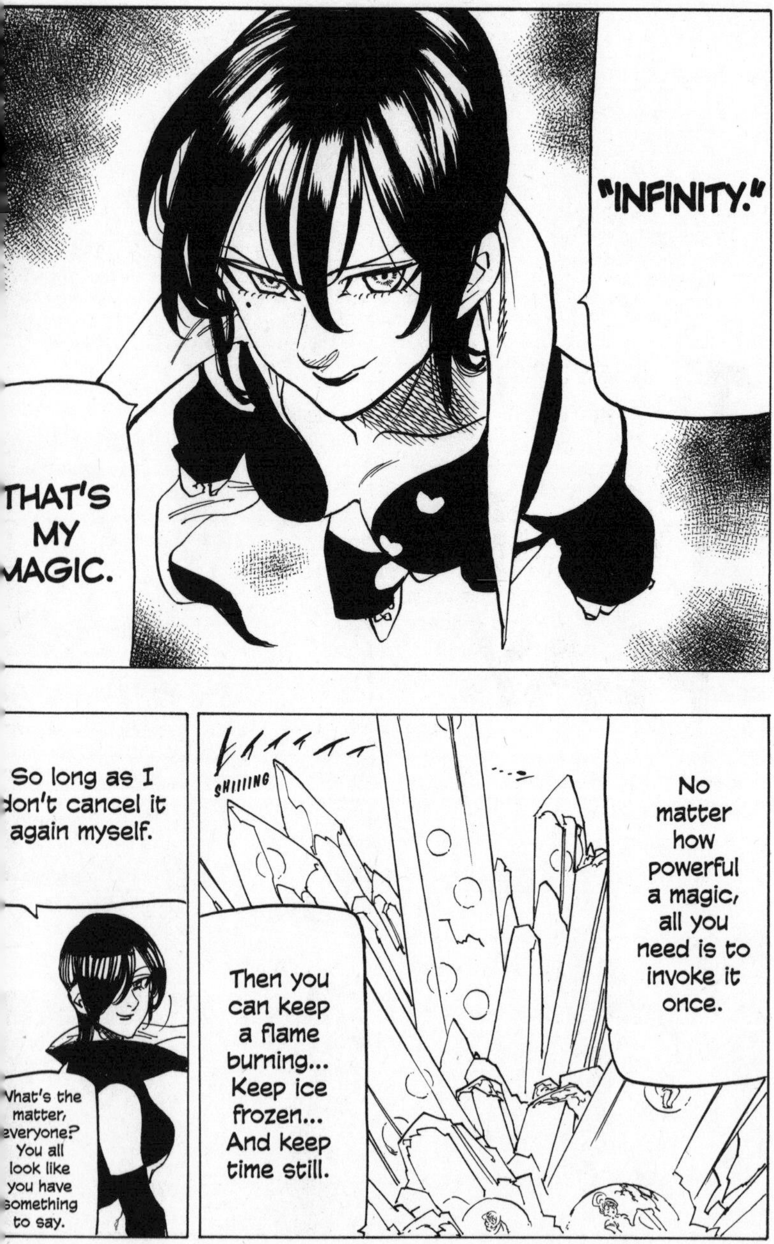
"INFINITY."
THAT'S MY MAGIC.
No matter how powerful a magic, all you need is to invoke it once.
SHIIIING
Then you can keep a flame burning... Keep ice frozen... And keep time still.
So long as I don't cancel it again myself.
What's the matter, everyone? You all look like you have something to say.

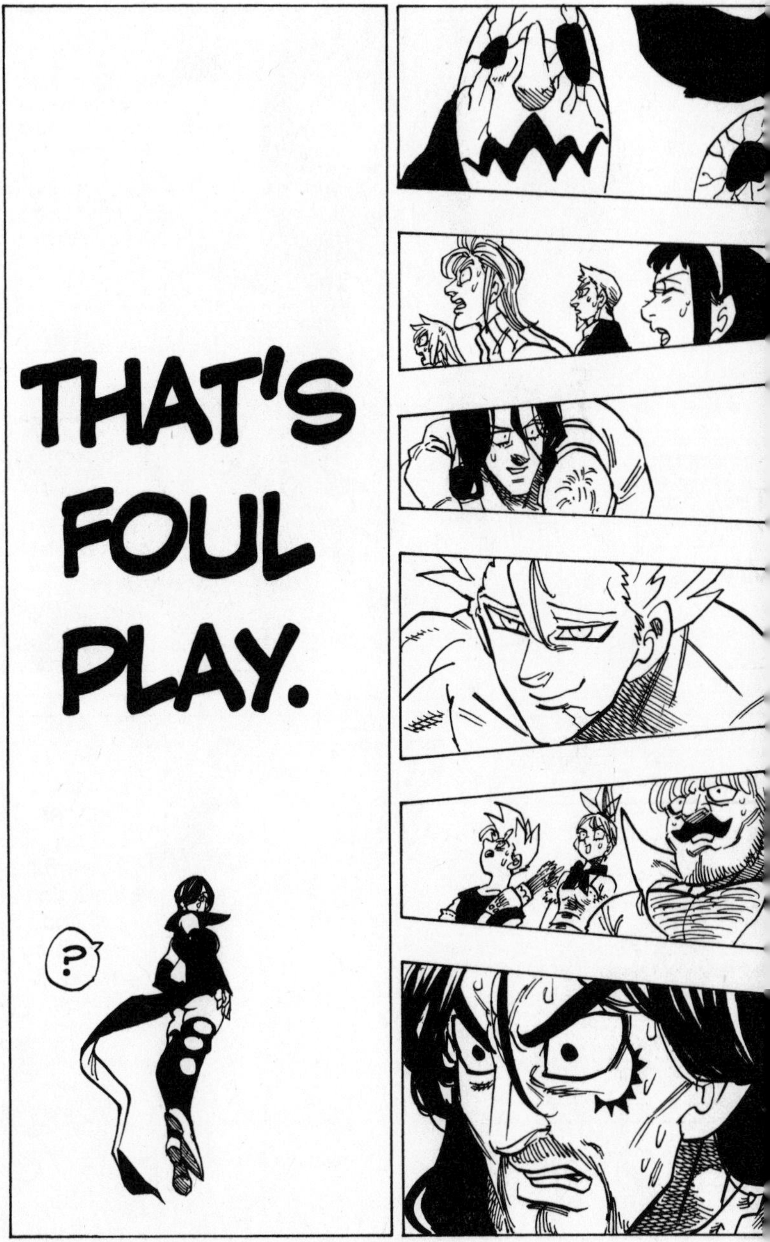
THAT'S FOUL PLAY.
?

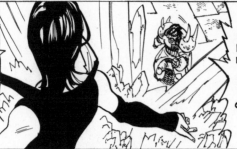

But! No matter how against the rules your magic is, it doesn't explain how you were able to cancel Galland's petrification.
Vell, it took some time for me to evert back to normal. Just as I'd xpect from a mmandment.
COMMANDMENTS ARE NO ORDINARY MAGIC. THEY ARE CURSES GRANTED TO THE TEN COMMANDMENTS BY THE DEMON LORD.
NO WIZARD, NO MATTER HOW MUCH TIME SHE HAD, SHOULD BE ABLE TO BREAK THEM!
I was nervous for a moment there too... But then I came back to my senses and it dawned on me.
I have a tolerance against Commandments.
?!
It's embarrassing, really. It'd just been so long...
...that I'd completely forgotten what my true form really is.

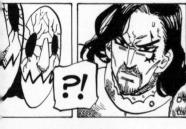

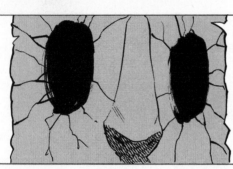

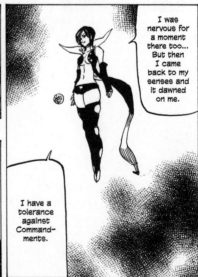

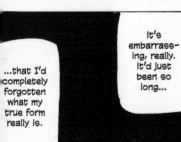

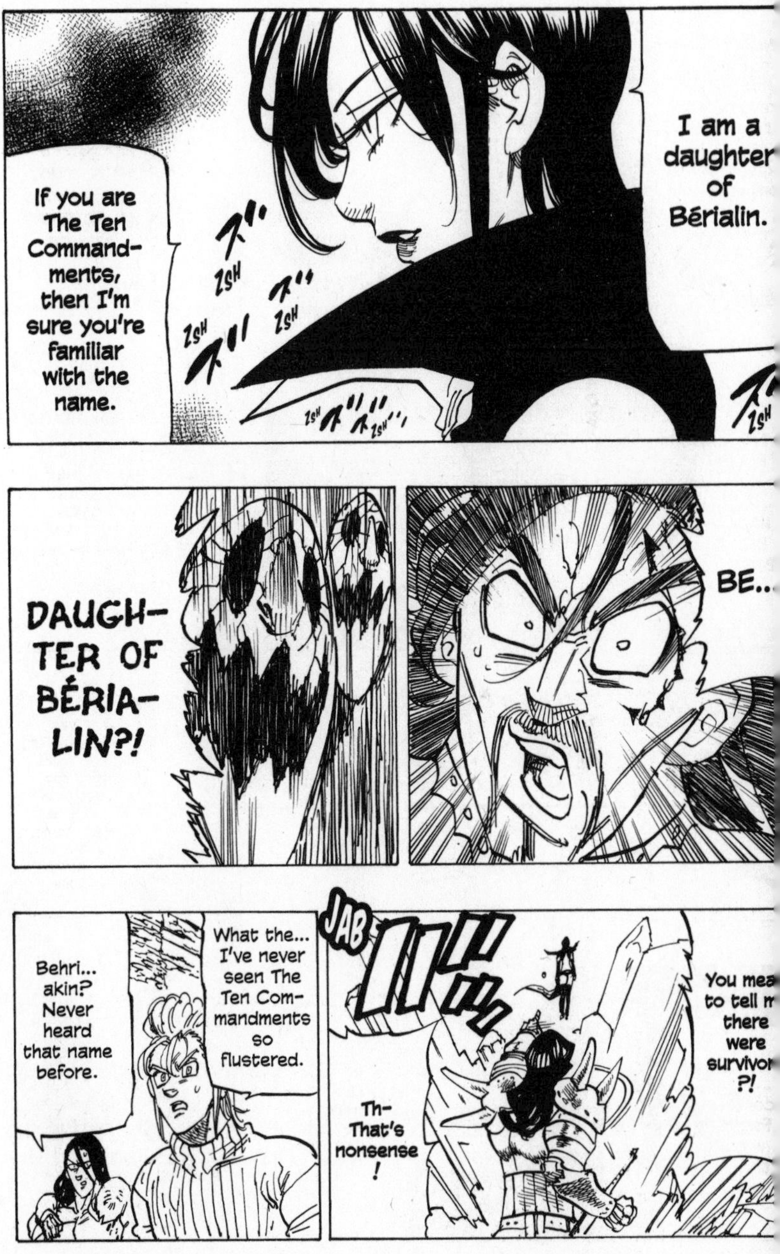
I am a daughter of Bérialin.
If you are The Ten Command- ments, then I'm sure you're familiar with the name.
ZSH ZSH ZSH ZSH ZSH ZSH
BE...
DAUGH- TER OF BÉRIA- LIN?!
You mea to tell m there were survivor ?!
JAB
Th- That's nonsense!
What the... I've never seen The Ten Com- mandments so flustered.
Behri... akin? Never heard that name before.

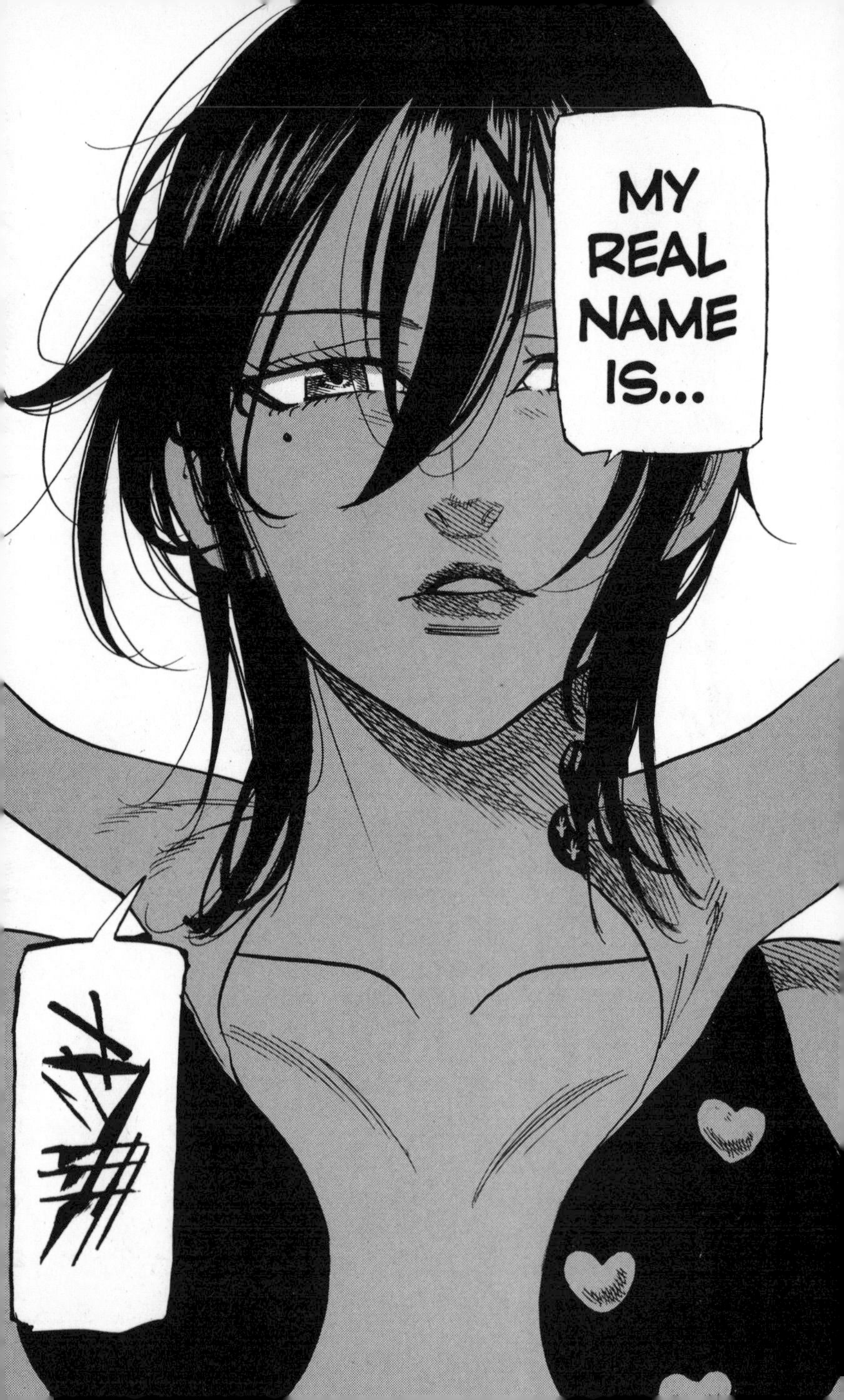
MY REAL NAME IS...

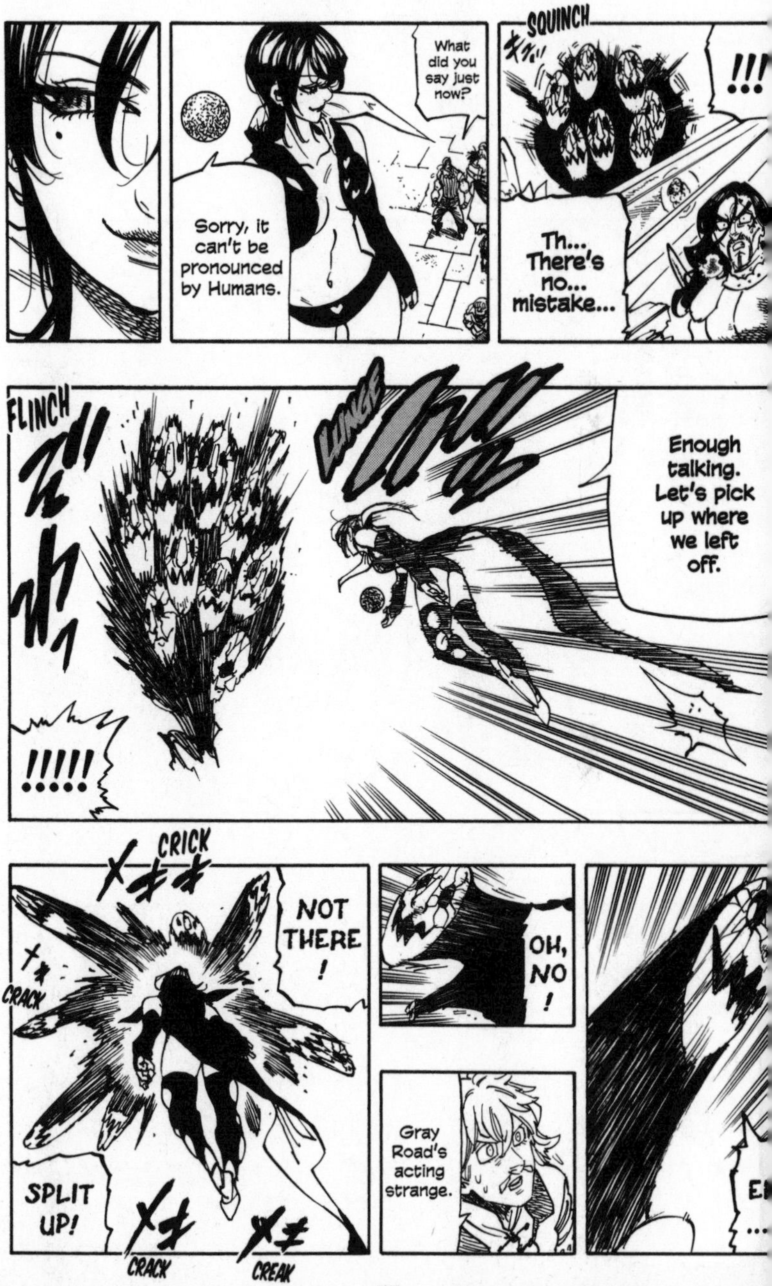
SQUINCH
!!!
Th... There's no... mistake...
What did you say just now?
Sorry, it can't be pronounced by Humans.
Enough talking. Let's pick up where we left off.
LUNGE
FLINCH
!!!!!
OH, NO!
Gray Road's acting strange.
CRICK
NOT THERE!
CRACK
SPLIT UP!
CRACK
CREAK

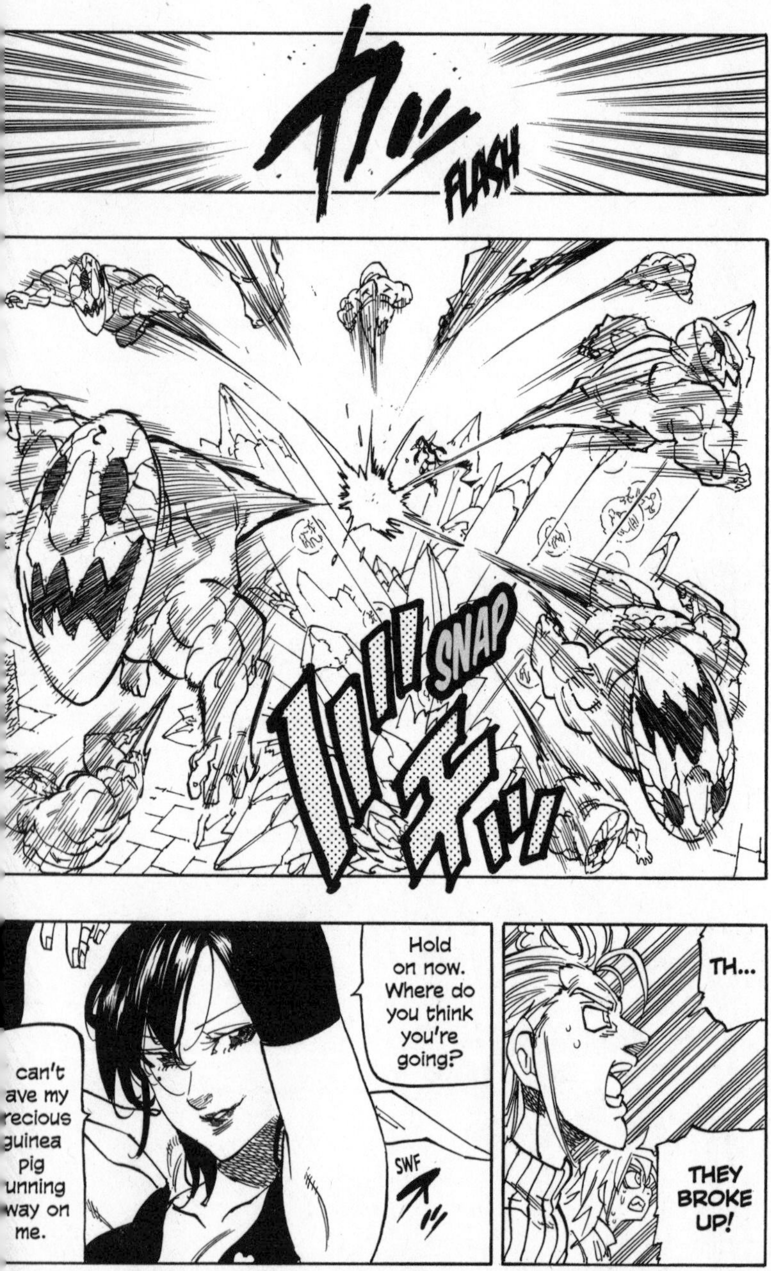
FLASH
SNAP
TH...
THEY BROKE UP!
Hold on now. Where do you think you're going?
SWF
can't ave my recious guinea pig unning way on me.

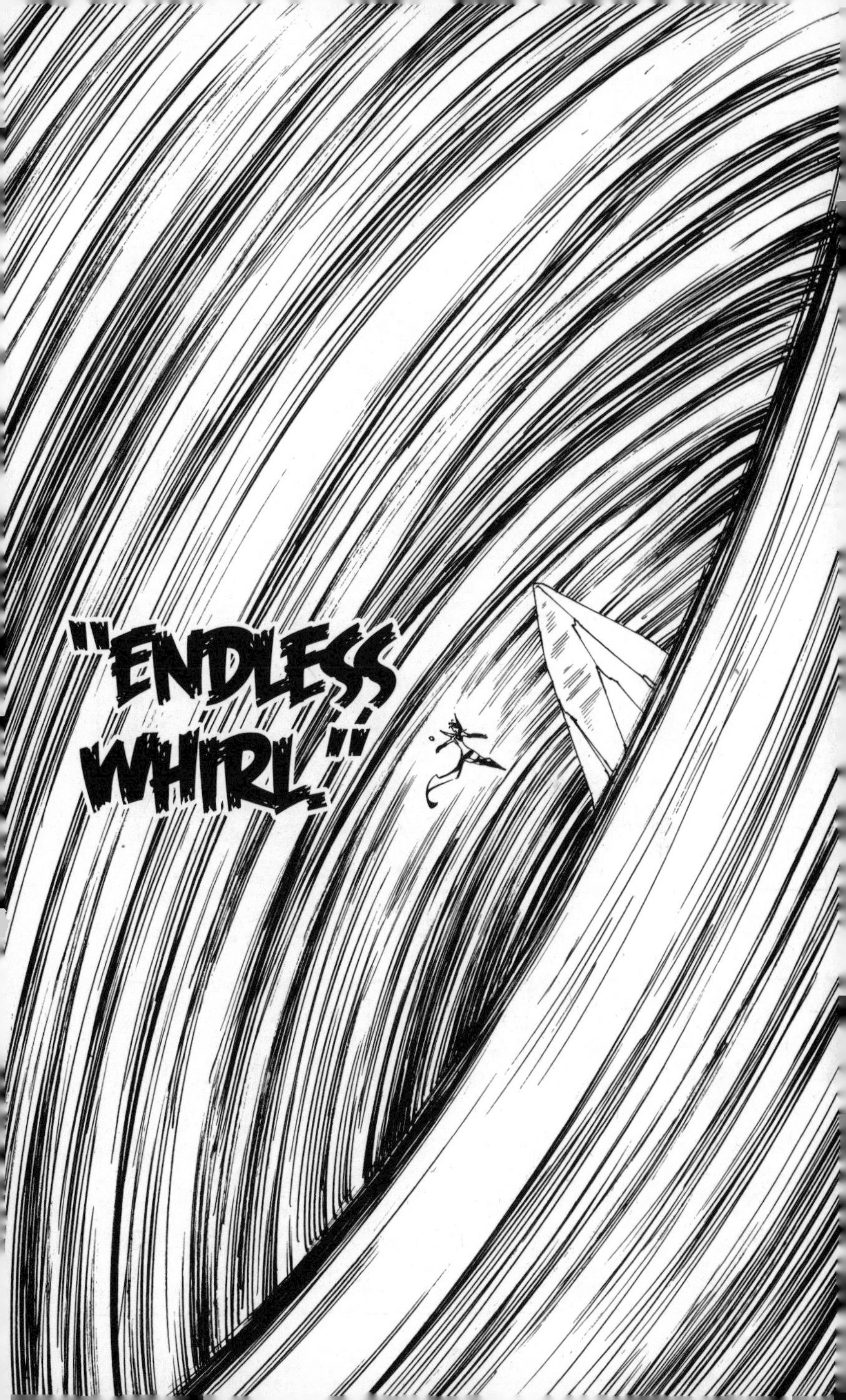
"ENDLESS WHIRL"

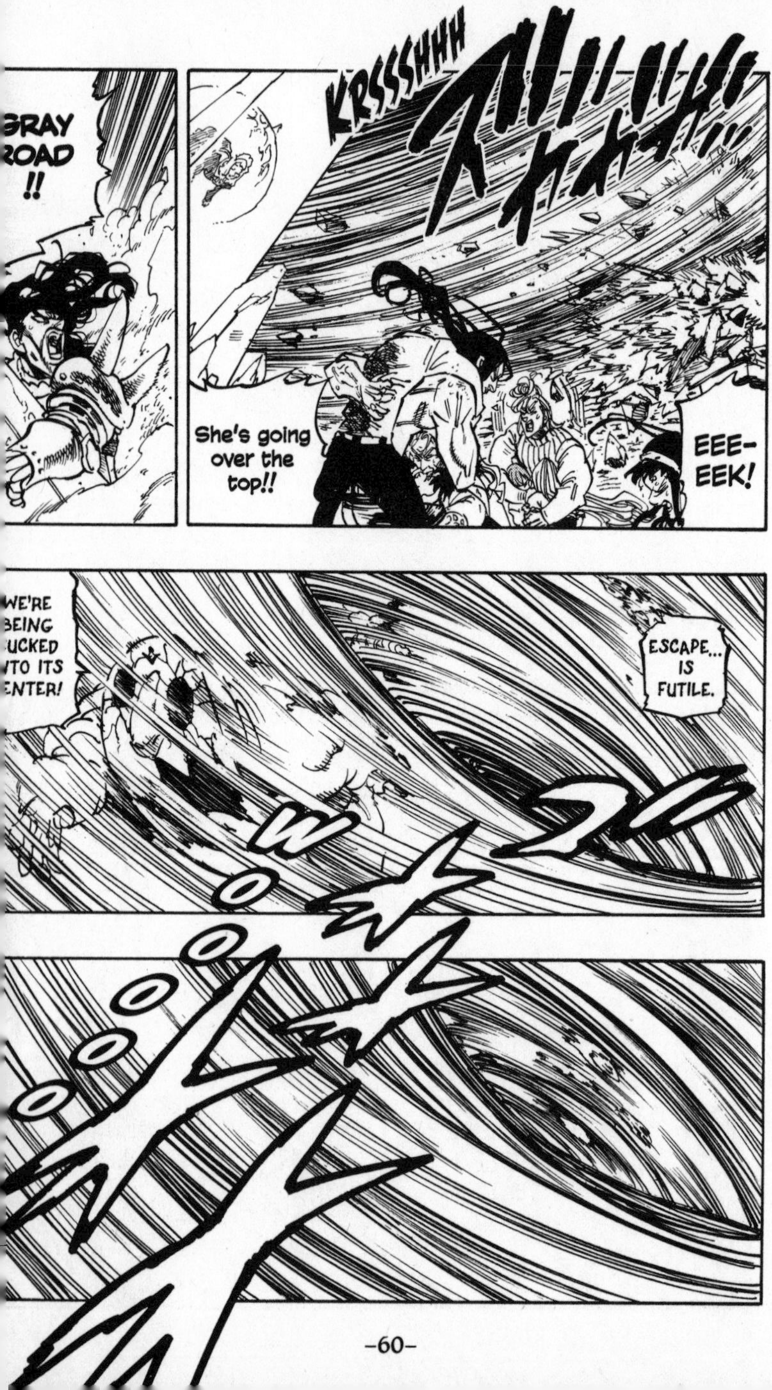
KRSSSHHH
She's going over the top!!
EEE-EEK!
GRAY ROAD !!
ESCAPE... IS FUTILE.
WE'RE BEING UCKED TO ITS ENTER!
WOOOOOO

TOP

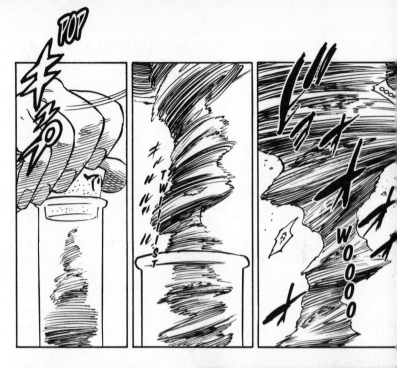

TWIST

WOOOO

Hm.
I got
myself
a good
guinea pig.

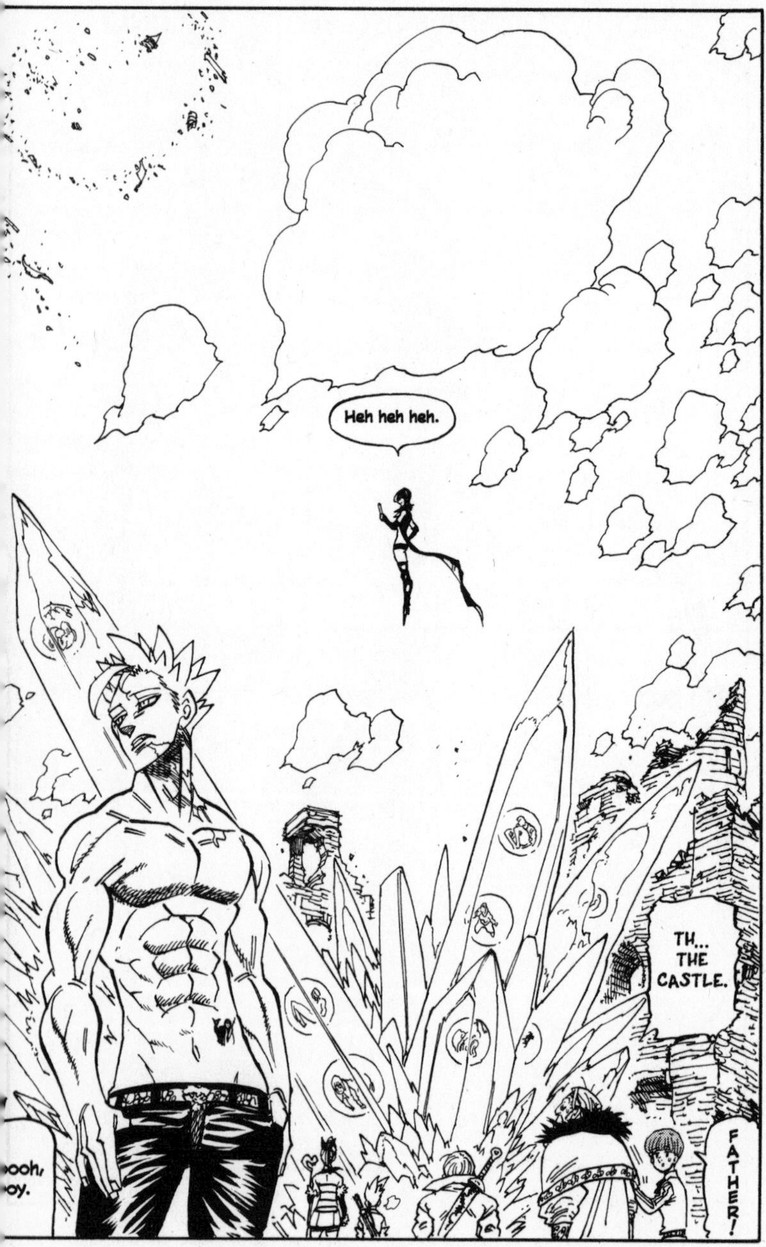
Heh heh heh.
TH... THE CASTLE.
FATHER!
ooh,
oy.

Chapter 192 - Hendrickson vs. Fraudrin

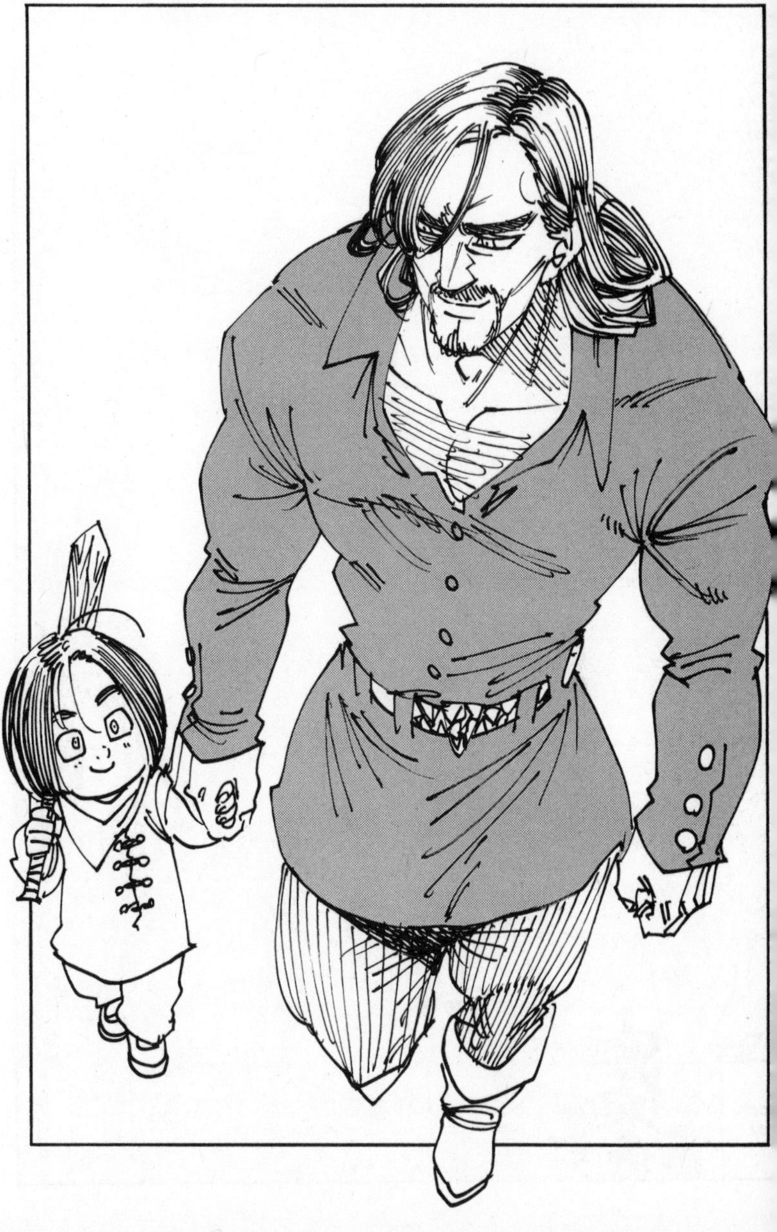

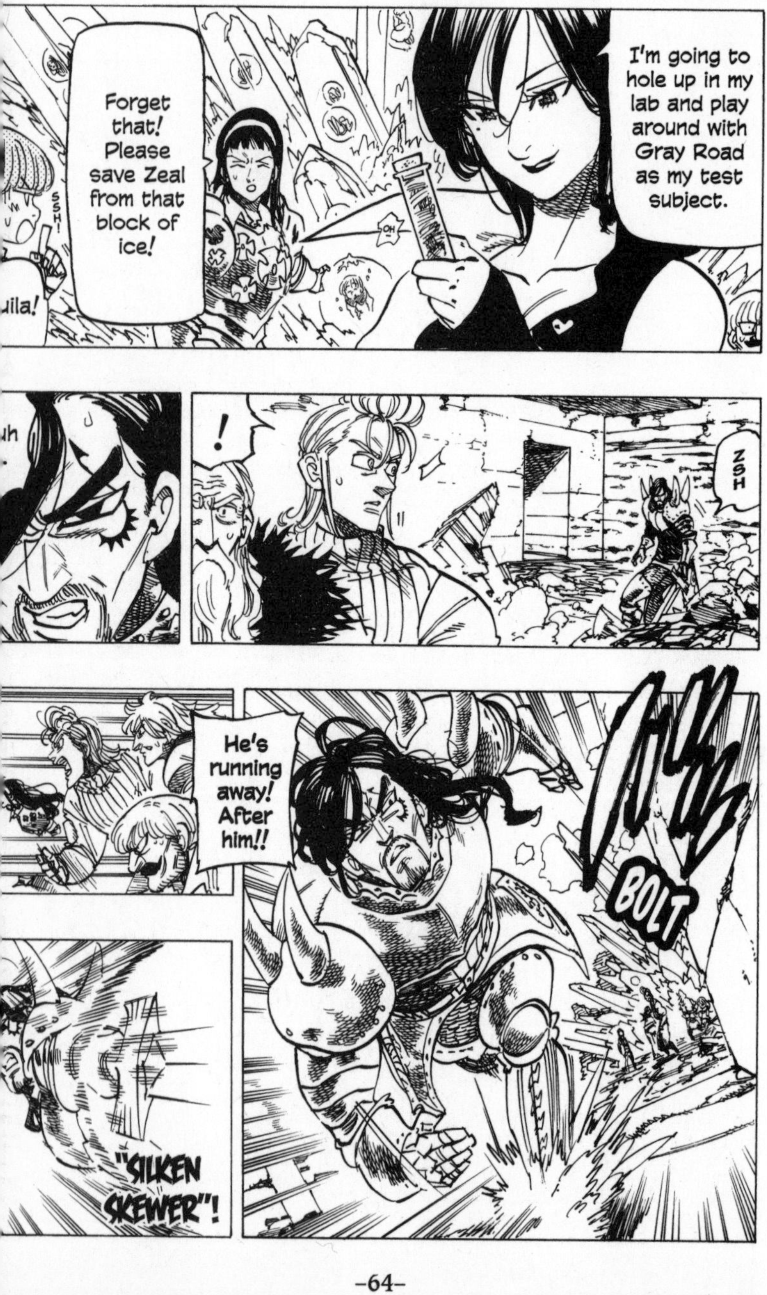
I'm going to hole up in my lab and play around with Gray Road as my test subject.
OH
Forget that! Please save Zeal from that block of ice!
SSH!
uila!
ZSH
!
uh
BOLT
He's running away! After him!!
"SILKEN SKEWER"!

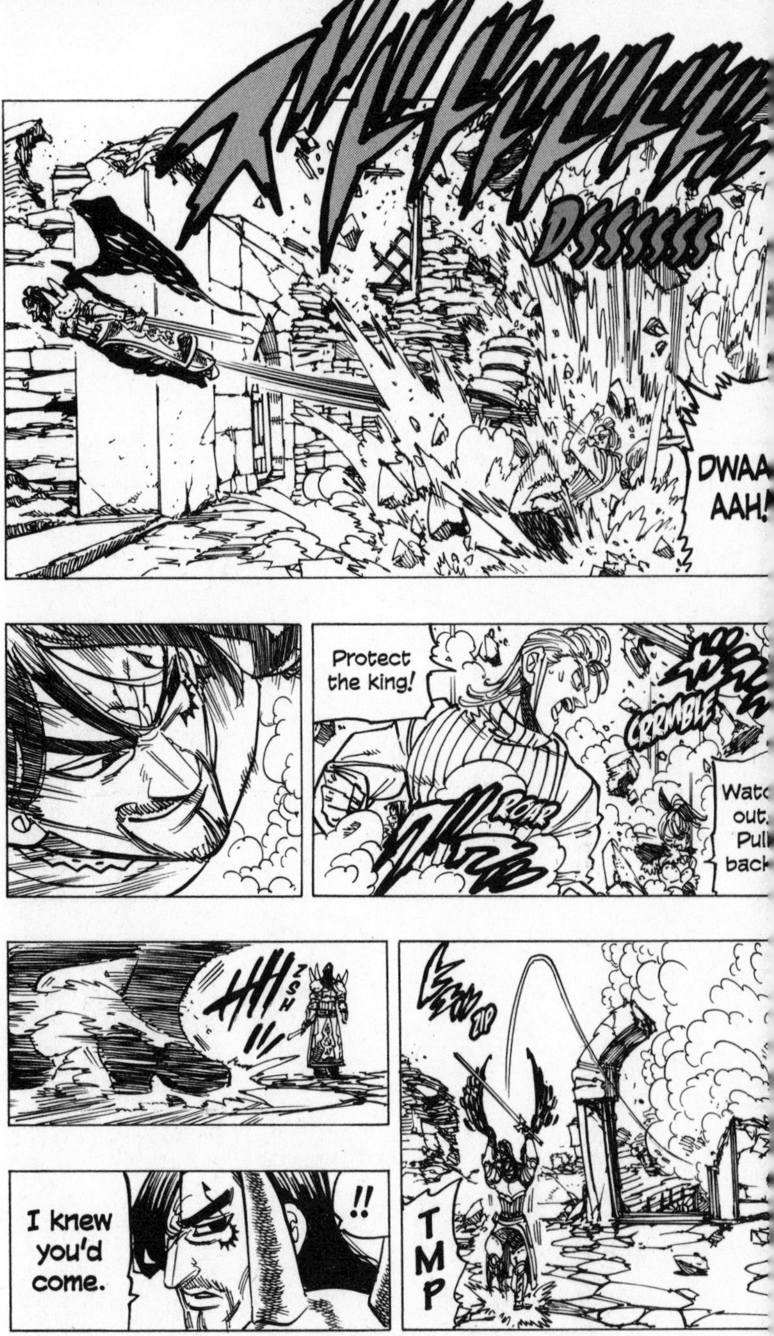
DSSSSS
DWAA AAH!
CRMBLE
Watc out. Pul back
Protect the king!
ROAR
ZIP
TMP
ZSH
!!
I knew you'd come.

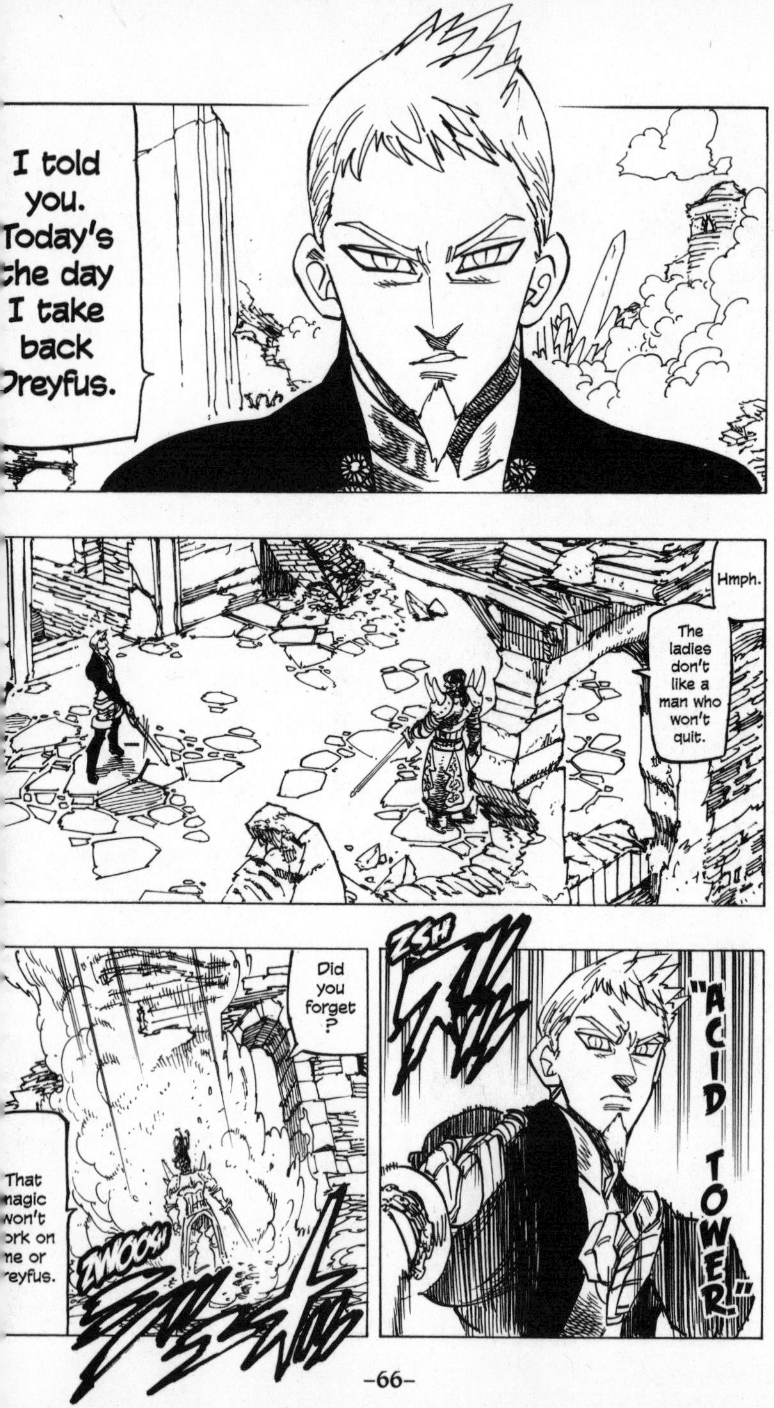

I told you. Today's the day I take back Dreyfus.
Hmph.
The ladies don't like a man who won't quit.
ZSH
"ACID TOWER"
Did you forget?
That magic won't work on me or Dreyfus.
ZWOOSH

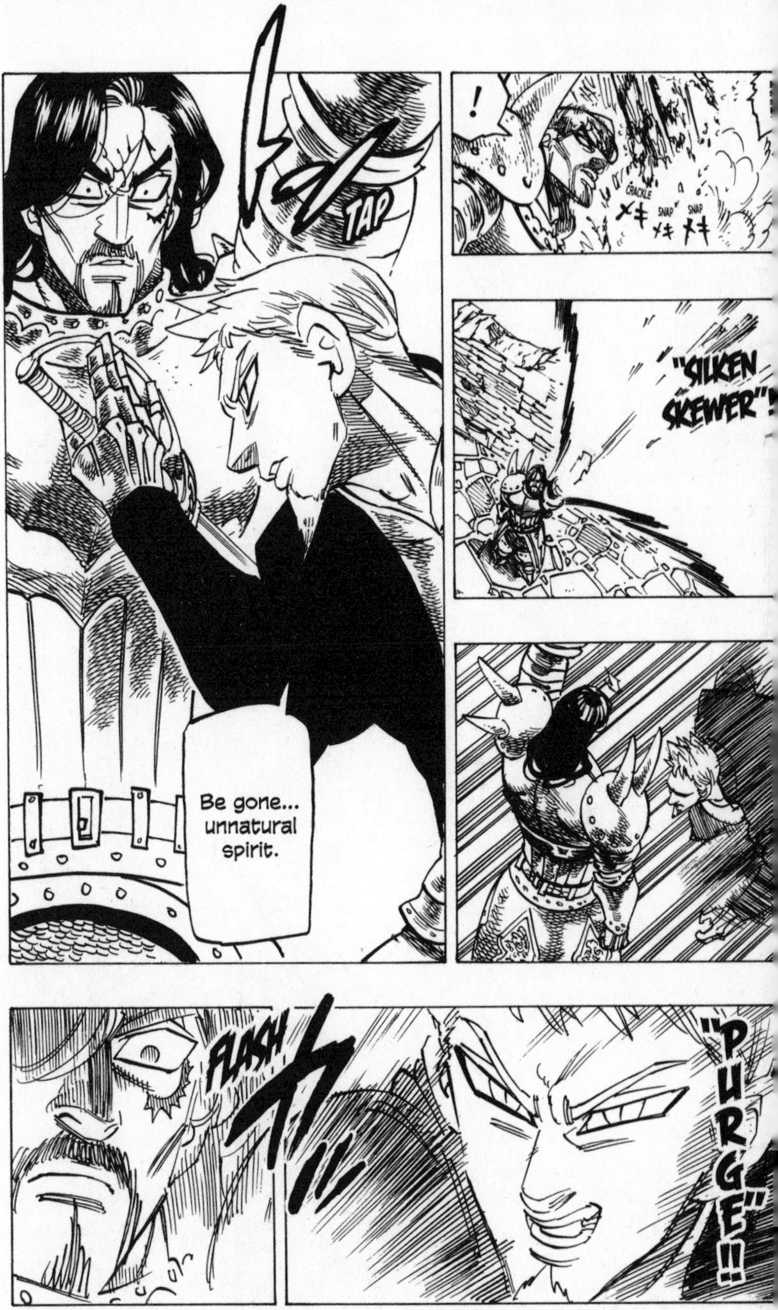
!
CRACKLE メキ
SNAP メキ
SNAP メキ
"SILKEN SKEWER"!
TAP
Be gone... unnatural spirit.
"PURGE"!!
FLASH

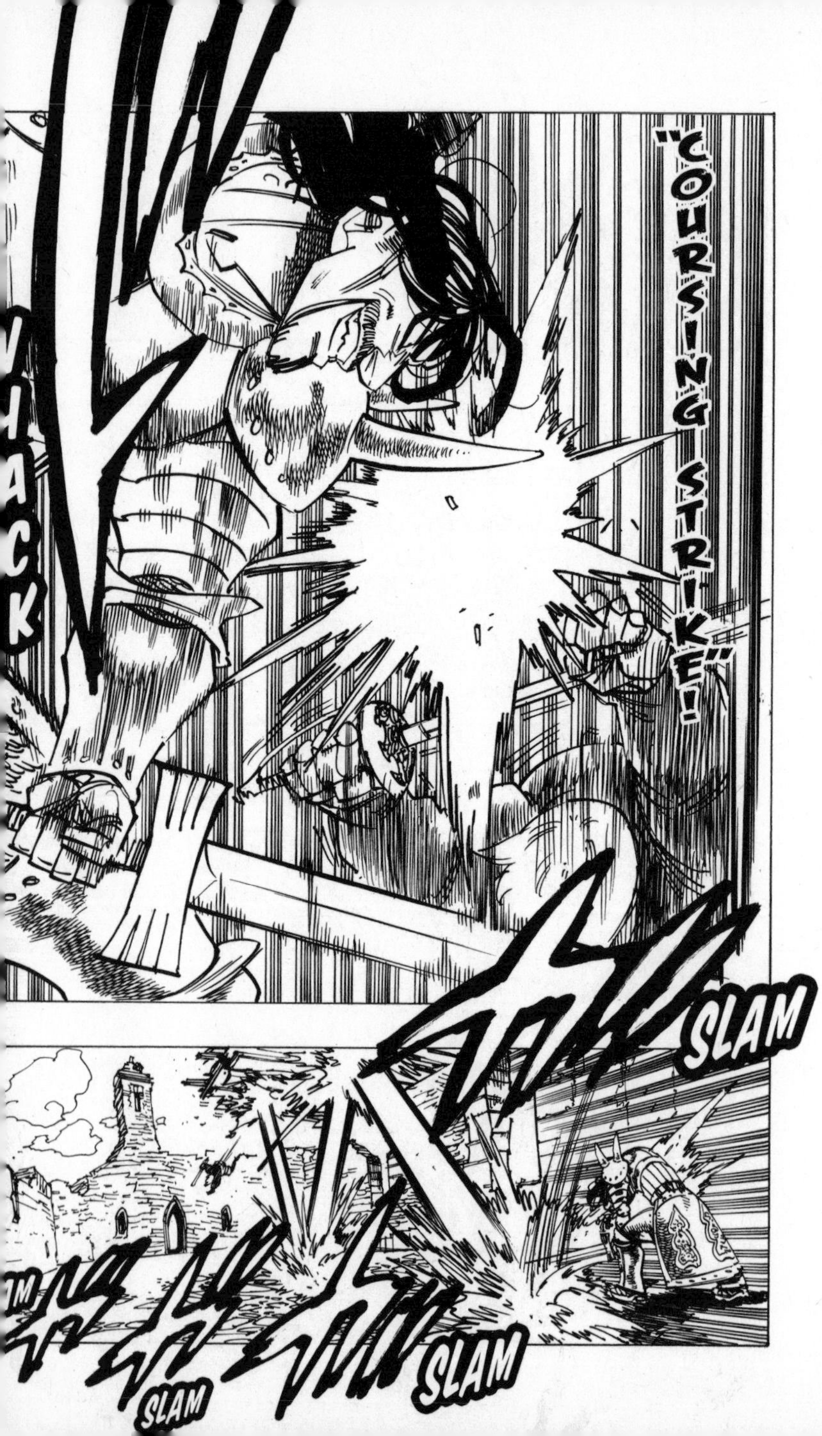

"COURSING STRIKE"!
WHACK
SLAM
SLAM
SLAM

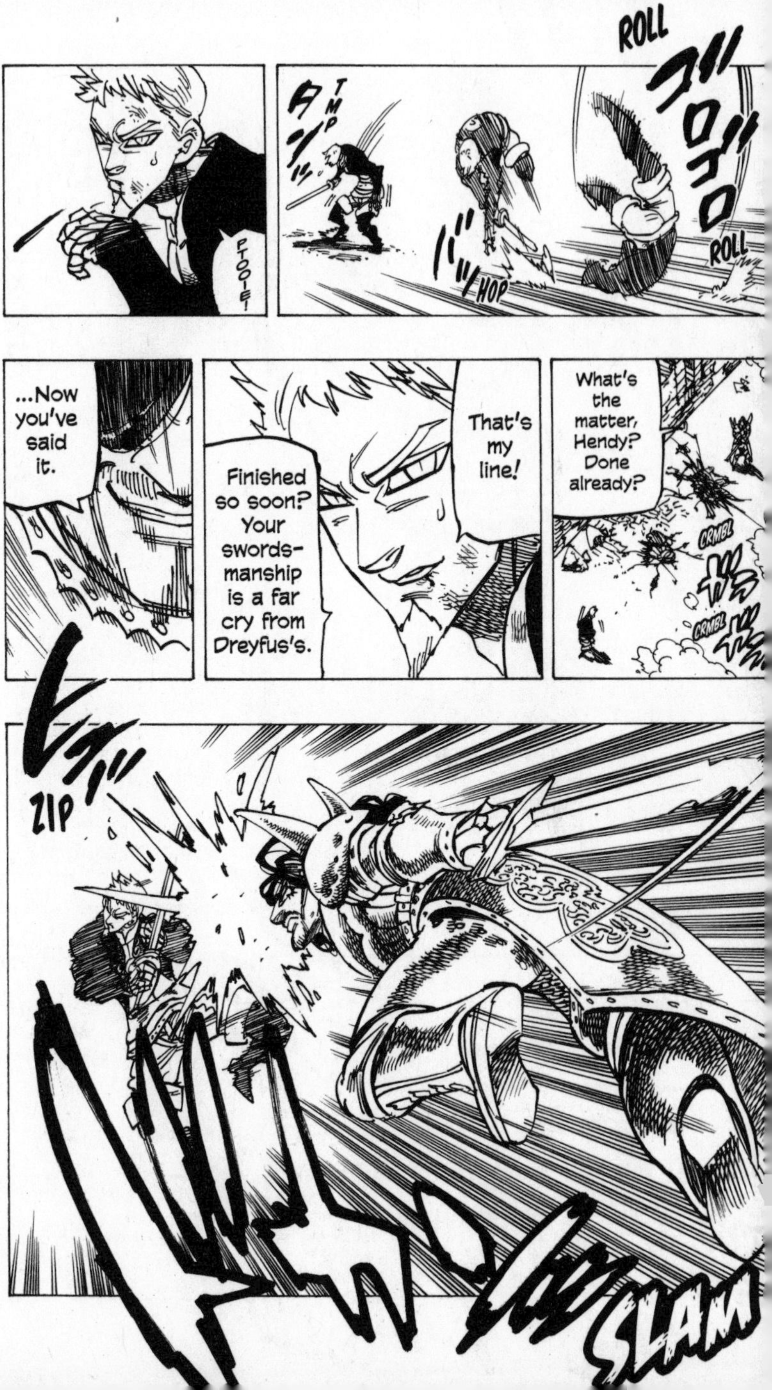
ROLL
ROLL
HOP
TMP
PTOOIE!
What's the matter, Hendy? Done already?
CRMBL
CRMBL
That's my line!
Finished so soon? Your swords-manship is a far cry from Dreyfus's.
...Now you've said it.
ZIP
SLAM

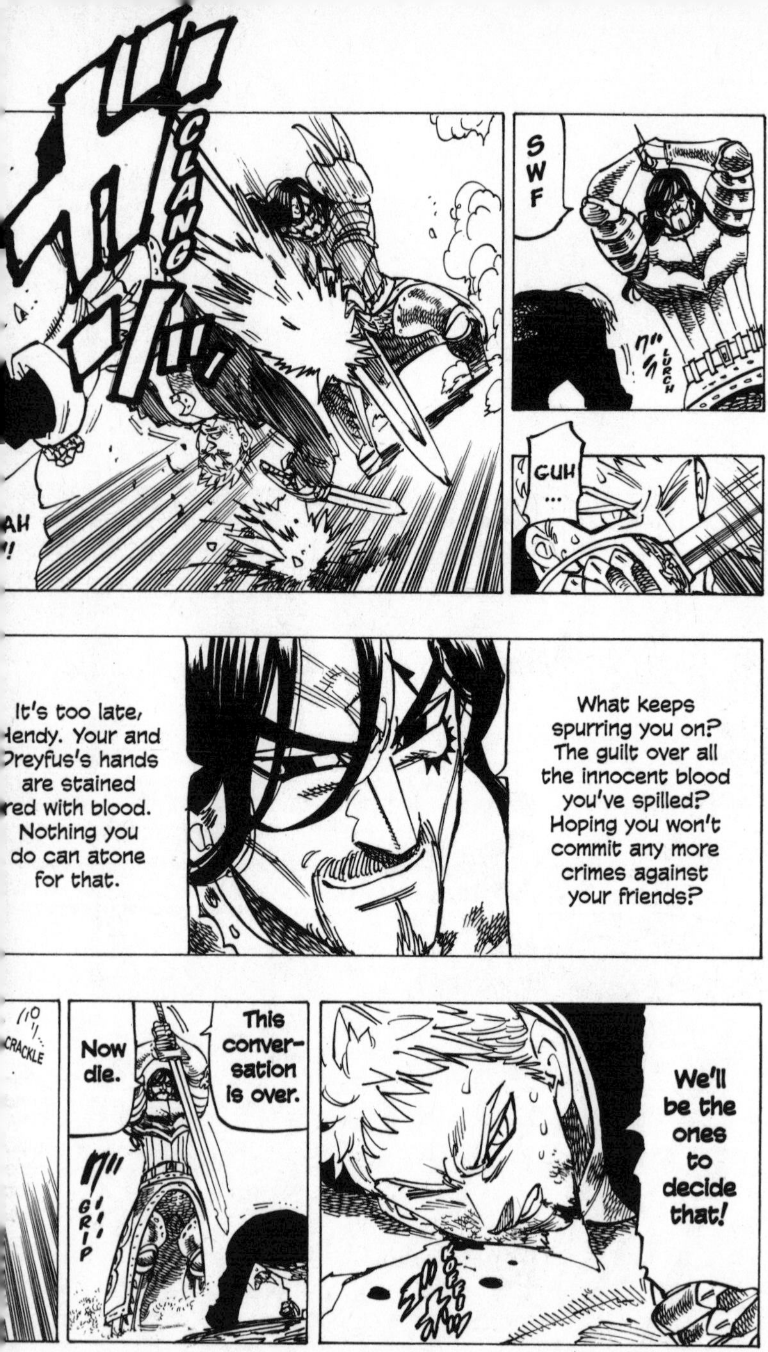

SWF
LURCH
GUH...
CLANG
AH!!
What keeps spurring you on? The guilt over all the innocent blood you've spilled? Hoping you won't commit any more crimes against your friends?
It's too late, Hendy. Your and Dreyfus's hands are stained red with blood. Nothing you do can atone for that.
We'll be the ones to decide that!
This conversation is over.
Now die.
GRIP
CRACKLE

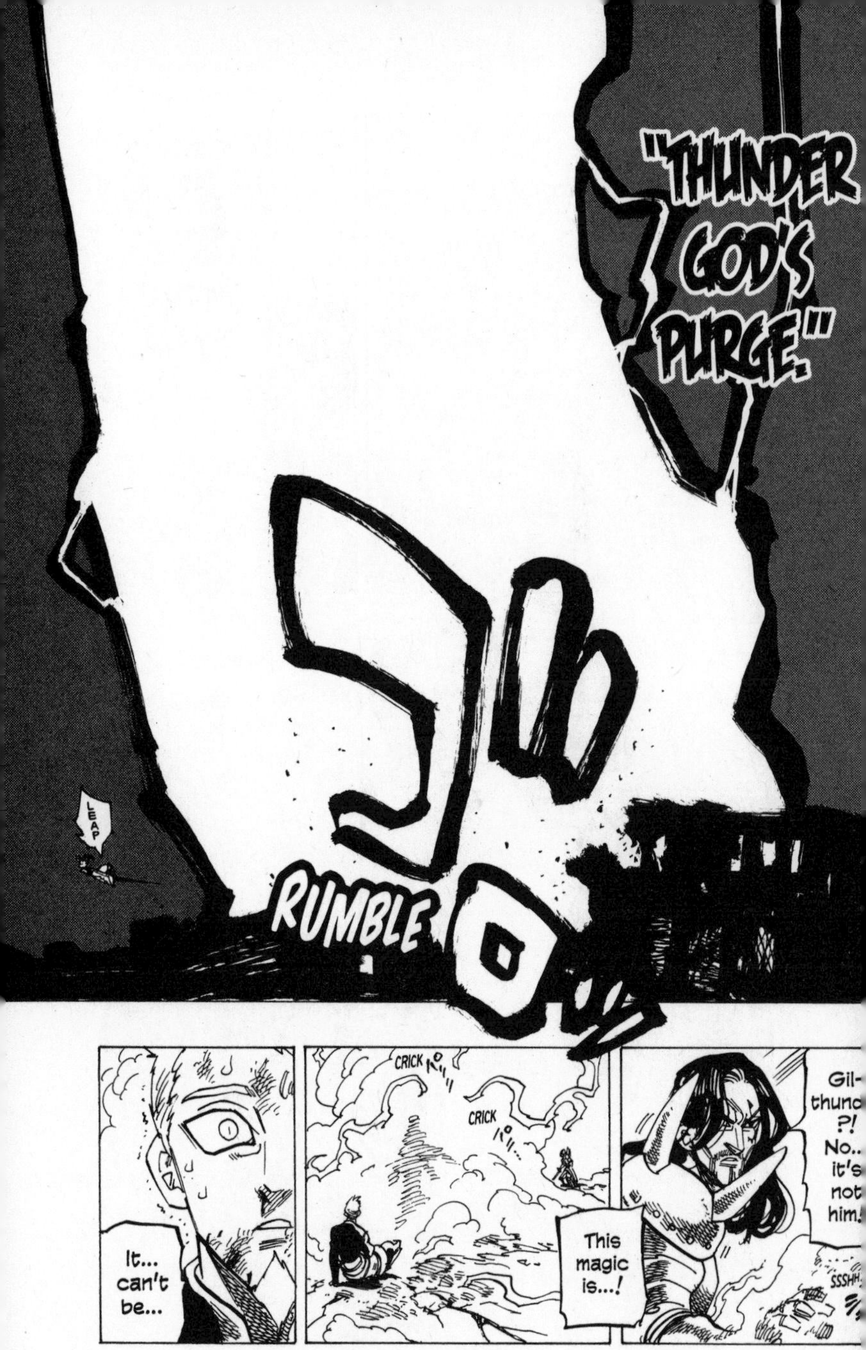
"THUNDER GOD'S PURGE."
LEAP
RUMBLE
Gil-thund ?! No.. it's not him.
SSSHH.
CRICK
CRICK
This magic is...!
It... can't be...

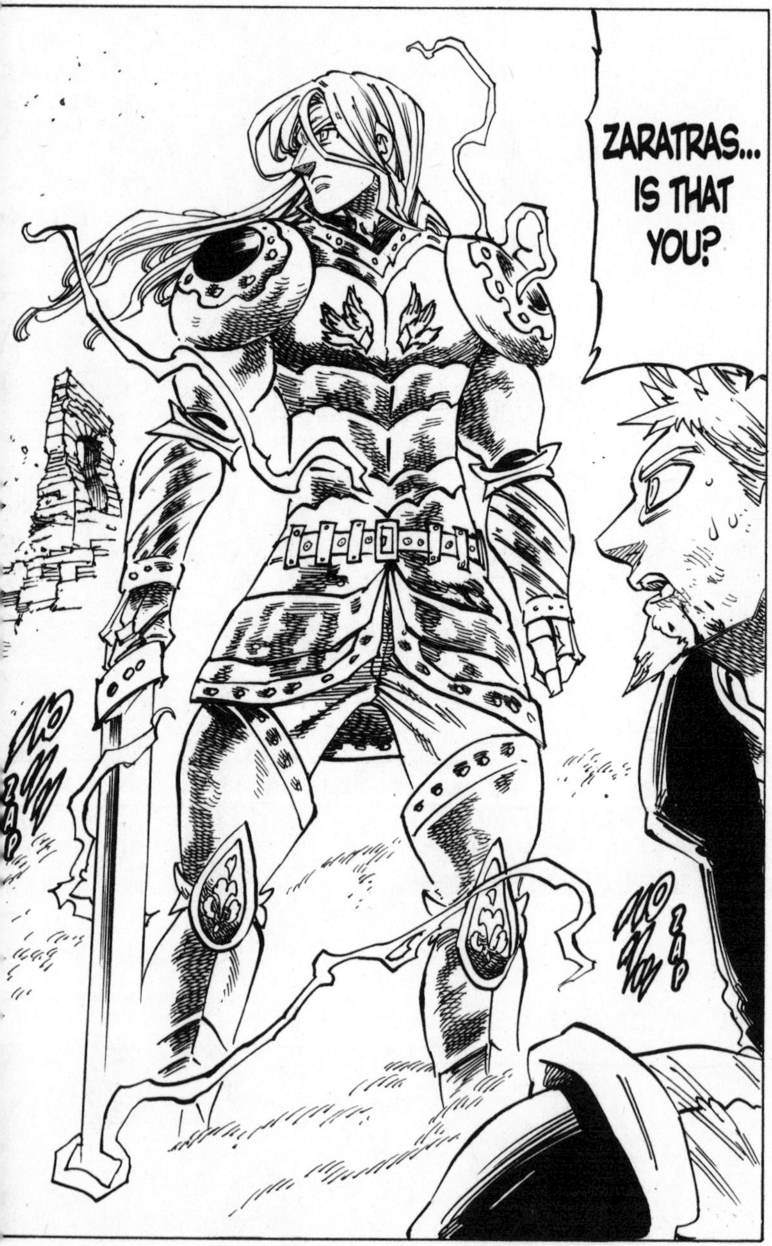
ZARATRAS... IS THAT YOU?
ZAP
ZAP

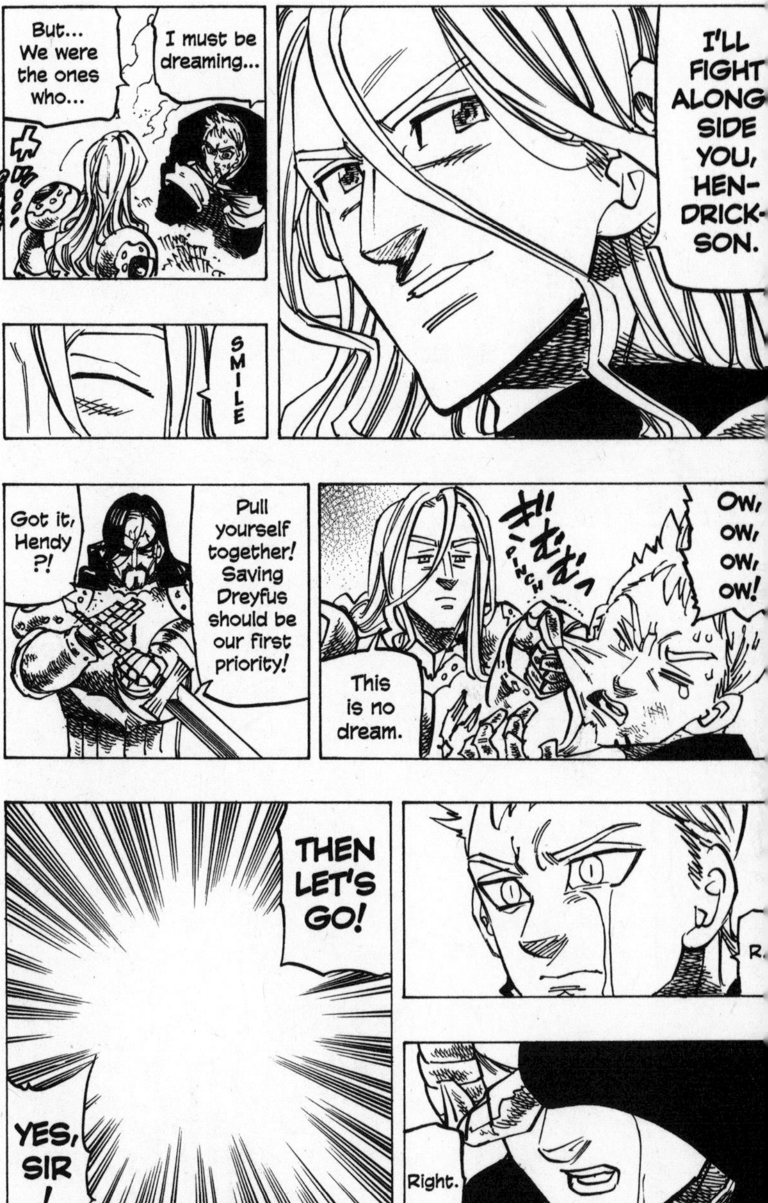
I'LL FIGHT ALONGSIDE YOU, HENDRICKSON.
I must be dreaming...
But... We were the ones who...
SMILE
Ow, ow, ow, ow!
PINCH
This is no dream.
Pull yourself together! Saving Dreyfus should be our first priority!
Got it, Hendy?!
R...
Right.
THEN LET'S GO!
YES, SIR!

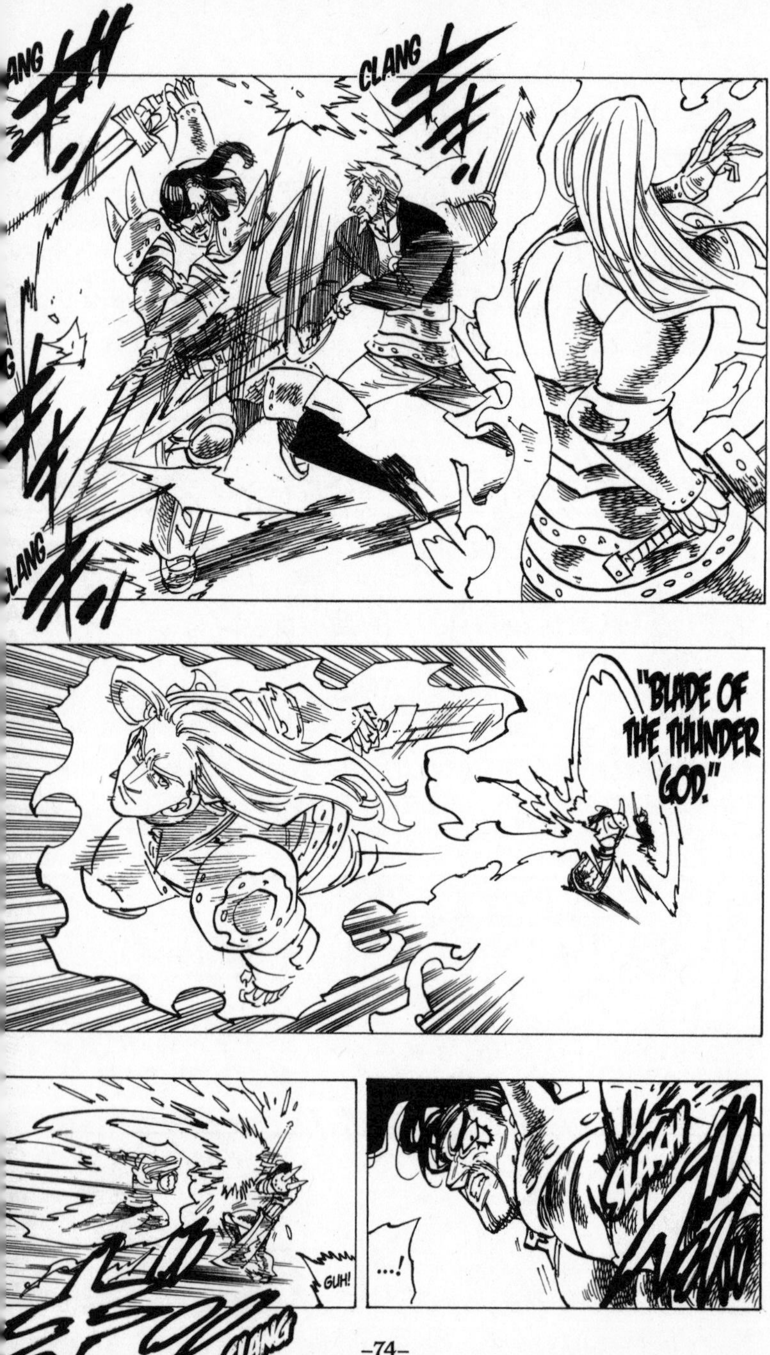
CLANG
CLANG
"BLADE OF THE THUNDER GOD."
SLASH
...!
GUH!
CLANG

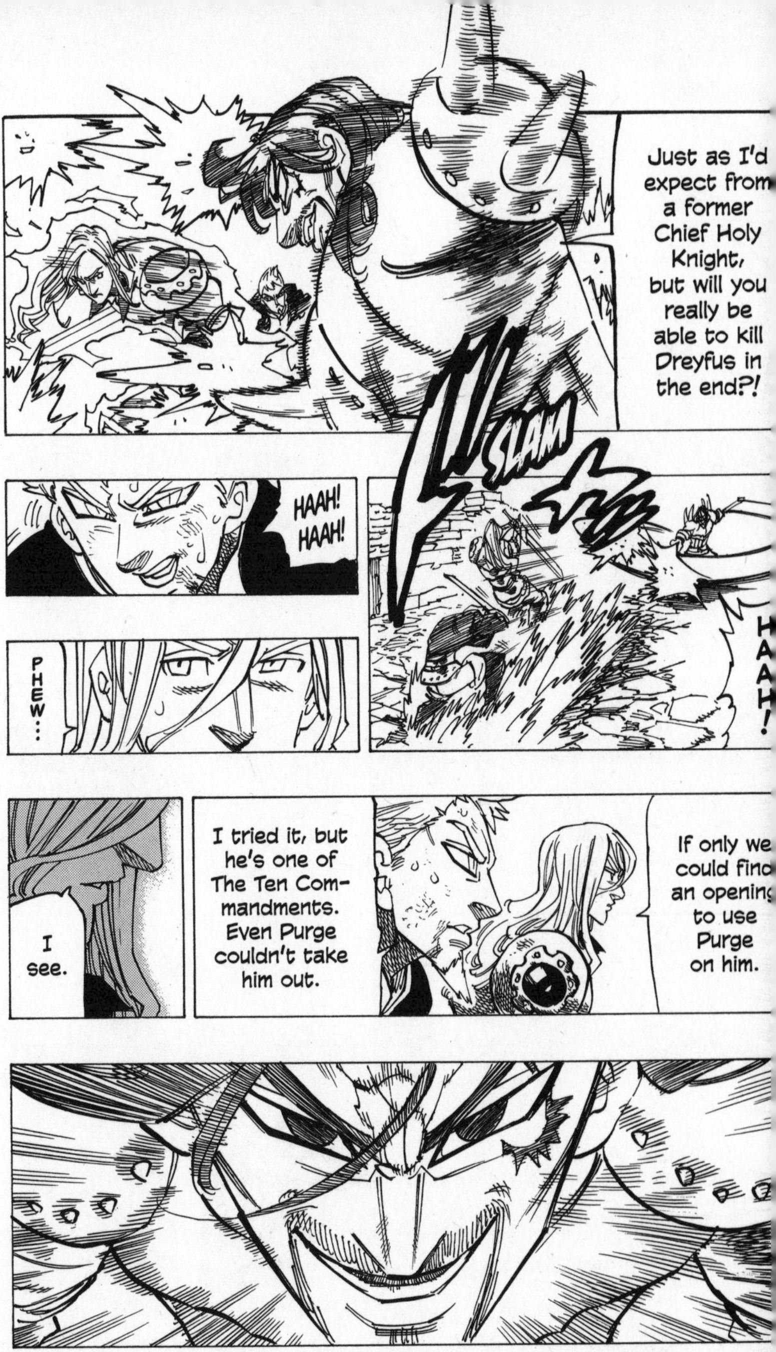
Just as I'd expect from a former Chief Holy Knight, but will you really be able to kill Dreyfus in the end?!
SLAM
HAAH!
HAAH! HAAH!
PHEW...
If only we could find an opening to use Purge on him.
I tried it, but he's one of The Ten Commandments. Even Purge couldn't take him out.
I see.

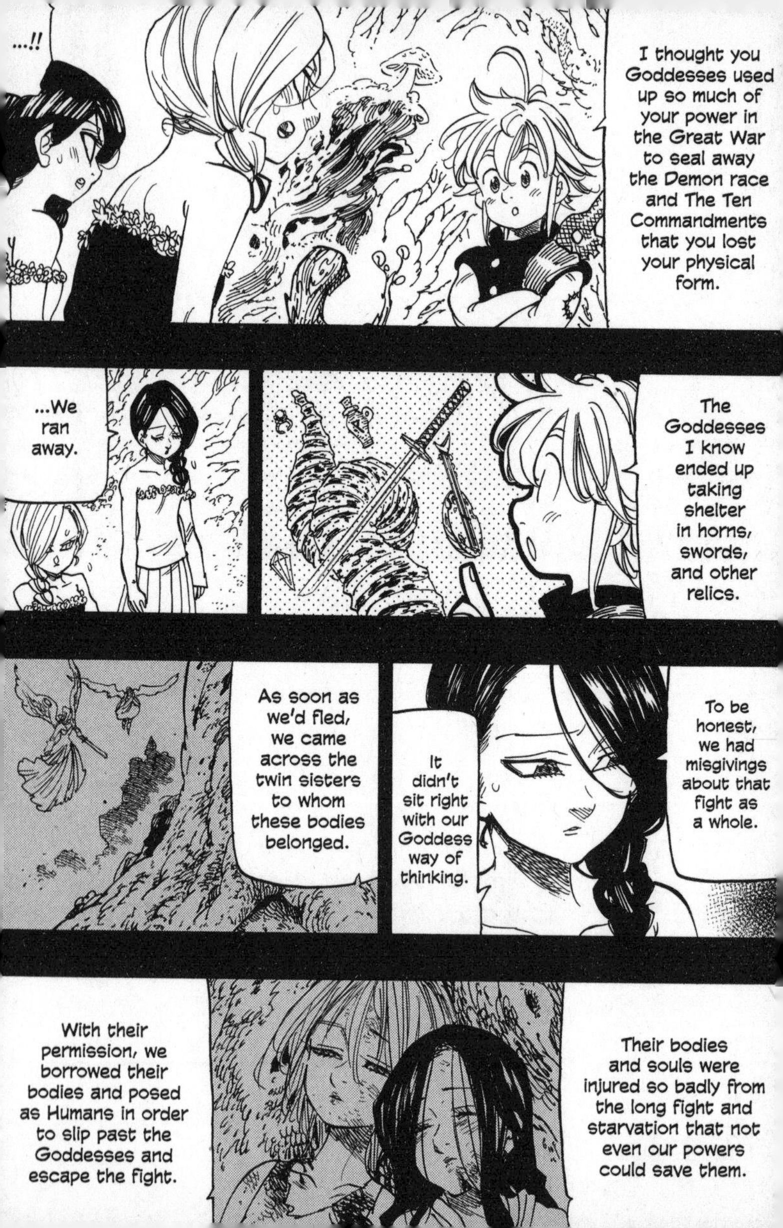
I thought you Goddesses used up so much of your power in the Great War to seal away the Demon race and The Ten Commandments that you lost your physical form.
...!!
The Goddesses I know ended up taking shelter in horns, swords, and other relics.
...We ran away.
To be honest, we had misgivings about that fight as a whole.
It didn't sit right with our Goddess way of thinking.
As soon as we'd fled, we came across the twin sisters to whom these bodies belonged.
Their bodies and souls were injured so badly from the long fight and starvation that not even our powers could save them.
With their permission, we borrowed their bodies and posed as Humans in order to slip past the Goddesses and escape the fight.

Chapter 195 – The Determined Chief Holy Knight

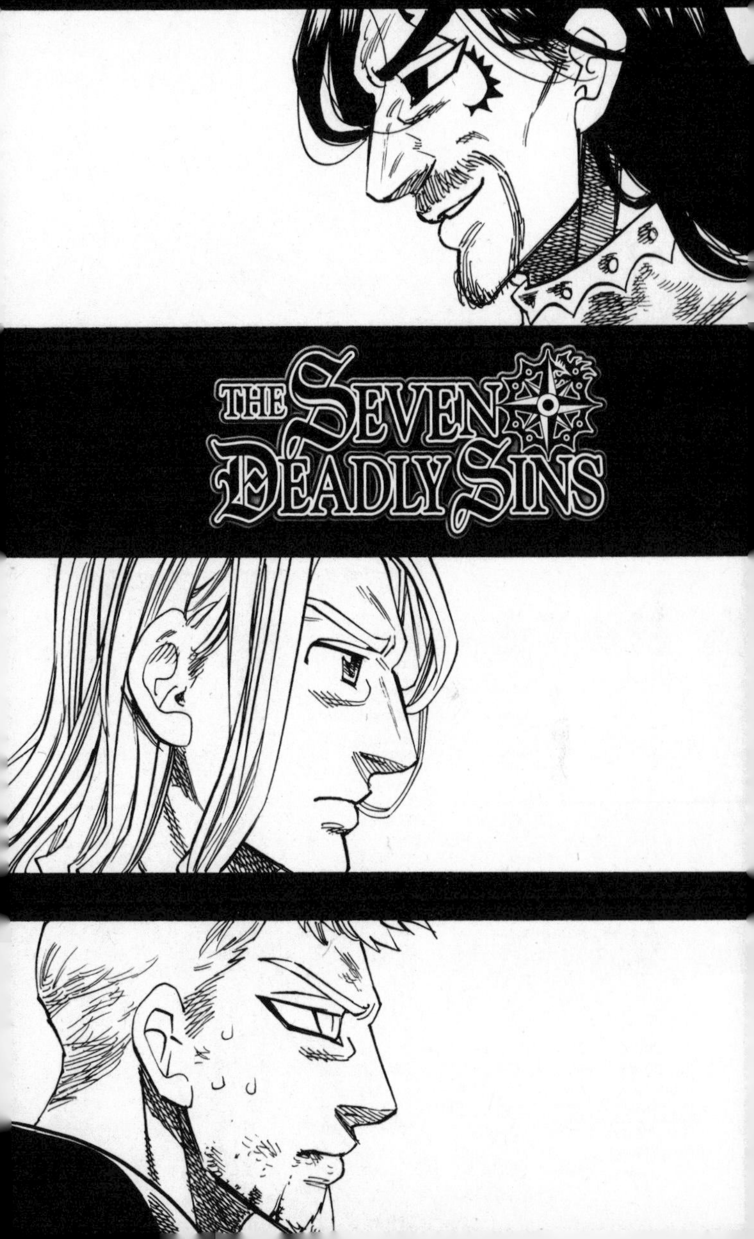
THE SEVEN DEADLY SINS

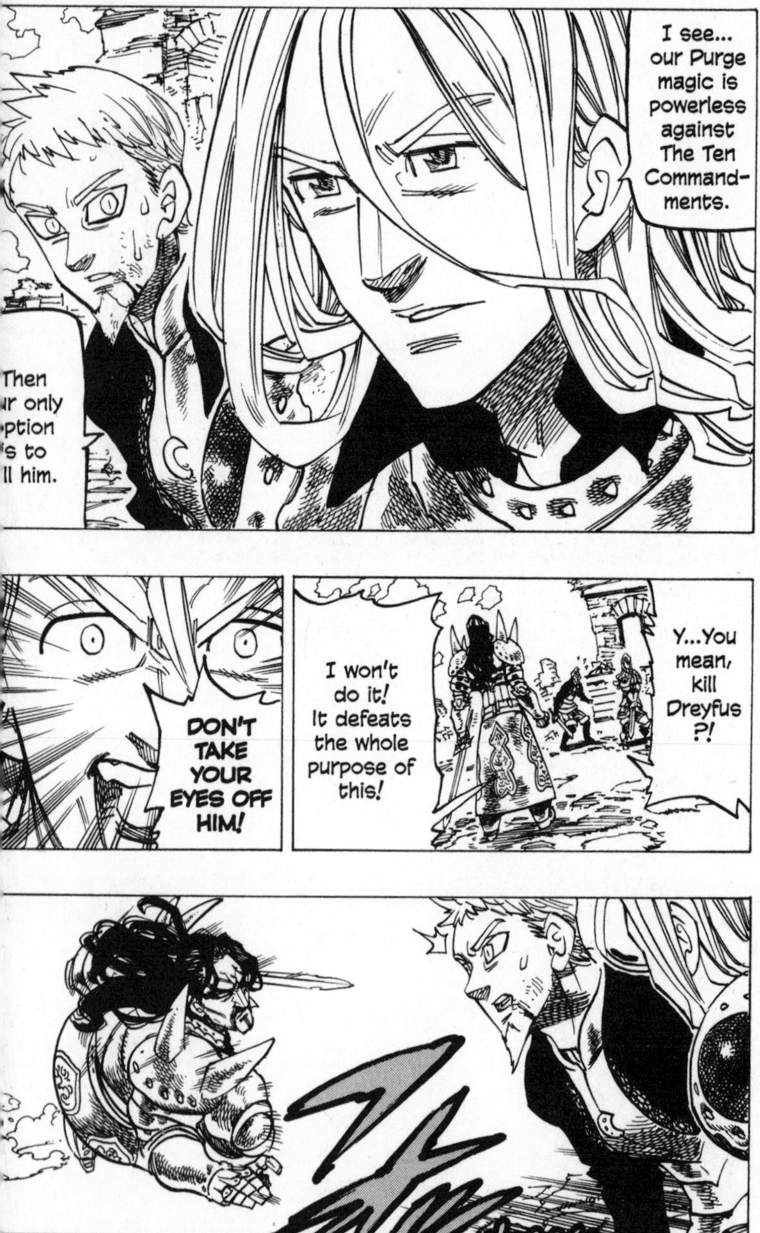
I see... our Purge magic is powerless against The Ten Command-ments.
Then r only ption 's to ll him.
Y...You mean, kill Dreyfus?!
I won't do it! It defeats the whole purpose of this!
DON'T TAKE YOUR EYES OFF HIM!
WHOOSH

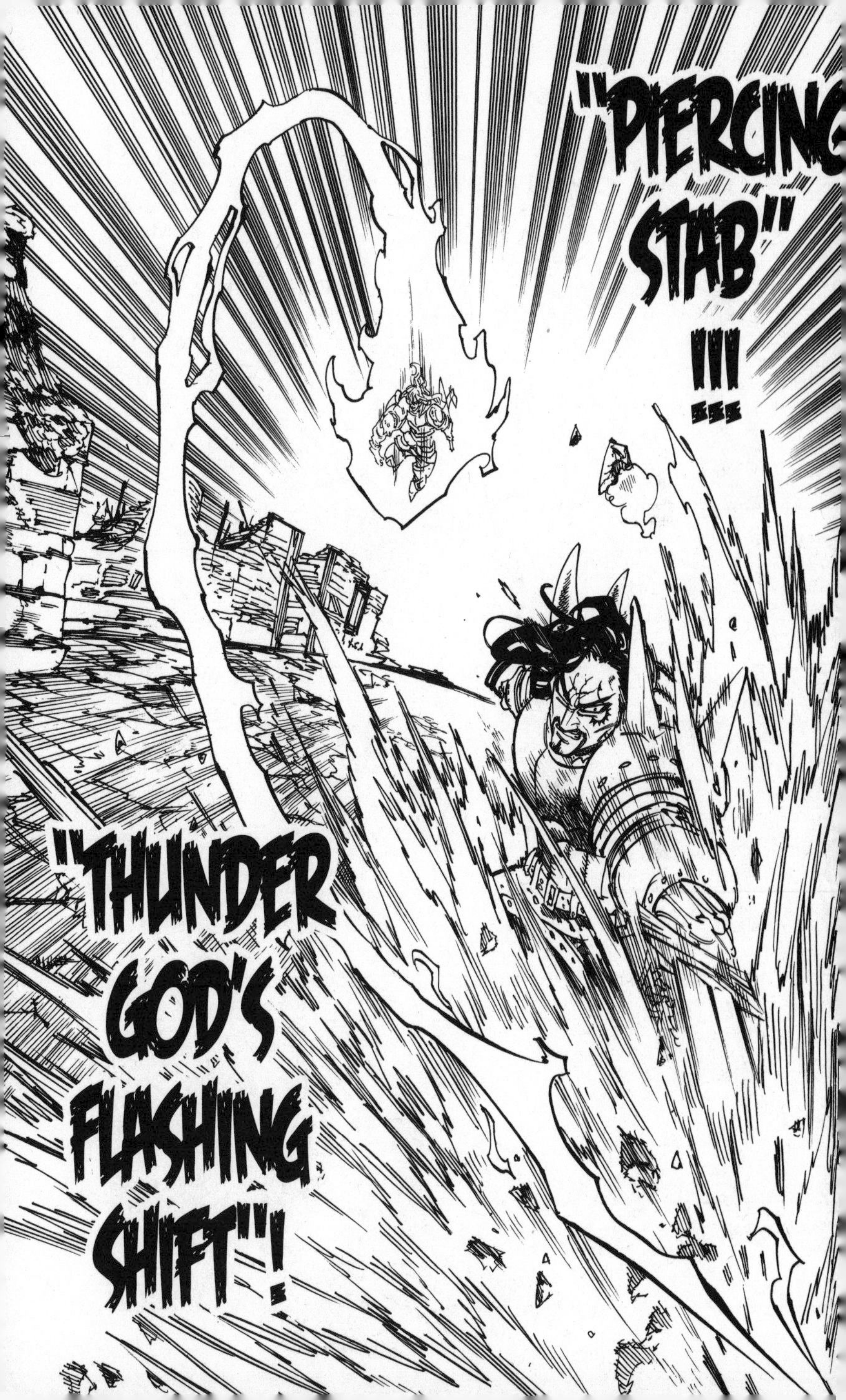
"PIERCING STAB"!!!
"THUNDER GOD'S FLASHING SHIFT"!

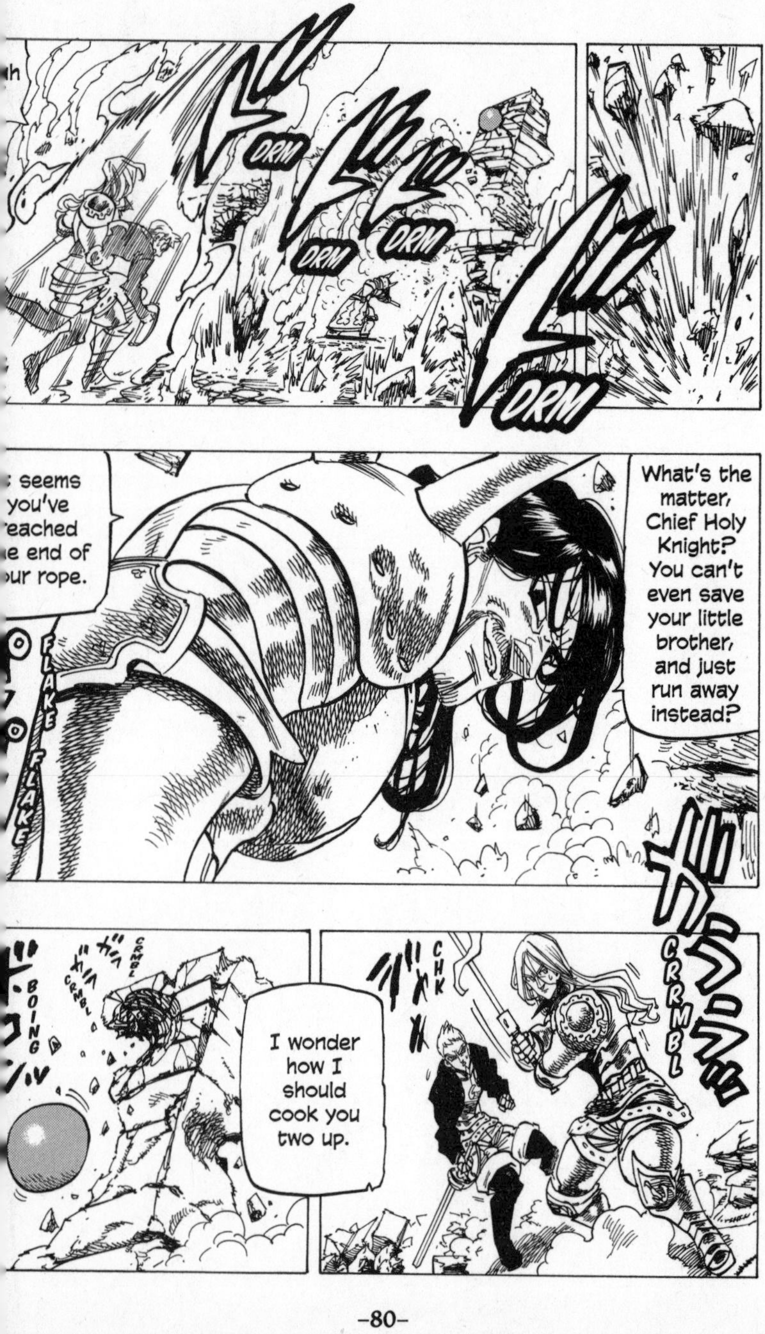
DRM
DRM
DRM
DRM
DRM
What's the matter, Chief Holy Knight? You can't even save your little brother, and just run away instead?
seems you've reached e end of ur rope.
FLAKE FLAKE
CRRMBL
CHK
I wonder how I should cook you two up.
CRMBL
CRMBL
BOING

YANK

What... is this?

That's ...

?

SPI...

FLOOMP

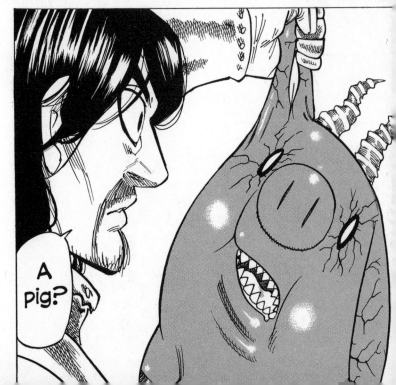

A pig?

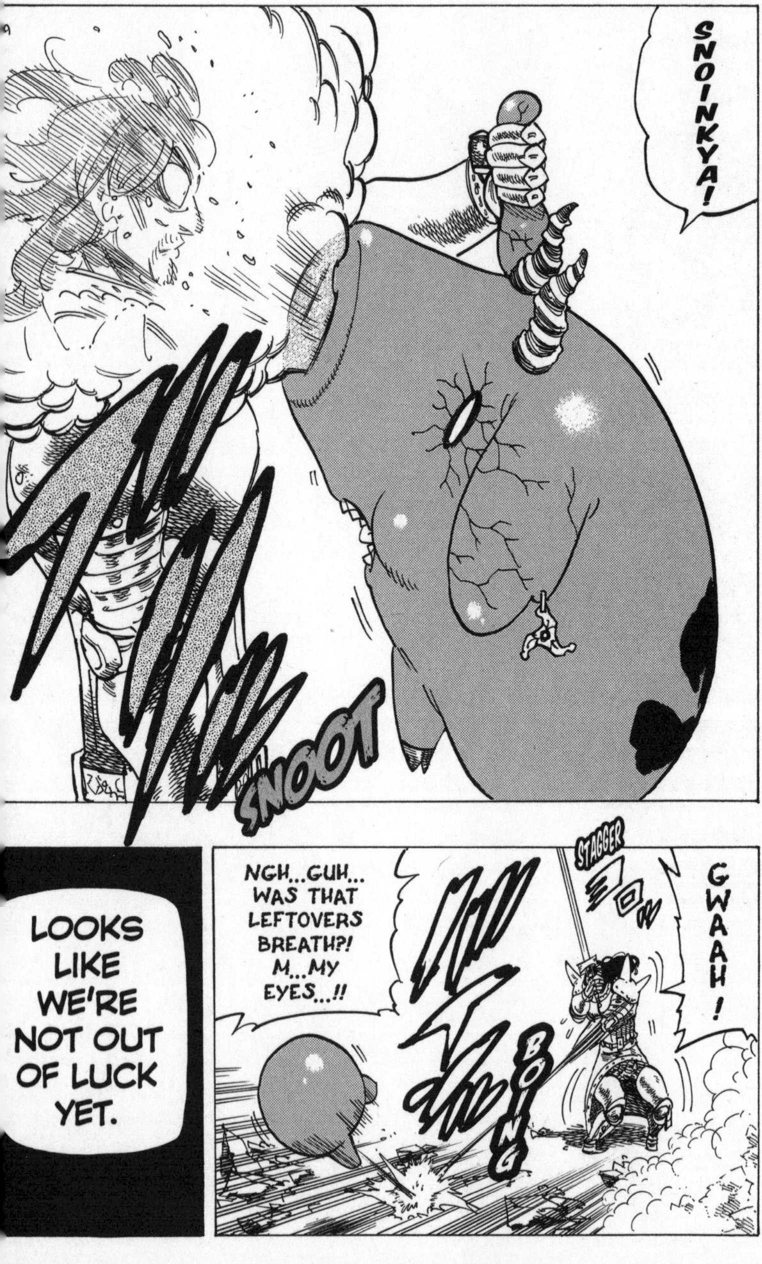
SNOINKYA!
SNOOT
GWAAH!
STAGGER
NGH...GUH... WAS THAT LEFTOVERS BREATH?! M...MY EYES...!!
BOING
LOOKS LIKE WE'RE NOT OUT OF LUCK YET.

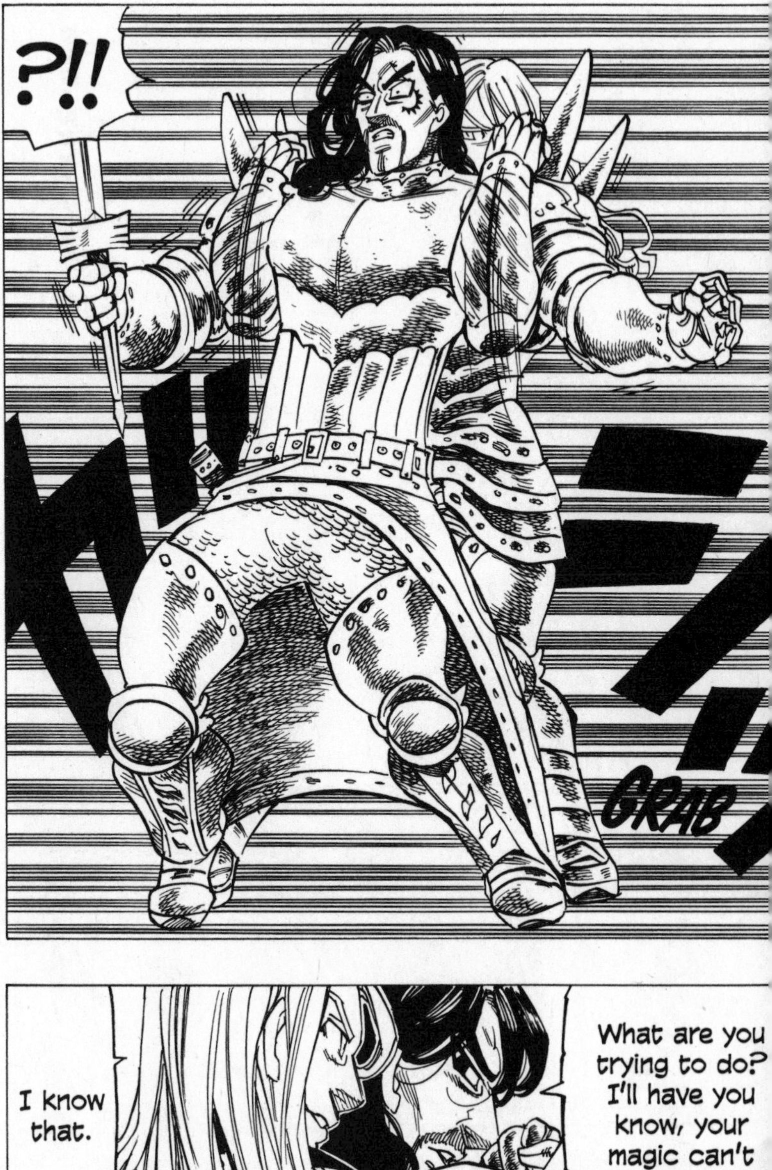
?!!
GRAB
What are you trying to do? I'll have you know, your magic can't kill me.
I know that.

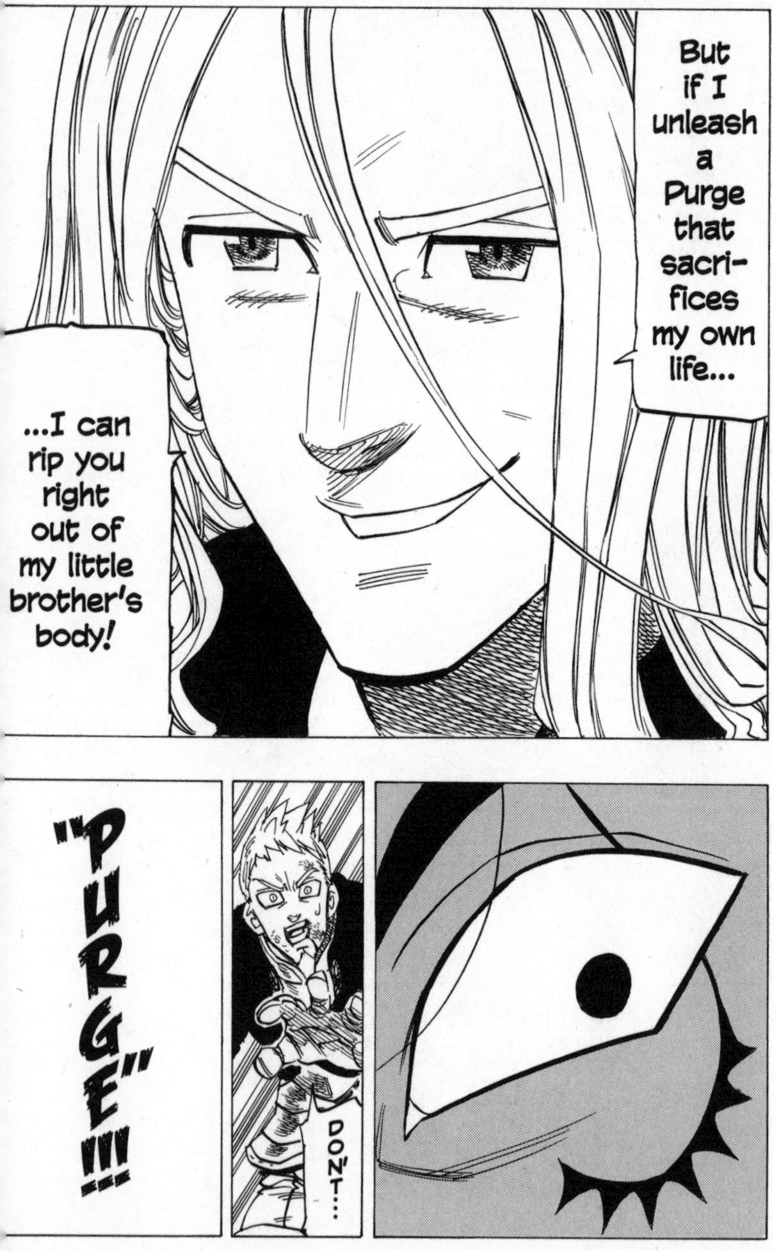
But if I unleash a Purge that sacri-fices my own life...
...I can rip you right out of my little brother's body!
DON'T...
"PURGE"!!!

Ow...
My
eyes.

Wh...
What
was
that...?

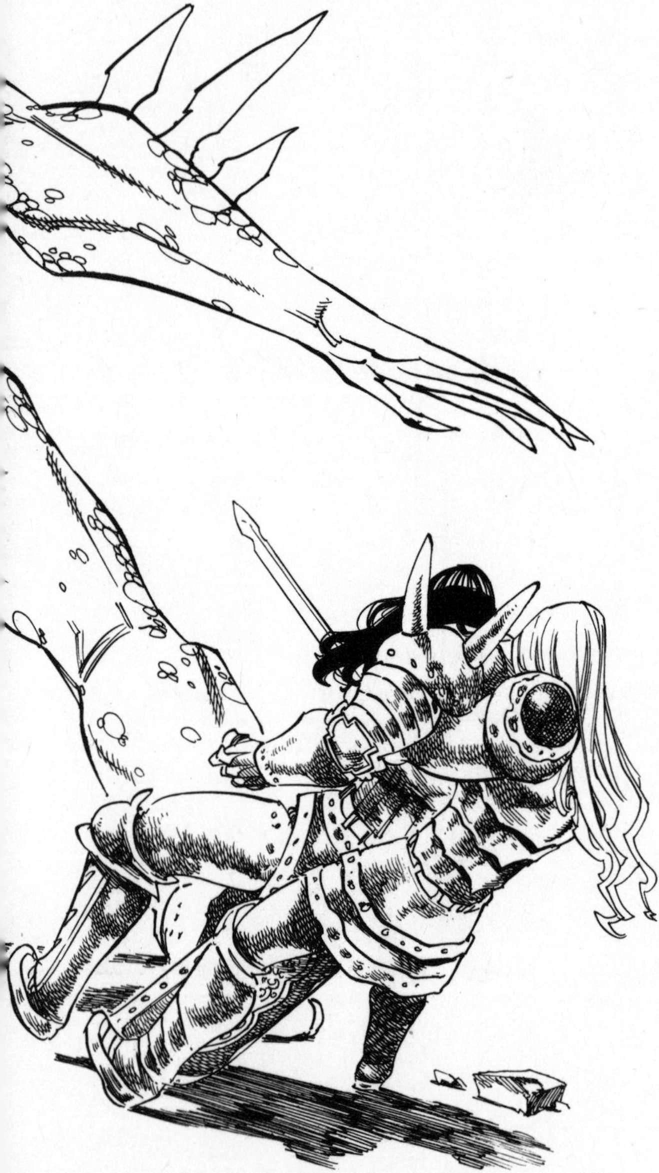

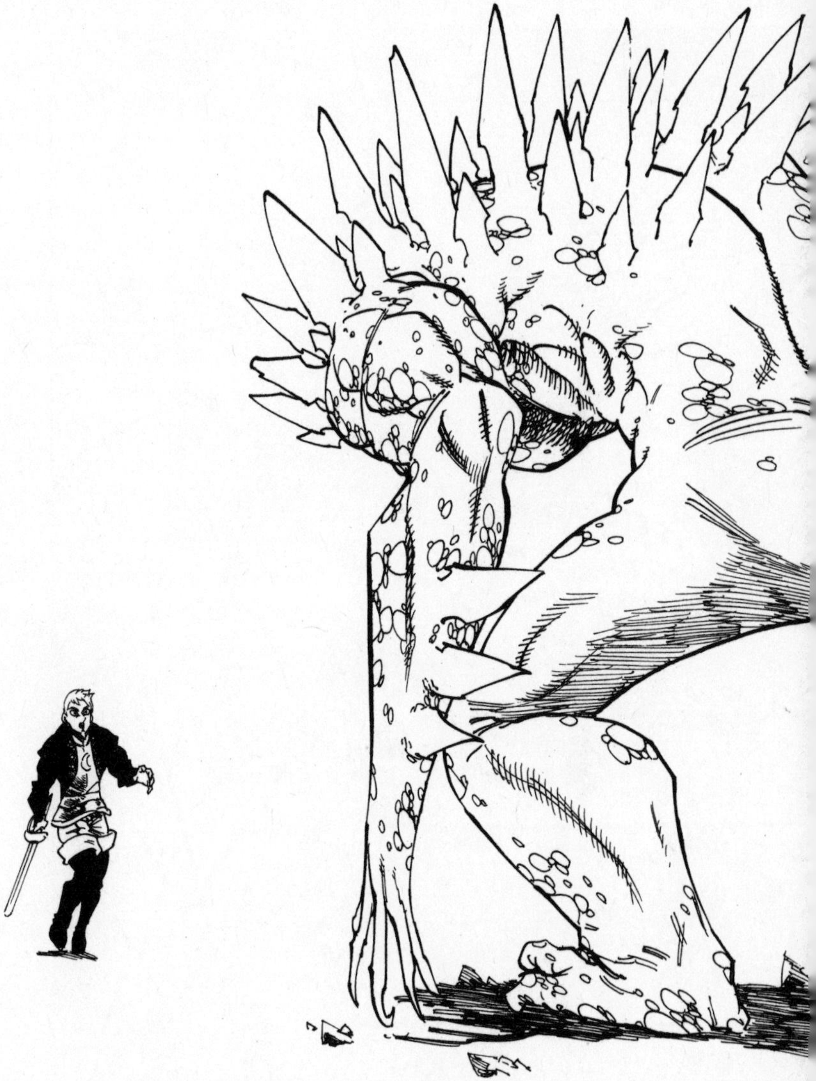

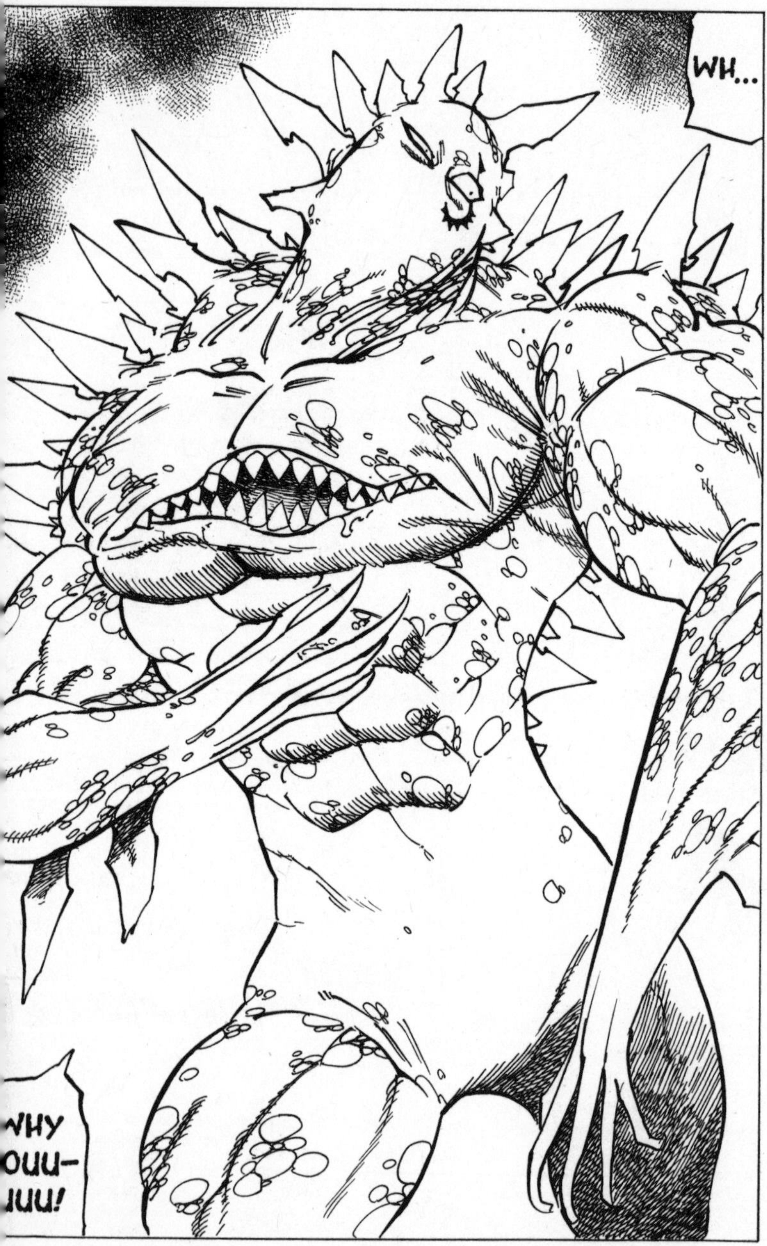
WH...
WHY
OUU-
UUU!

!!
How hideous! So this is the true form of The Ten Command-ments' Fraudrin!
DREYFUS!
ZARATRAS!
YOU'D WASTE YOUR LIFE FOR ANOTHER? HOW UTTERLY FOOLISH!
RRRUMBLE
YOU MAY HAVE EXCHANGED YOUR LIFE TO DRIVE ME OUT OF DREYFUS, BUT I'LL JUST GO RIGHT BACK IN.
NOT ON MY WATCH !!

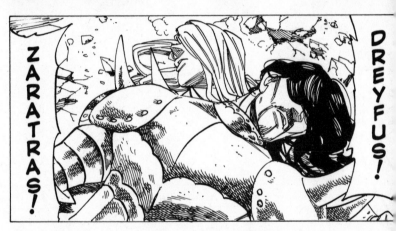

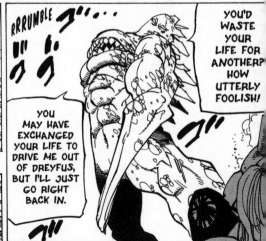

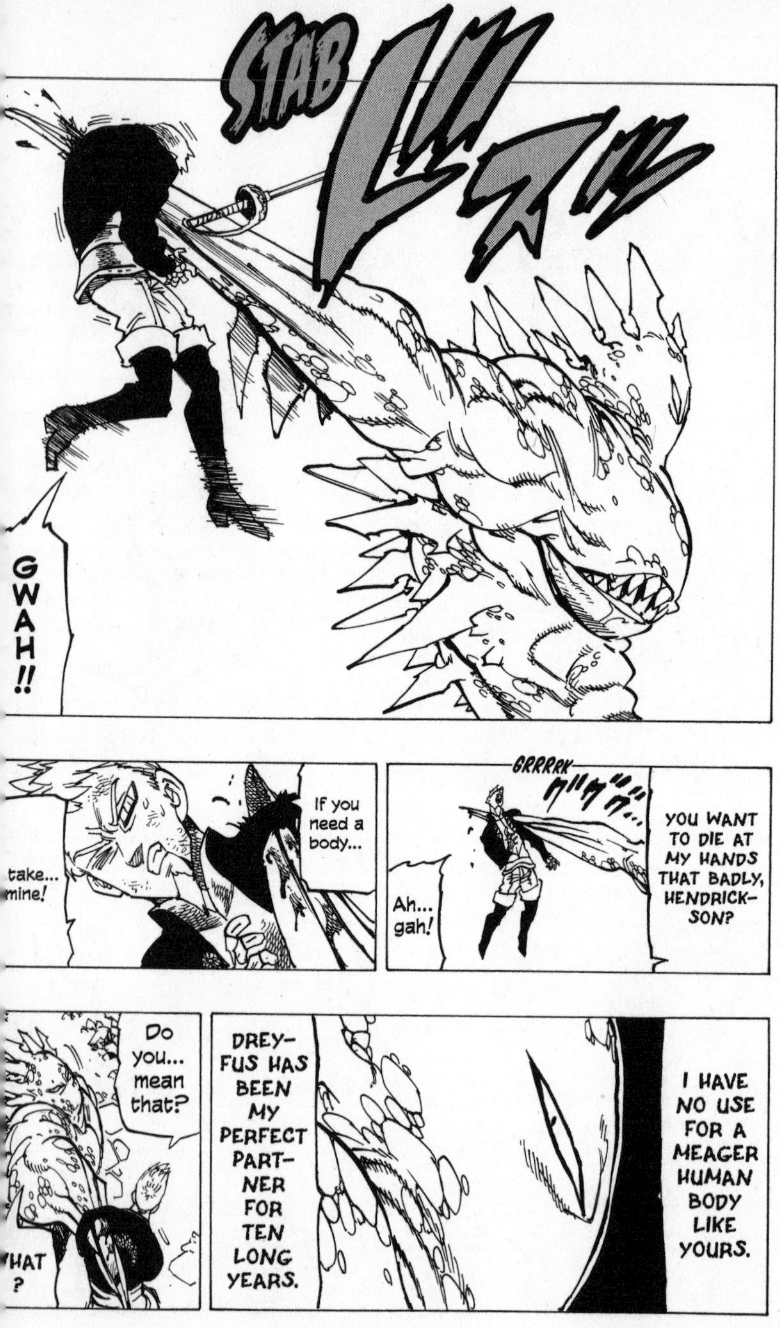
STAB
GWAH!!
GRRRRK
YOU WANT TO DIE AT MY HANDS THAT BADLY, HENDRICKSON?
Ah... gah!
If you need a body...
take... mine!
I HAVE NO USE FOR A MEAGER HUMAN BODY LIKE YOURS.
DREYFUS HAS BEEN MY PERFECT PARTNER FOR TEN LONG YEARS.
Do you... mean that?
HAT ?

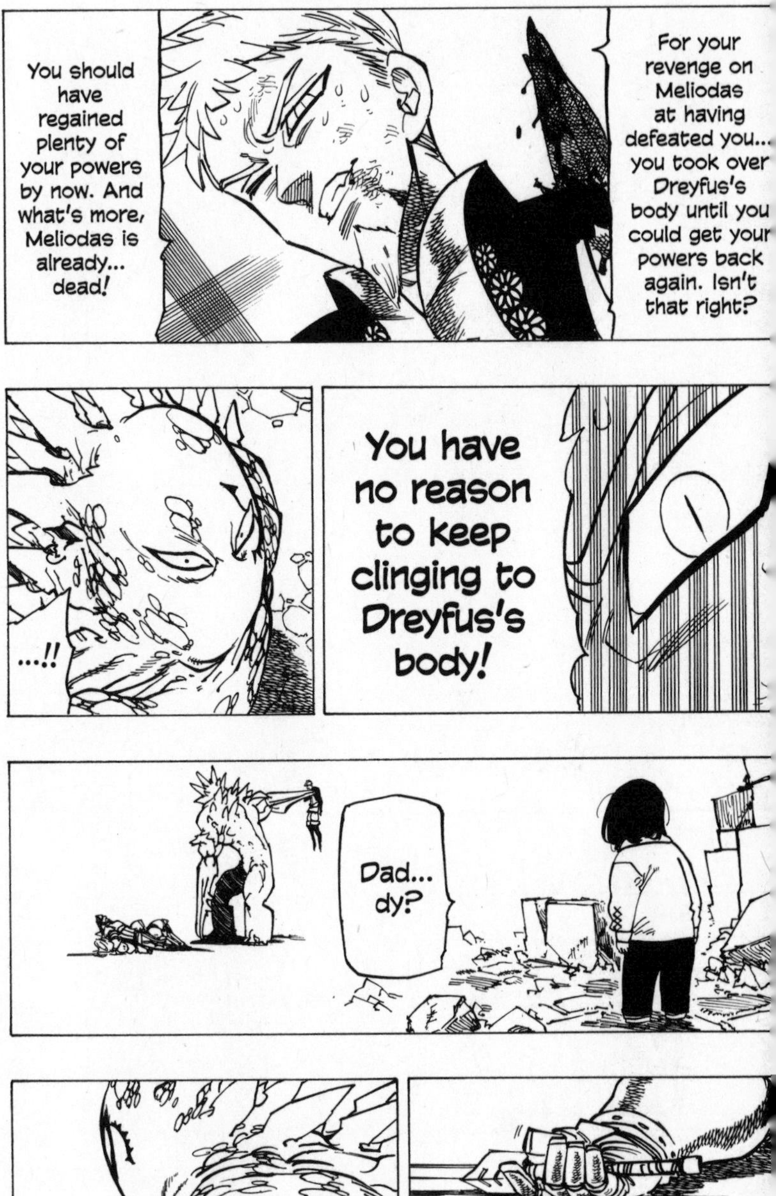
For your revenge on Meliodas at having defeated you... you took over Dreyfus's body until you could get your powers back again. Isn't that right?
You should have regained plenty of your powers by now. And what's more, Meliodas is already... dead!
You have no reason to keep clinging to Dreyfus's body!
...!!
Dad... dy?

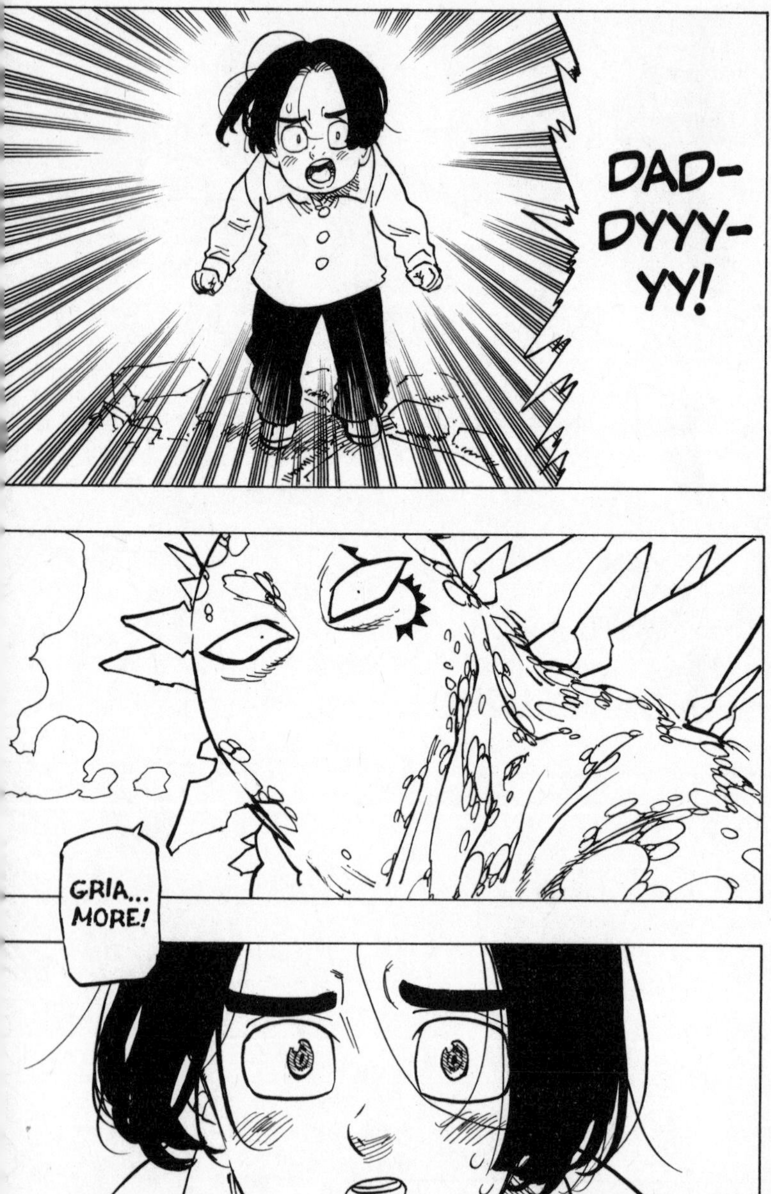
DAD-
DYYY-
YY!
GRIA...
MORE!

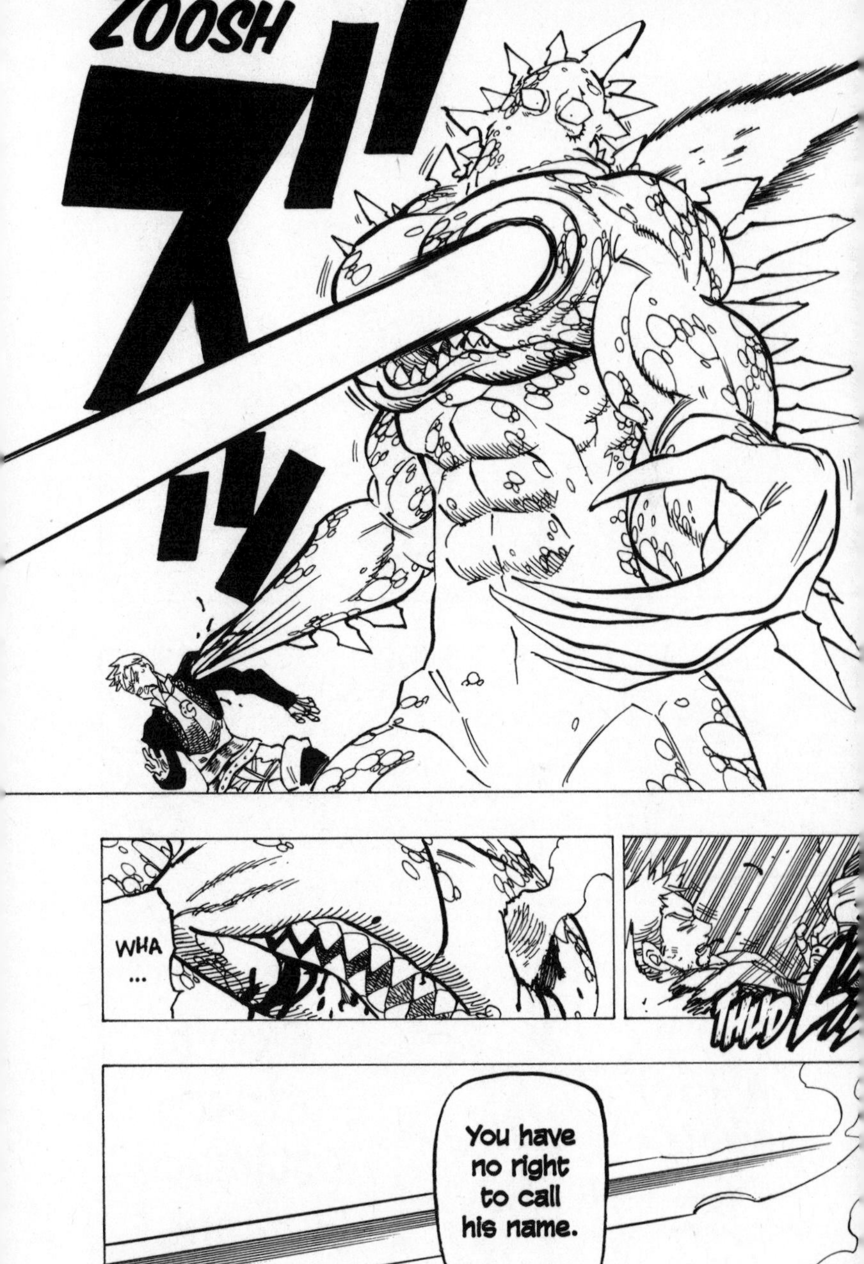
ZOOSH
ズバッ
THUD
WHA
...
You have no right to call his name.

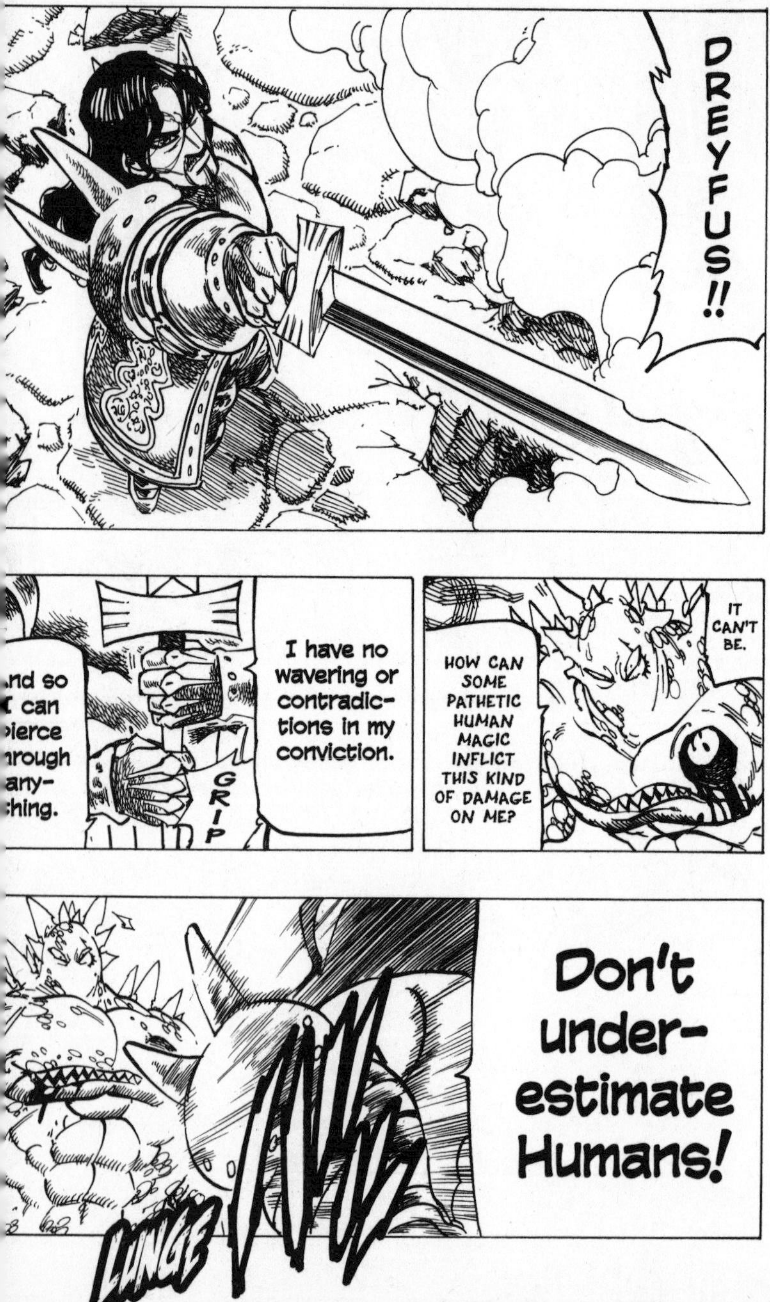
DREYFUS!!
IT CAN'T BE.
HOW CAN SOME PATHETIC HUMAN MAGIC INFLICT THIS KIND OF DAMAGE ON ME?
I have no wavering or contradictions in my conviction.
nd so can ierce hrough any-hing.
GRIP
Don't under-estimate Humans!
LUNGE

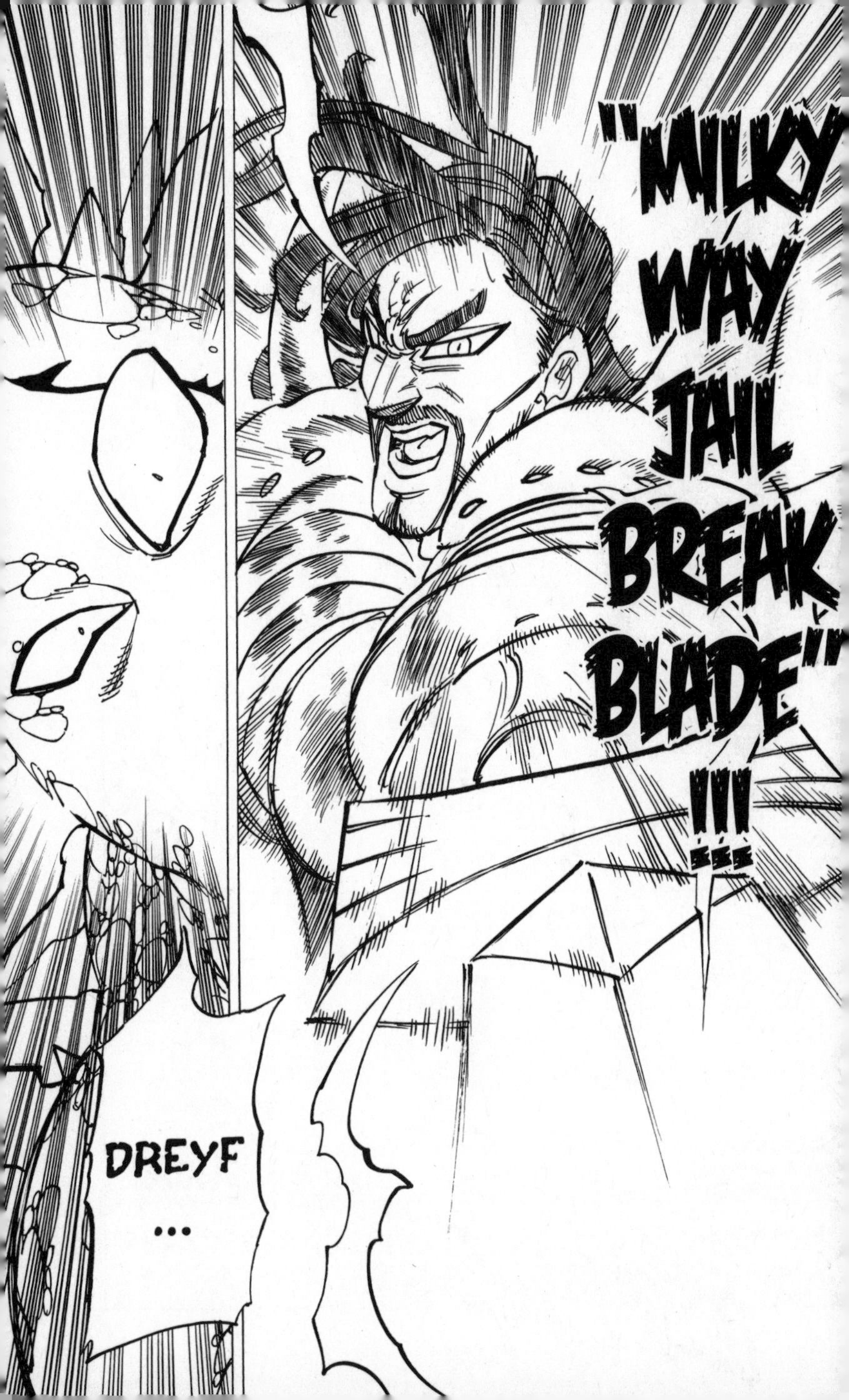
"MILKY WAY JAIL BREAK BLADE"!!!
DREYF
...

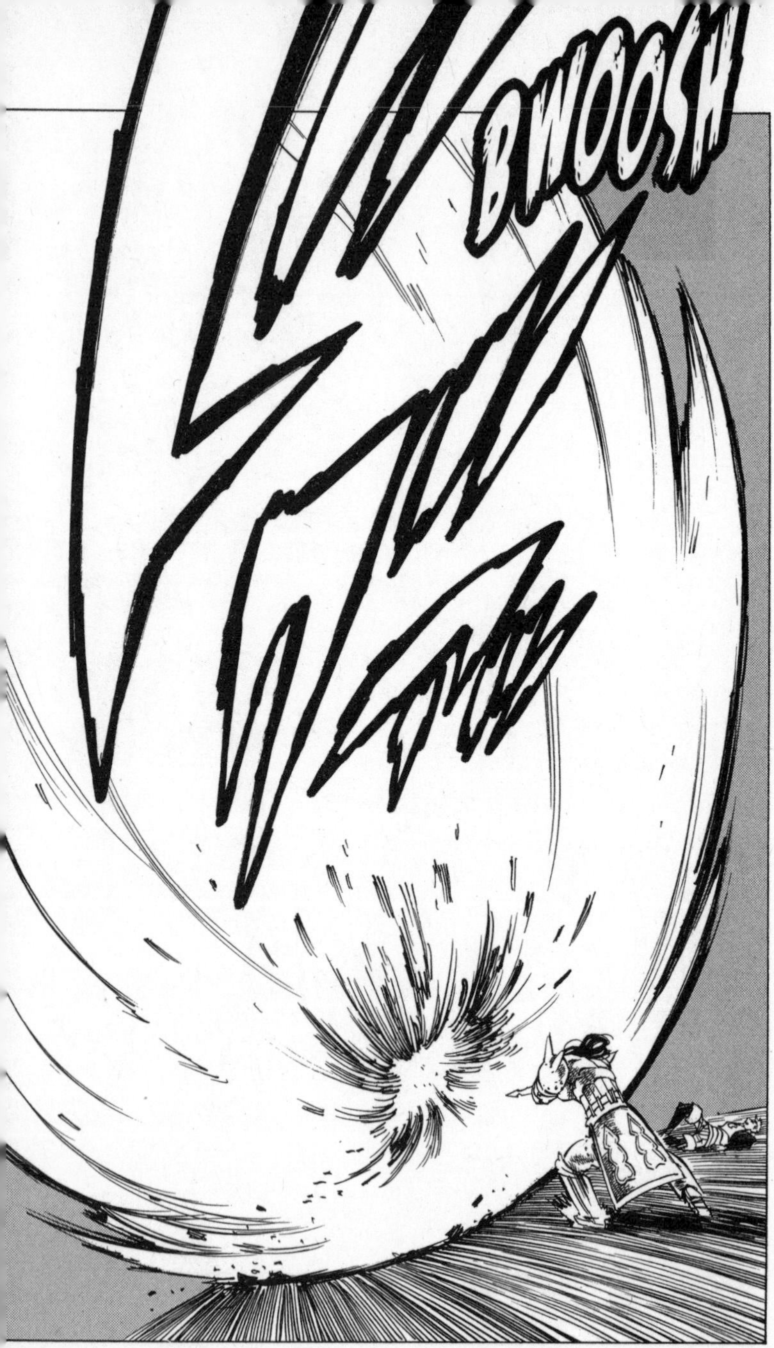
BWOOSH

Chapter 194 - Cruel Hop

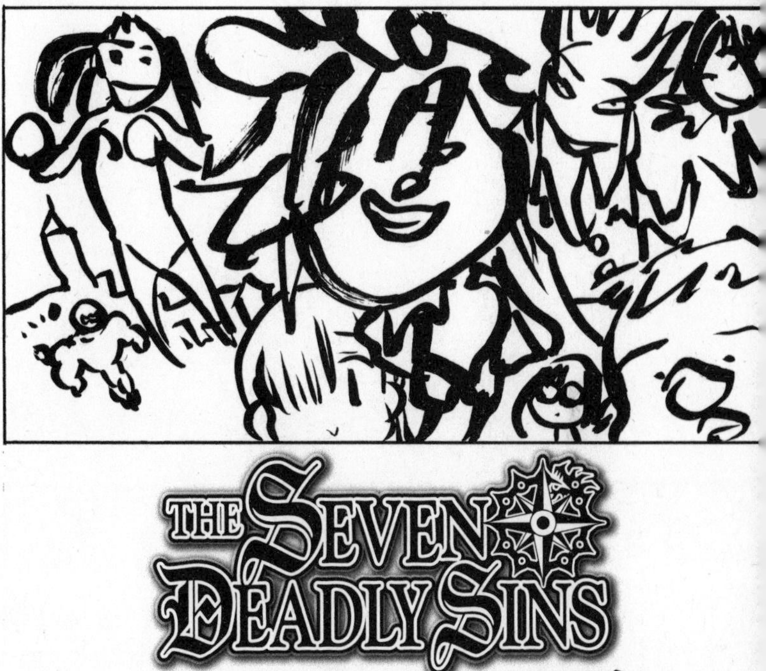

THE SEVEN DEADLY SINS

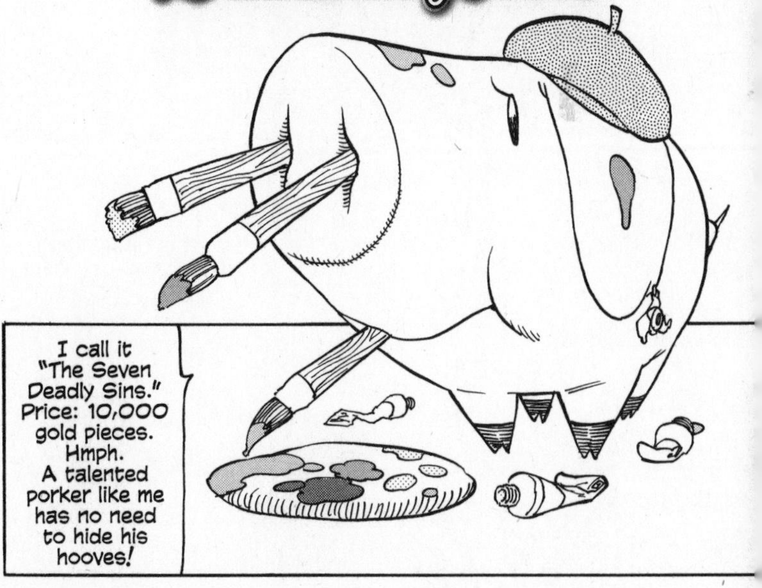
I call it "The Seven Deadly Sins." Price: 10,000 gold pieces. Hmph. A talented porker like me has no need to hide his hooves!

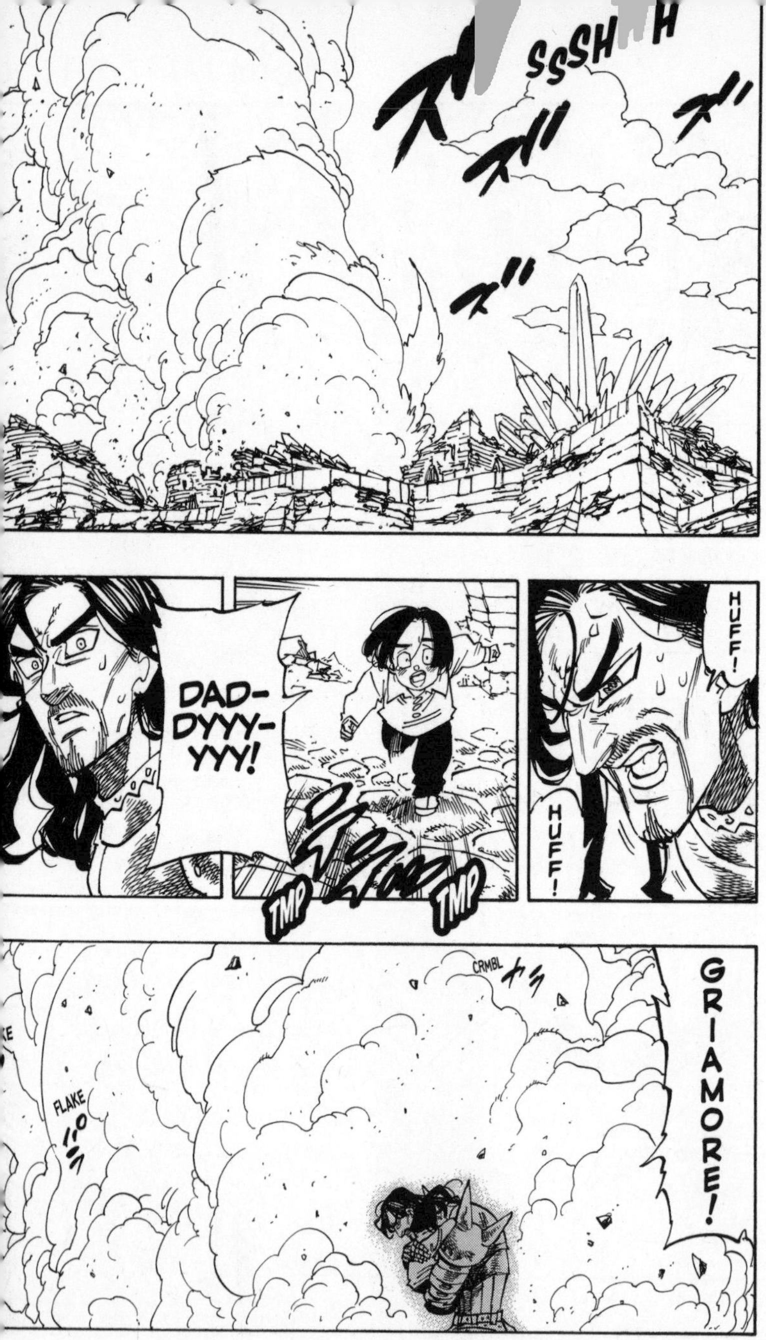
SSSH H
HUFF!
HUFF!
DAD-DYYY-YYY!
TMP
TMP
GRIAMORE!
CRMBL
FLAKE

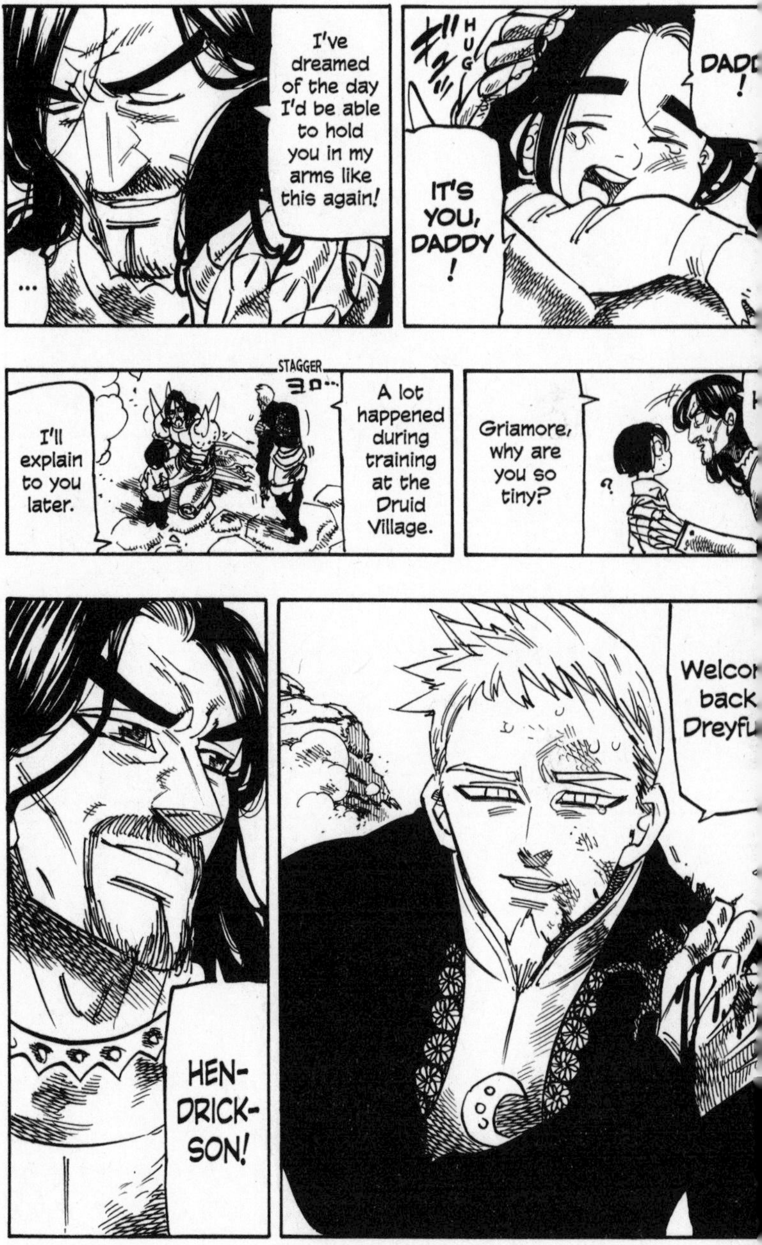
DADD
HUG
IT'S YOU, DADDY!
I've dreamed of the day I'd be able to hold you in my arms like this again!
...
Griamore, why are you so tiny?
?
A lot happened during training at the Druid Village.
STAGGER
I'll explain to you later.
Welco back Dreyfu
HEN-DRICK-SON!

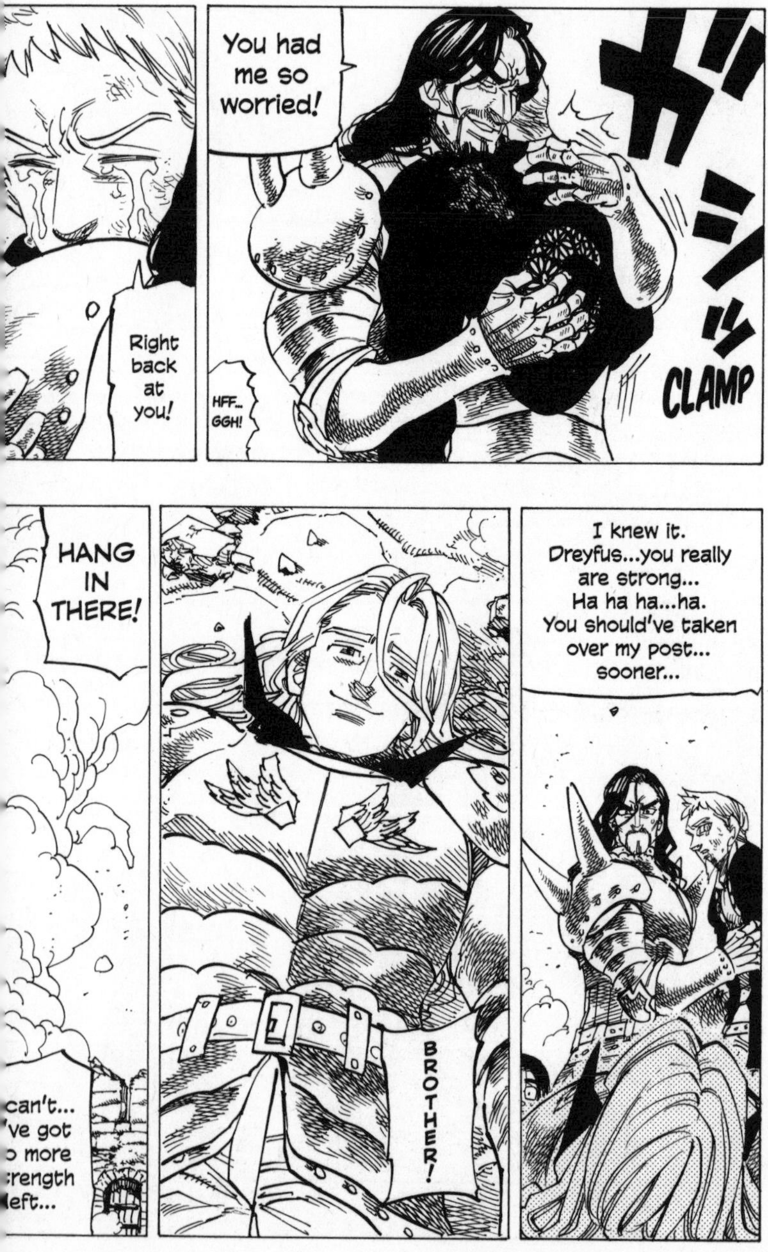
You had me so worried!
HFF... GGH!
CLAMP
Right back at you!
I knew it. Dreyfus...you really are strong... Ha ha ha...ha. You should've taken over my post... sooner...
BROTHER!
HANG IN THERE!
can't... 've got o more rength left...

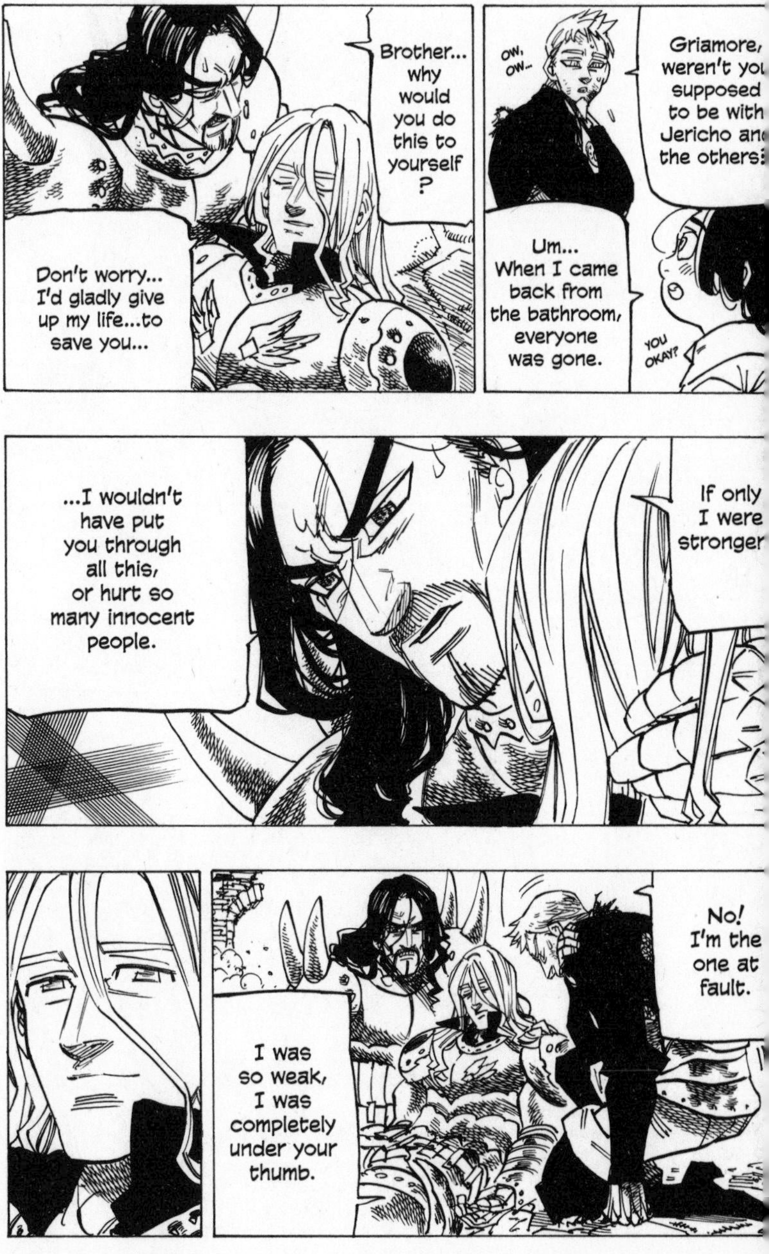
Griamore, weren't you supposed to be with Jericho an the others?
OW, OW...
YOU OKAY?
Um... When I came back from the bathroom, everyone was gone.
Brother... why would you do this to yourself?
Don't worry... I'd gladly give up my life...to save you...
If only I were stronger
...I wouldn't have put you through all this, or hurt so many innocent people.
No! I'm the one at fault.
I was so weak, I was completely under your thumb.

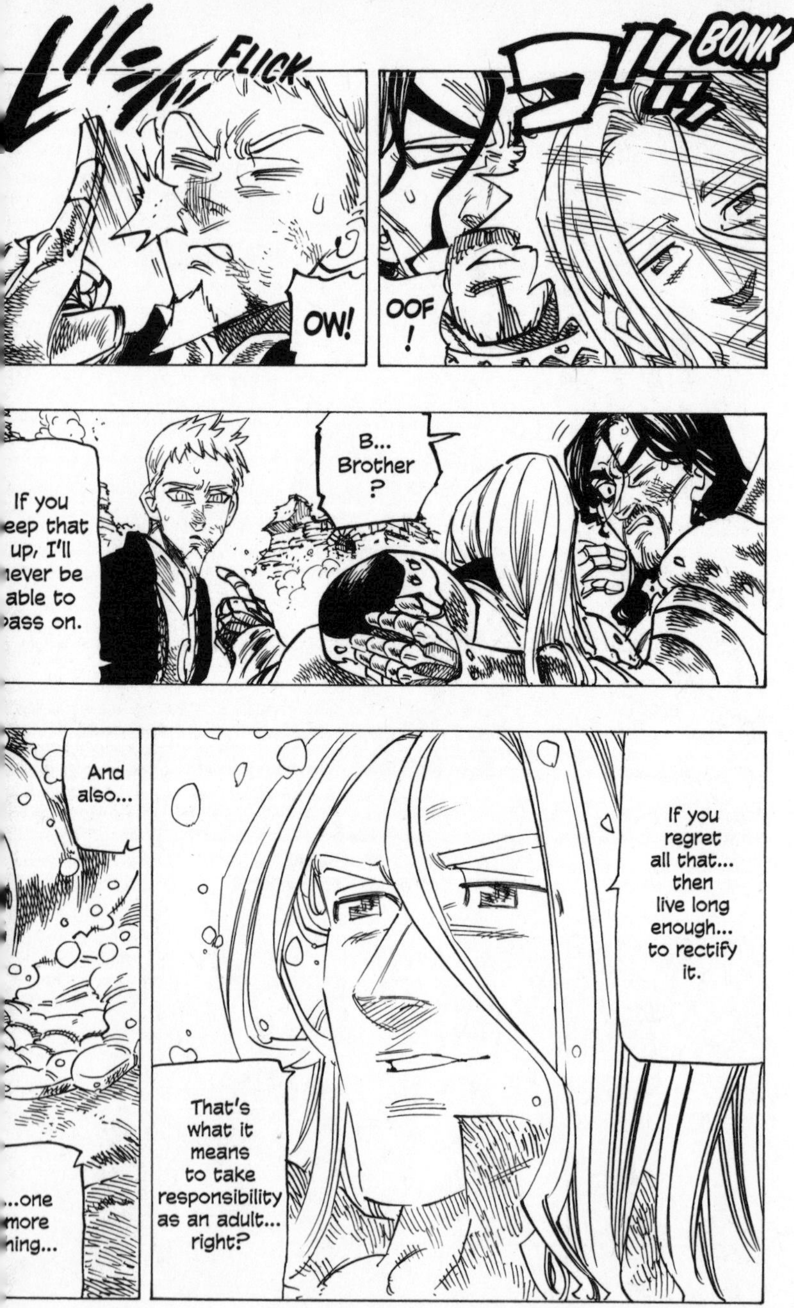
BONK
OOF!
FLICK
OW!
B... Brother?
If you eep that up, I'll ever be able to ass on.
If you regret all that... then live long enough... to rectify it.
That's what it means to take responsibility as an adult... right?
And also...
...one more hing...

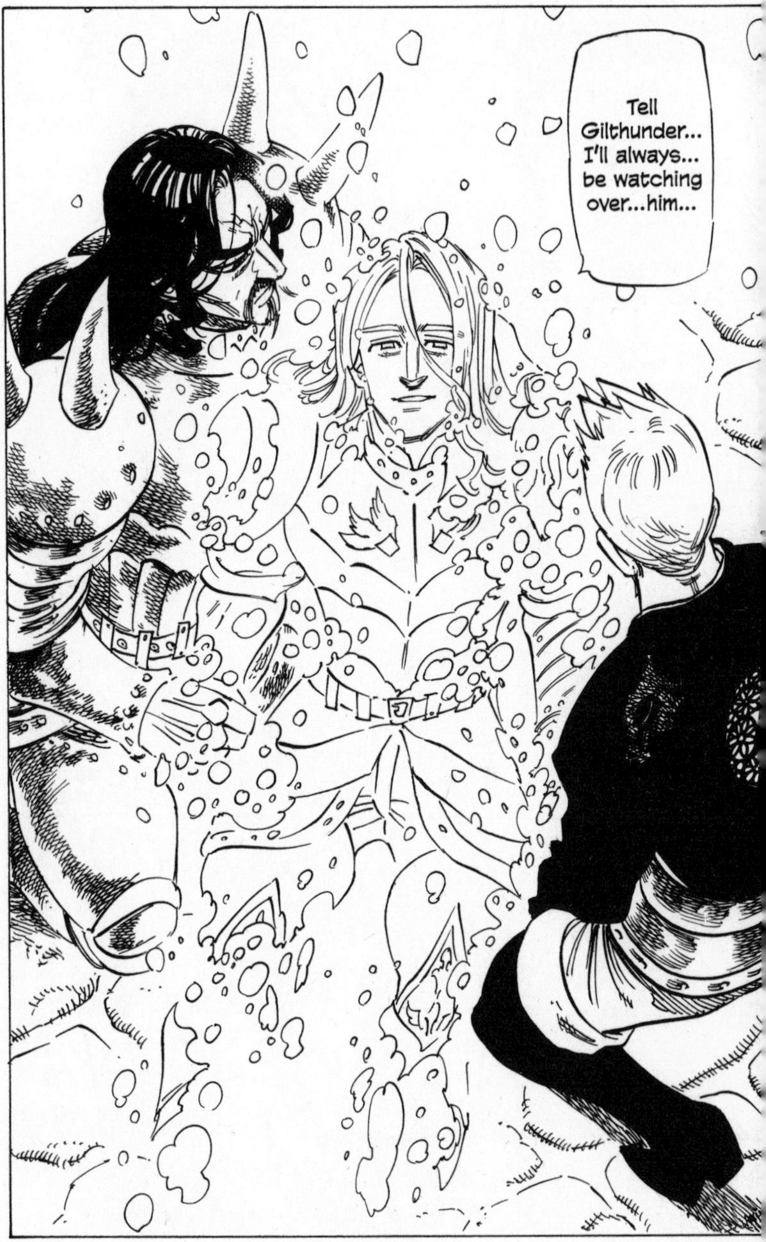
Tell Gilthunder... I'll always... be watching over...him...

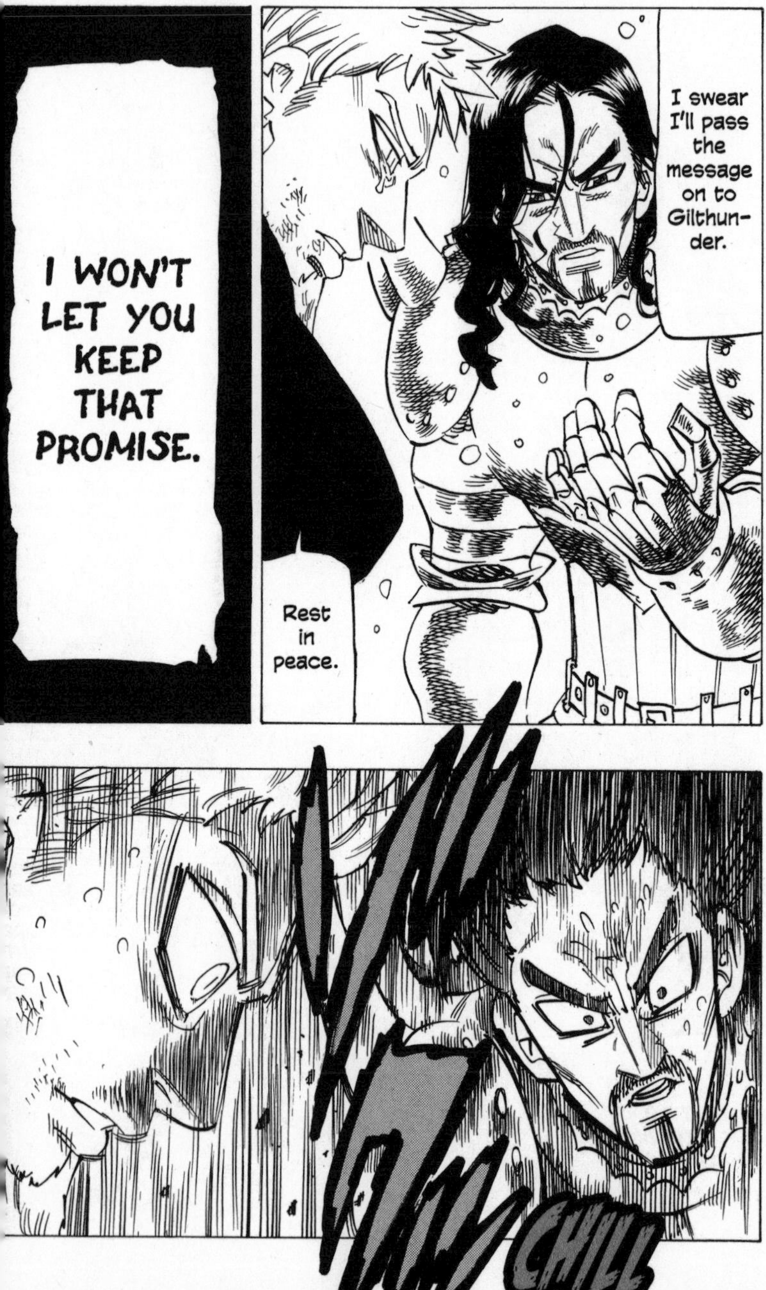
I swear I'll pass the message on to Gilthunder.
Rest in peace.
I WON'T LET YOU KEEP THAT PROMISE.
CHILL

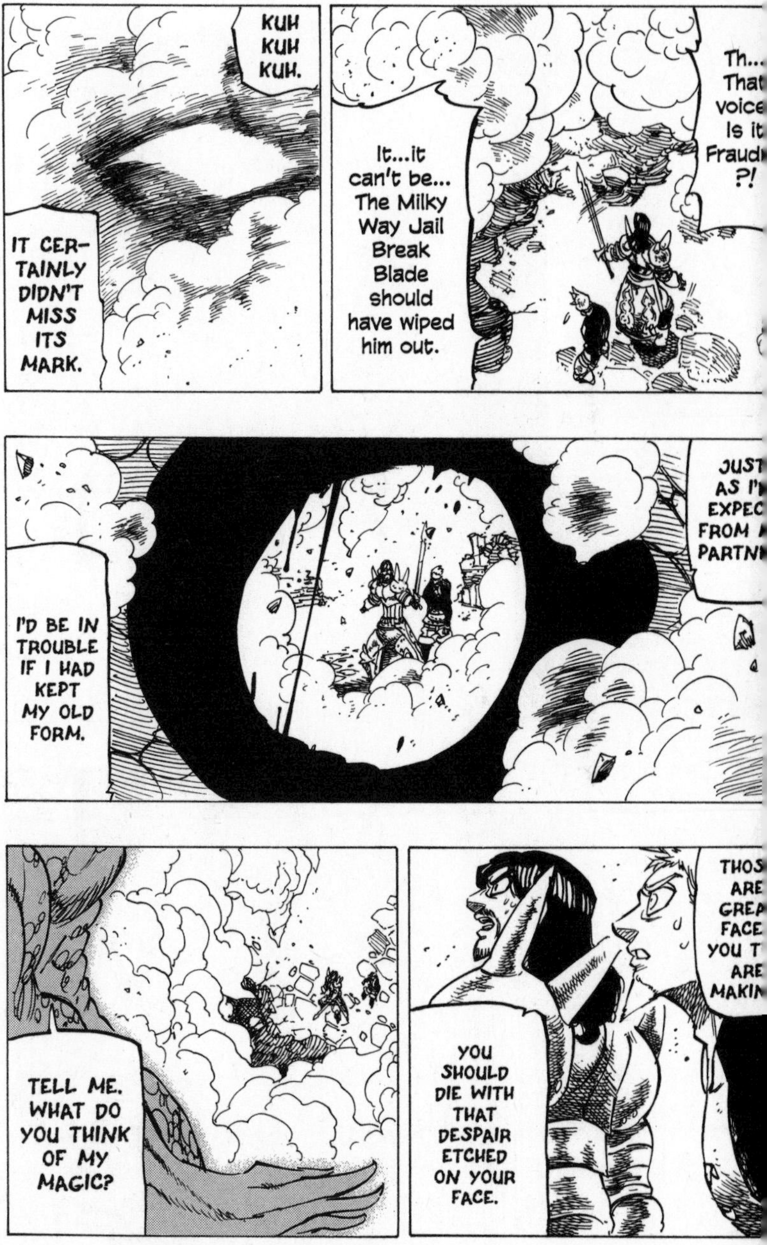

Th... That voice Is it Fraud ?!
It...it can't be... The Milky Way Jail Break Blade should have wiped him out.
KUH KUH KUH.
IT CERTAINLY DIDN'T MISS ITS MARK.
JUST AS I' EXPEC FROM PARTN
I'D BE IN TROUBLE IF I HAD KEPT MY OLD FORM.
THOS ARE GREA FACE YOU T ARE MAKIN
YOU SHOULD DIE WITH THAT DESPAIR ETCHED ON YOUR FACE.
TELL ME. WHAT DO YOU THINK OF MY MAGIC?

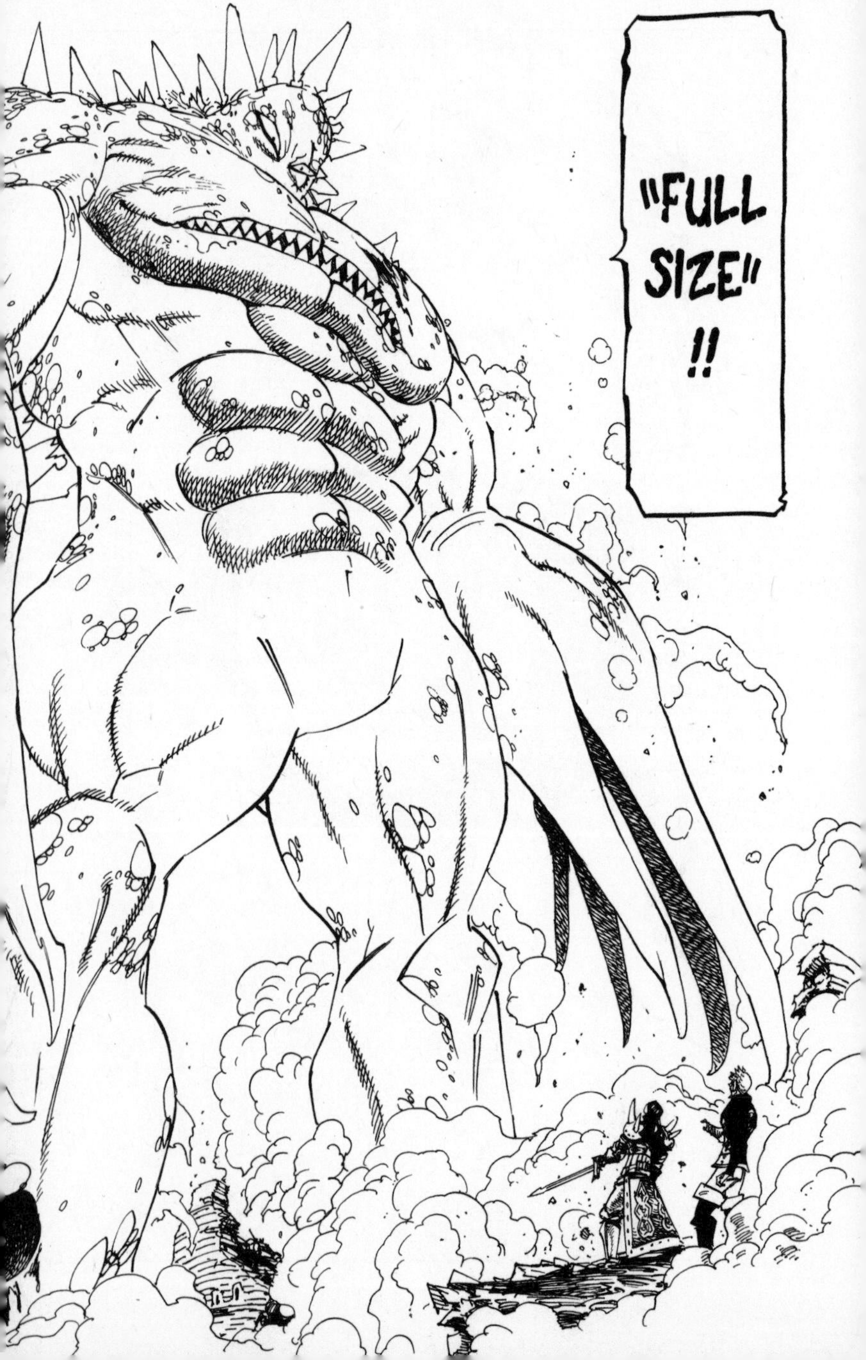
"FULL SIZE" !!

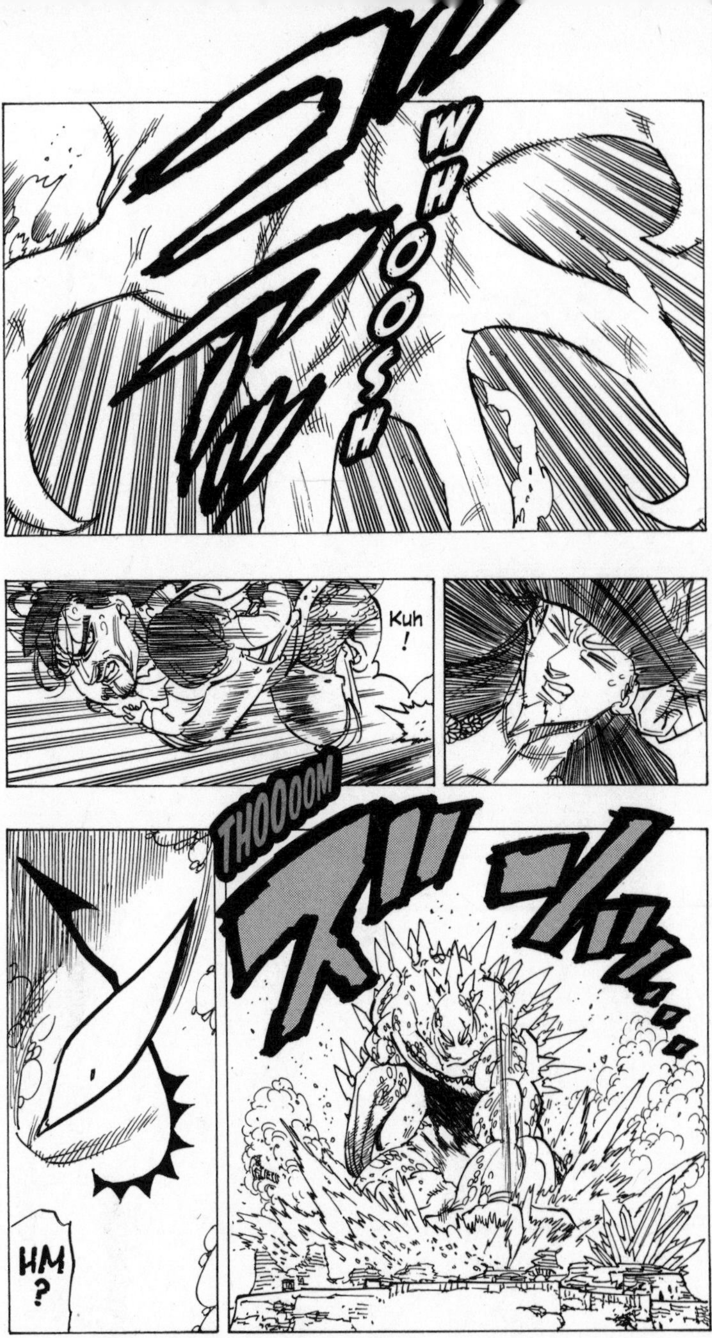
WHOOOSH
Kuh!
THOOOOM
HM?

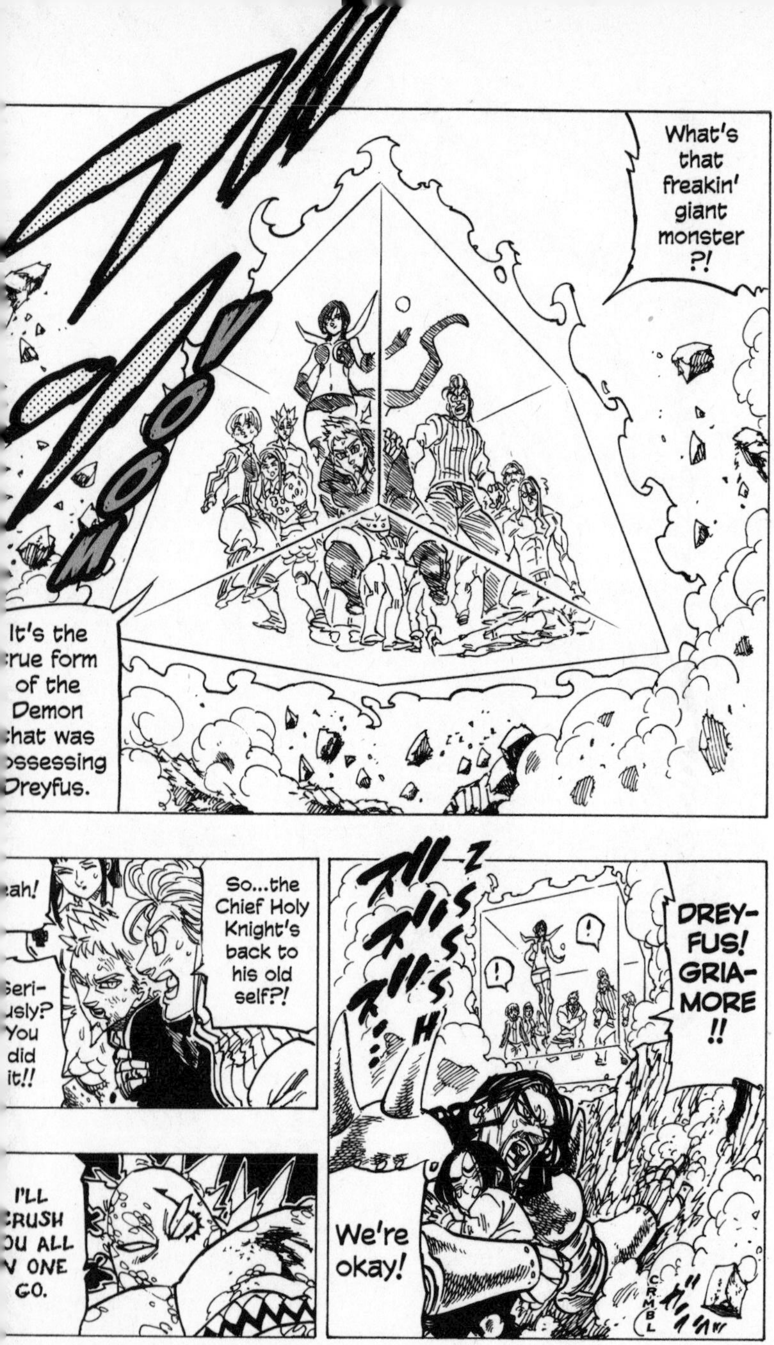
What's that freakin' giant monster?!
It's the rue form of the Demon hat was ossessing Dreyfus.
ZSSSSH
DREY-FUS! GRIA-MORE!!
We're okay!
CRMBL
So...the Chief Holy Knight's back to his old self?!
eah!
Seri-usly? You did it!!
I'LL RUSH OU ALL N ONE GO.

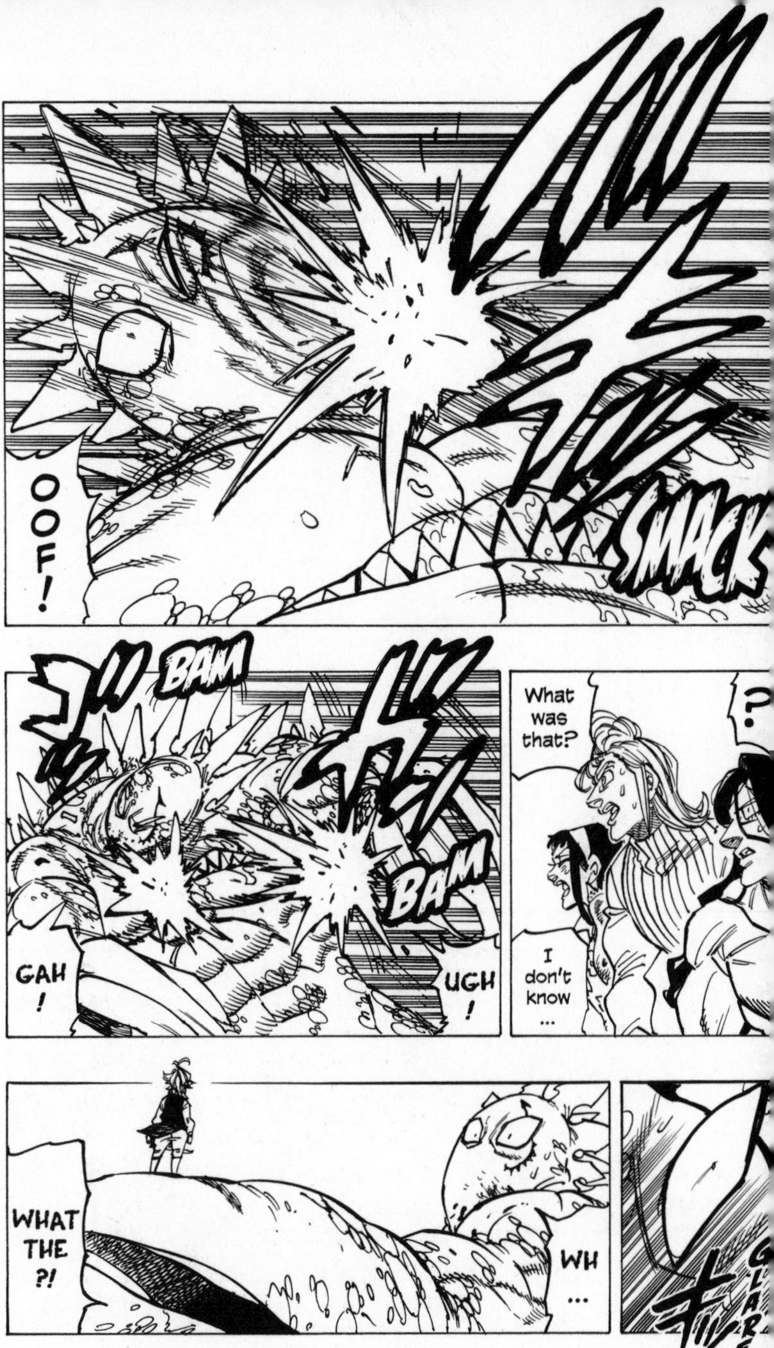
SMACK
OOF!
?
What was that?
I don't know...
BAM
BAM
UGH!
GAH!
GLARE
WH...
WHAT THE?!

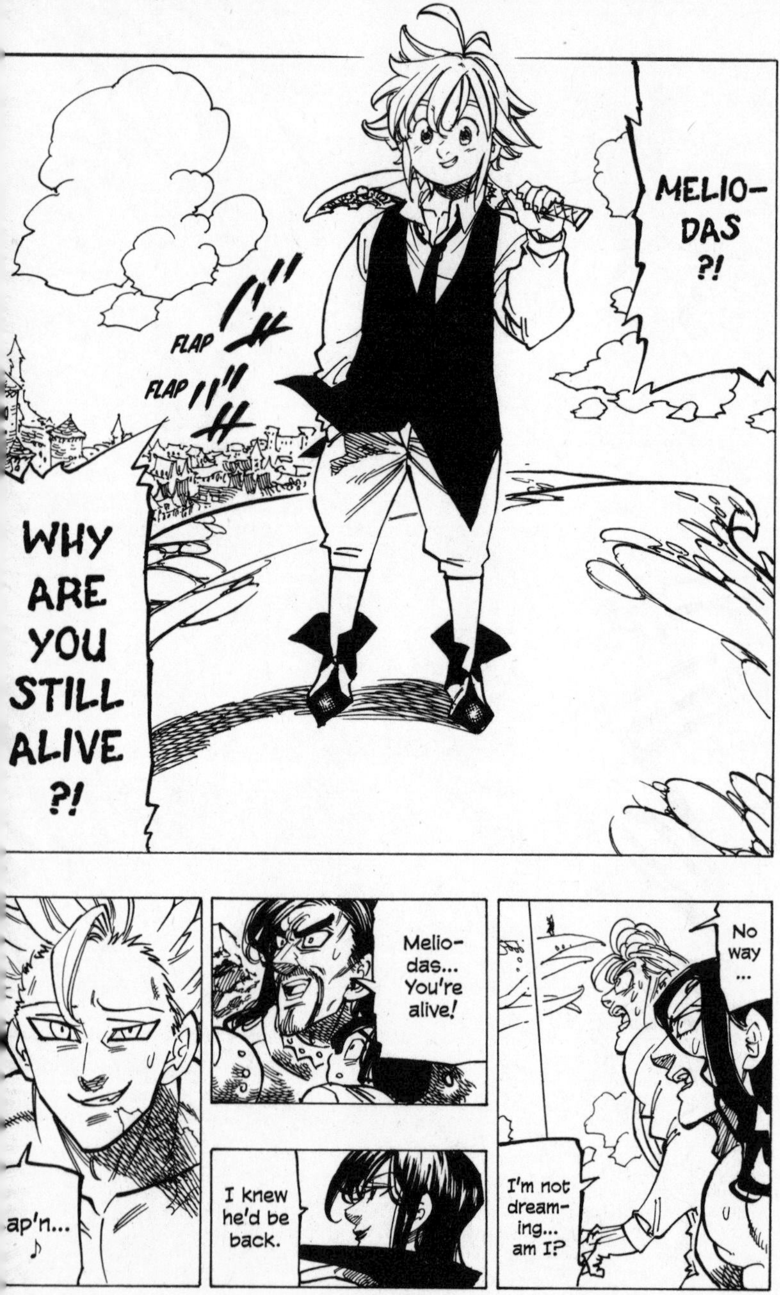
MELIO-DAS ?!
FLAP
FLAP
WHY ARE YOU STILL ALIVE ?!
No way ...
I'm not dreaming... am I?
Melio-das... You're alive!
I knew he'd be back.
ap'n... ♪

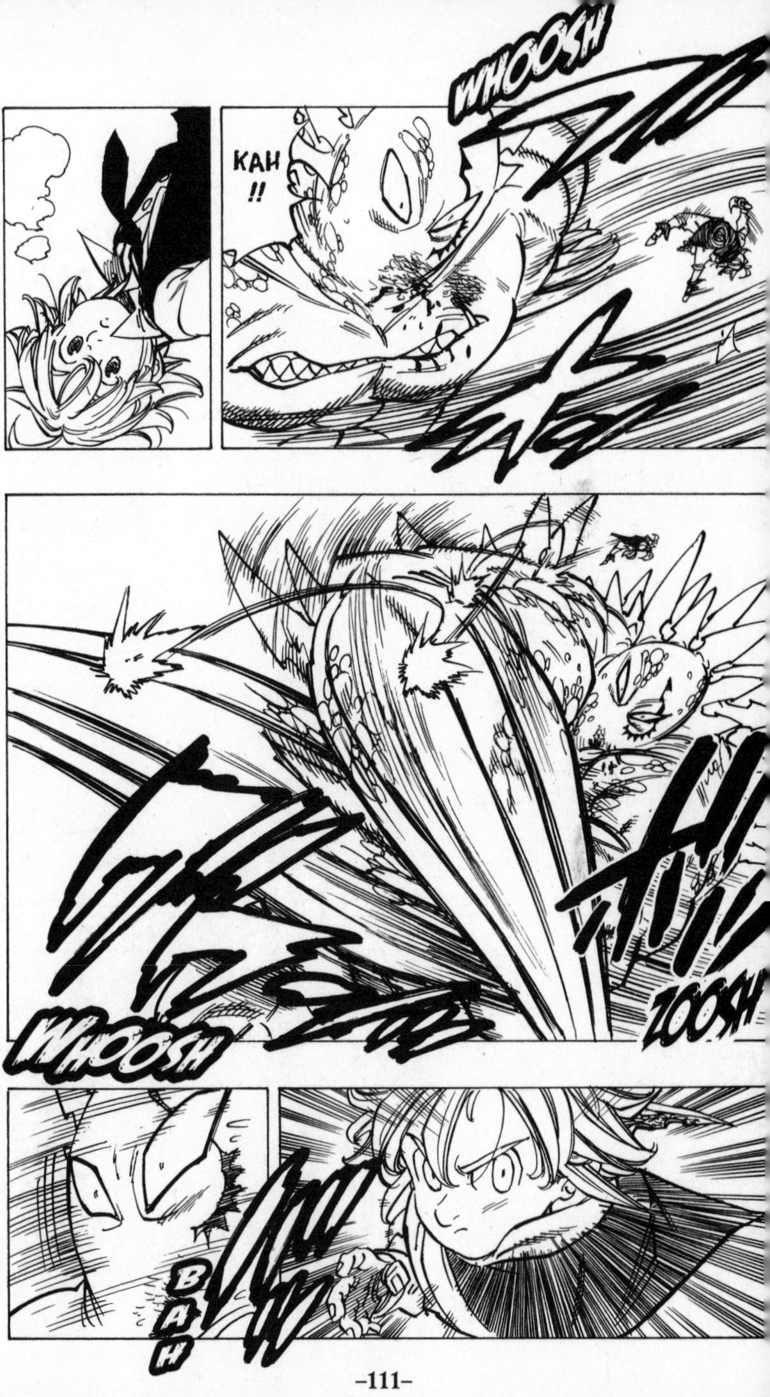
WHOOSH
KAH !!
ZOOSH
WHOOSH
BAH

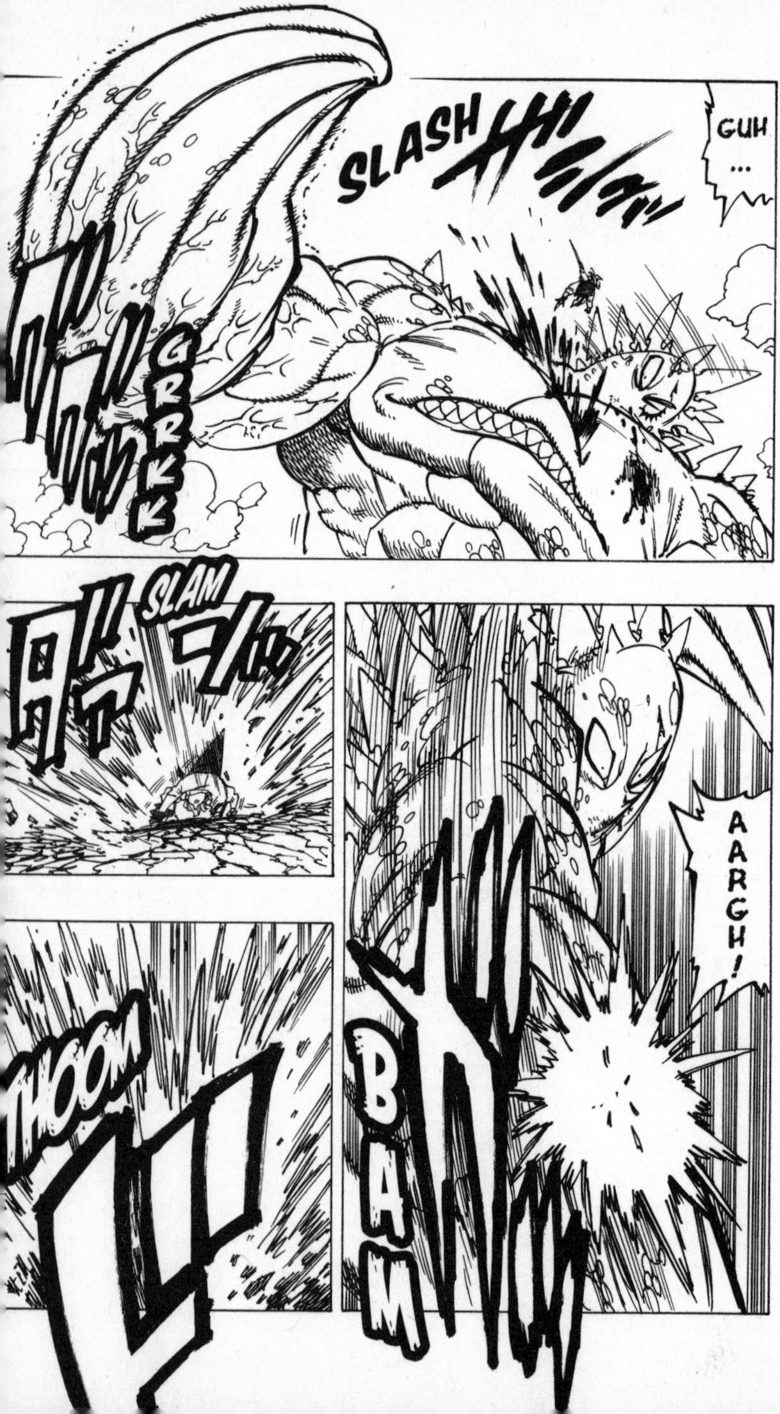
GUH ...
SLASH
GRRR
AARGH!
BAM
SLAM
THOOM

WHOOSH!

NGAH!

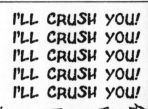

I'LL CRUSH YOU!
I'LL CRUSH YOU!
I'LL CRUSH YOU!
I'LL CRUSH YOU!
I'LL CRUSH YOU!

NOT BAD... BUT YOUR STRENGTH IS NO MATCH FOR ME NOW!

LET'S FINISH WHAT WE STARTED 16 YEARS AGO!

TAK

How odd.

Whoa... It's an almost equal match.

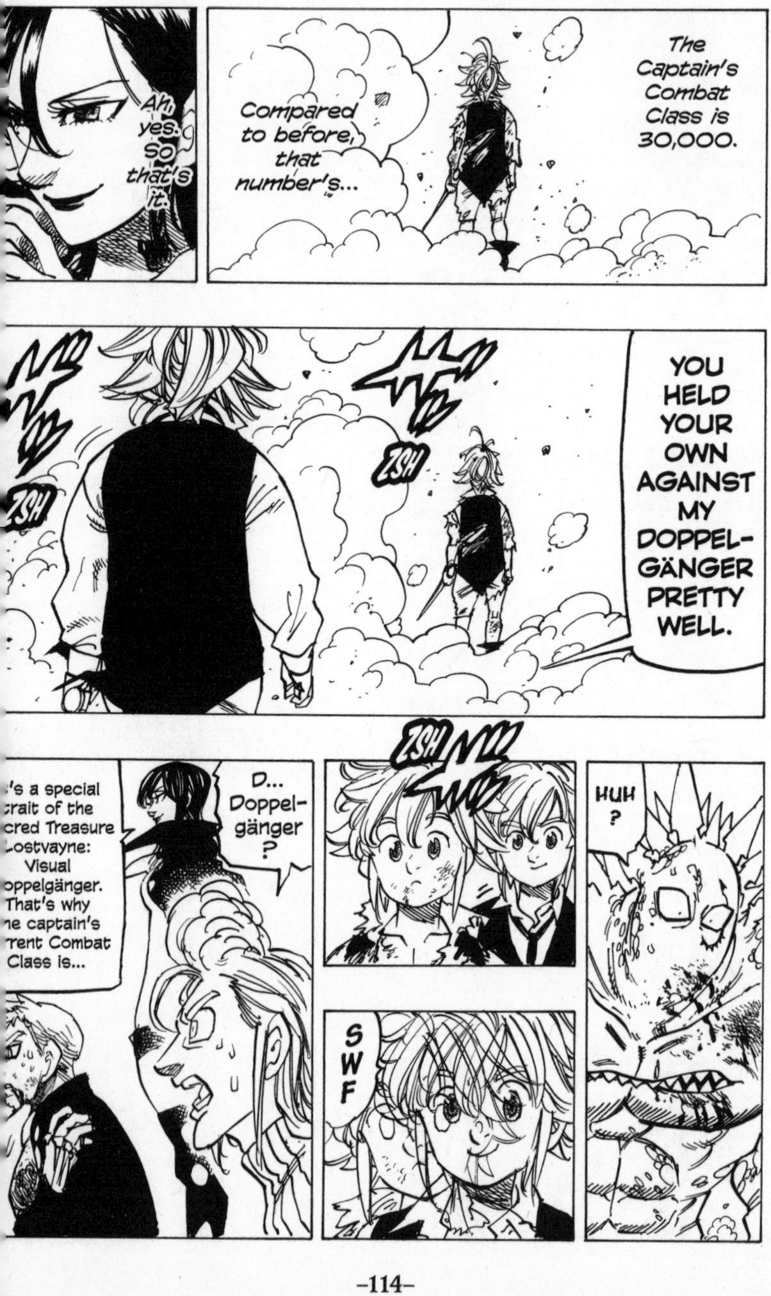
The Captain's Combat Class is 30,000.
Compared to before, that number's...
Ah, yes. So that's it.
YOU HELD YOUR OWN AGAINST MY DOPPEL-GÄNGER PRETTY WELL.
ZSH
ZSH
HUH ?
ZSH
SWF
D... Doppel-gänger ?
's a special trait of the cred Treasure Lostvayne: Visual oppelgänger. That's why ne captain's rrent Combat Class is...

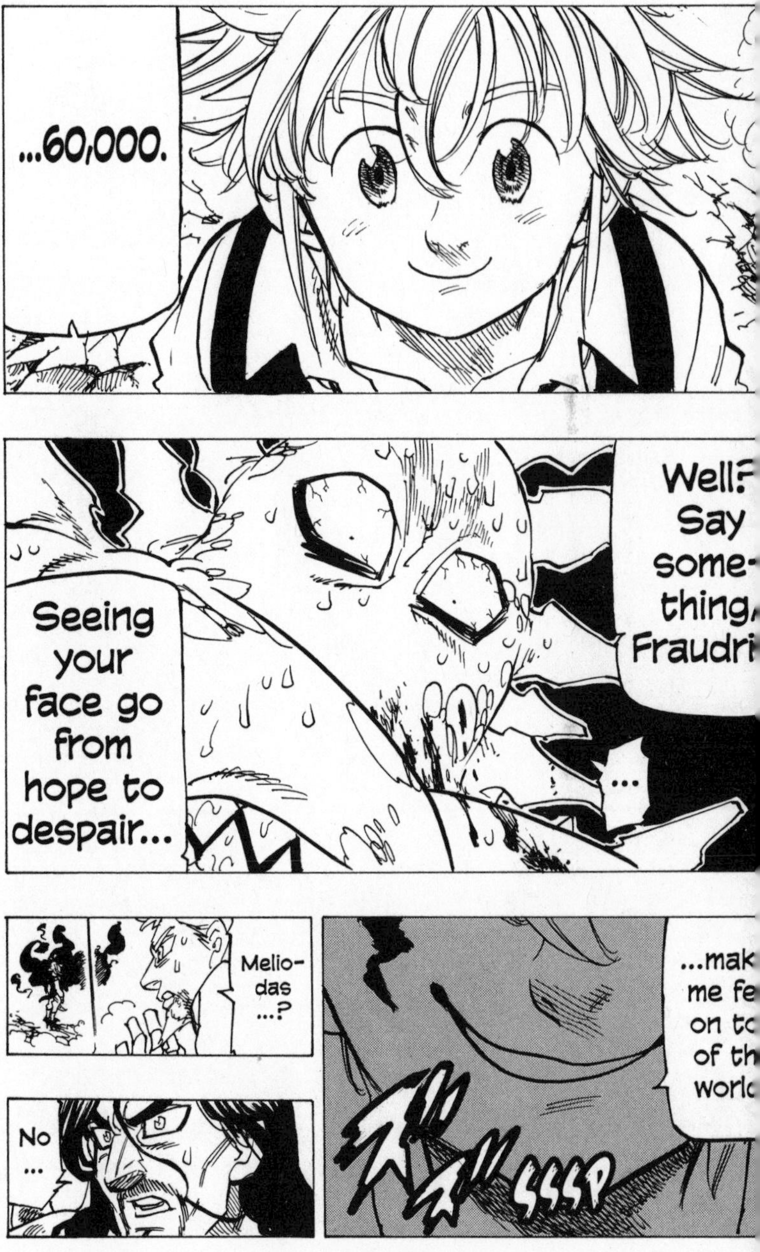
...60,000.
Well? Say some- thing, Fraudri
...
Seeing your face go from hope to despair...
...mak me fe on to of th worl
SSSP
Melio- das ...?
No ...

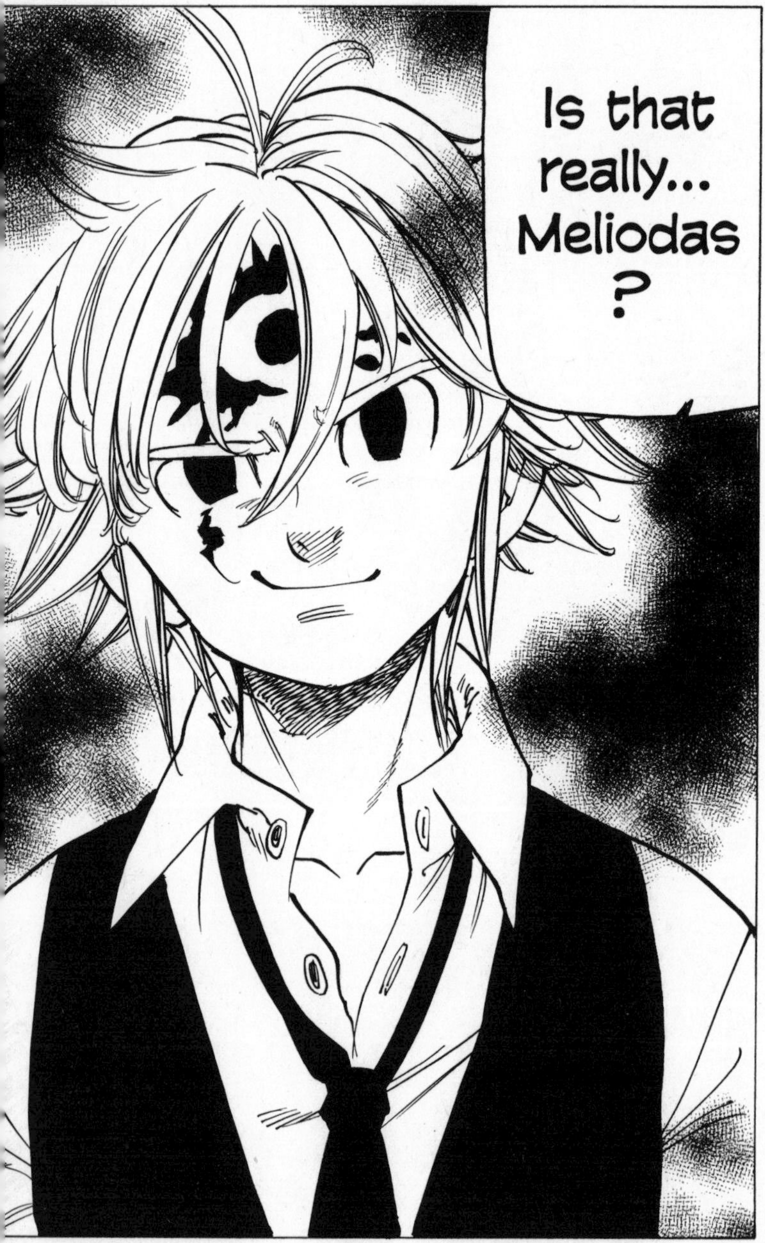
Is that really... Meliodas?

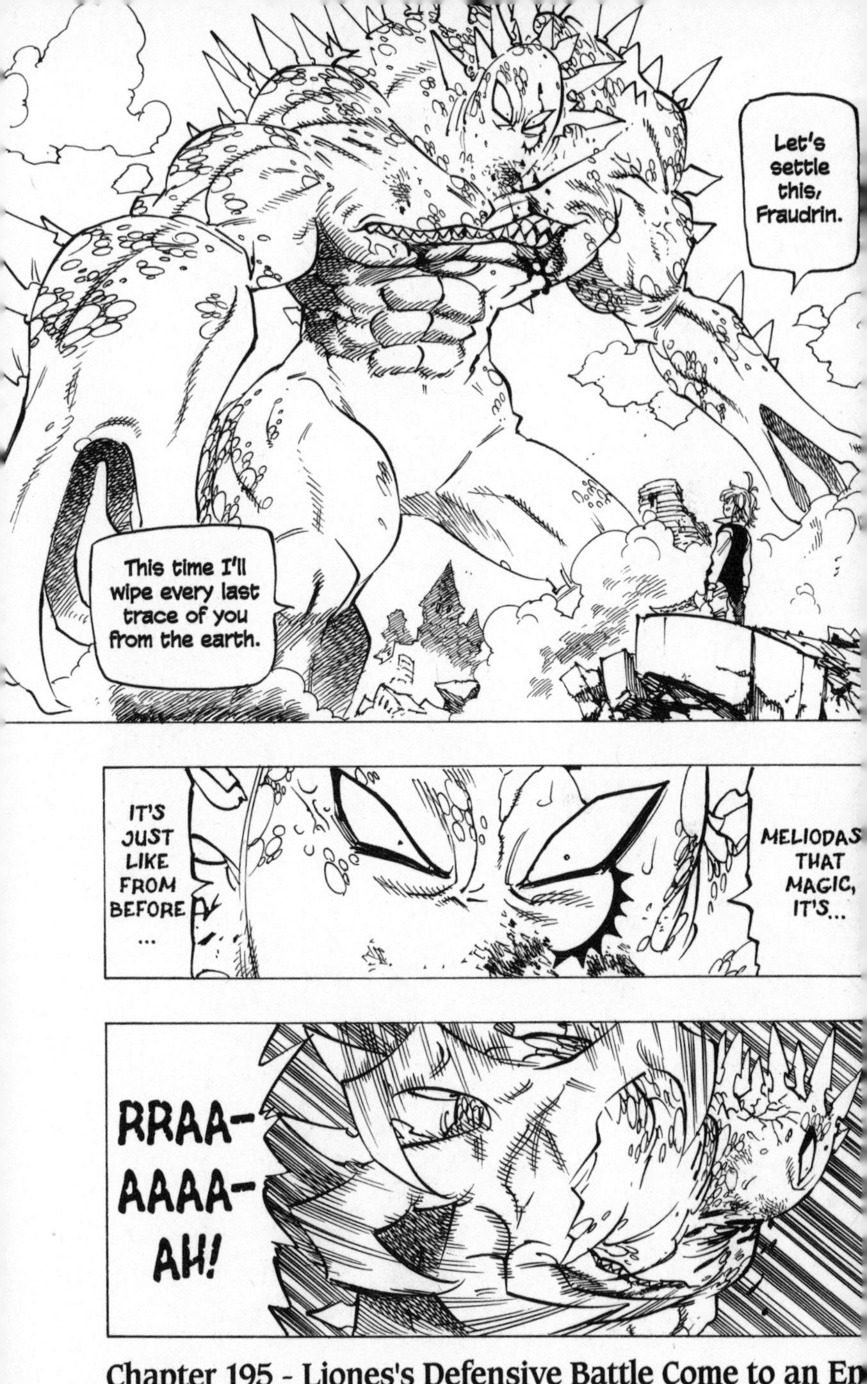
Let's settle this, Fraudrin.
This time I'll wipe every last trace of you from the earth.
MELIODAS THAT MAGIC, IT'S...
IT'S JUST LIKE FROM BEFORE ...
RRAA-AAAA-AH!

Chapter 195 - Liones's Defensive Battle Come to an En

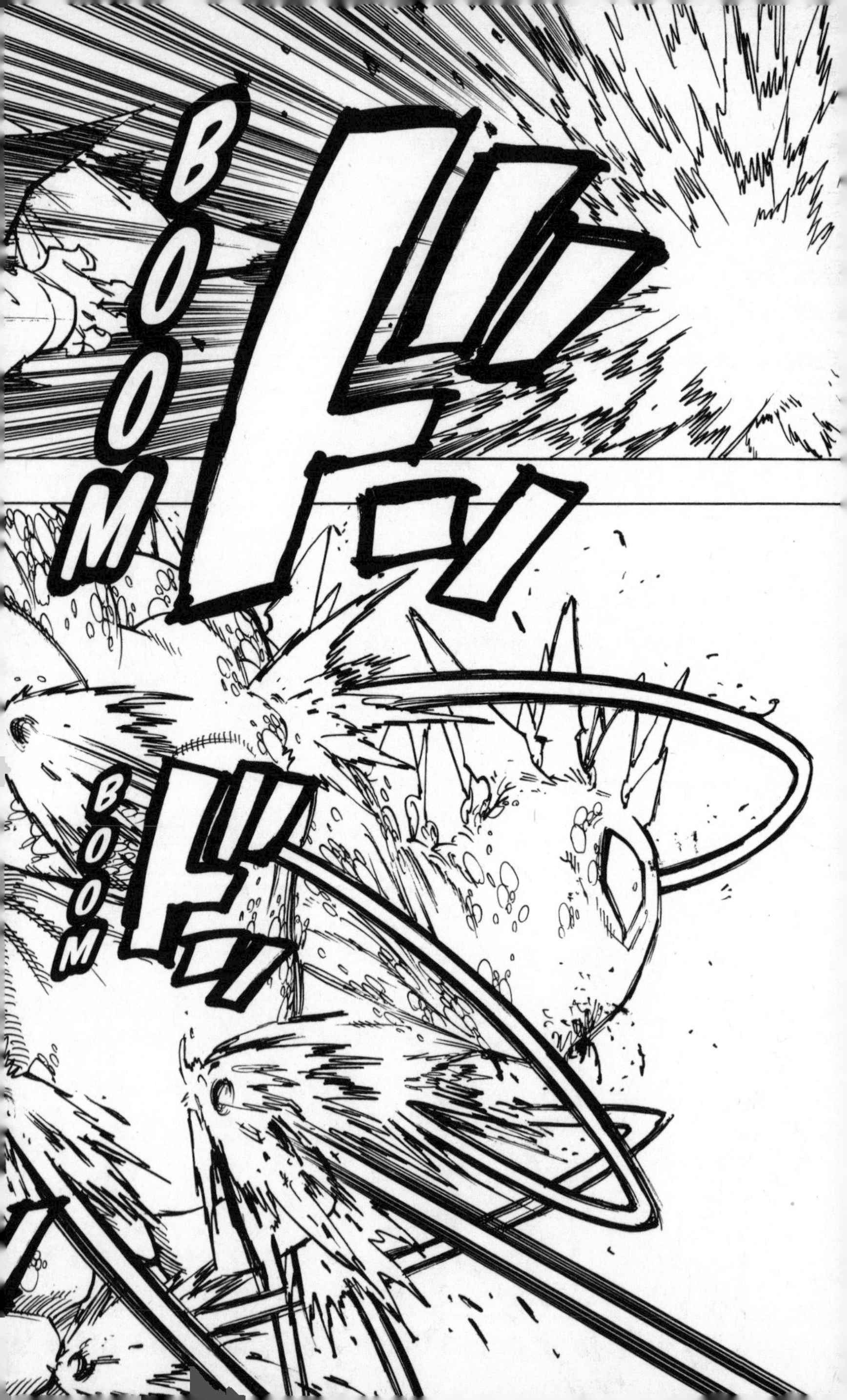
BOOM
BOOM

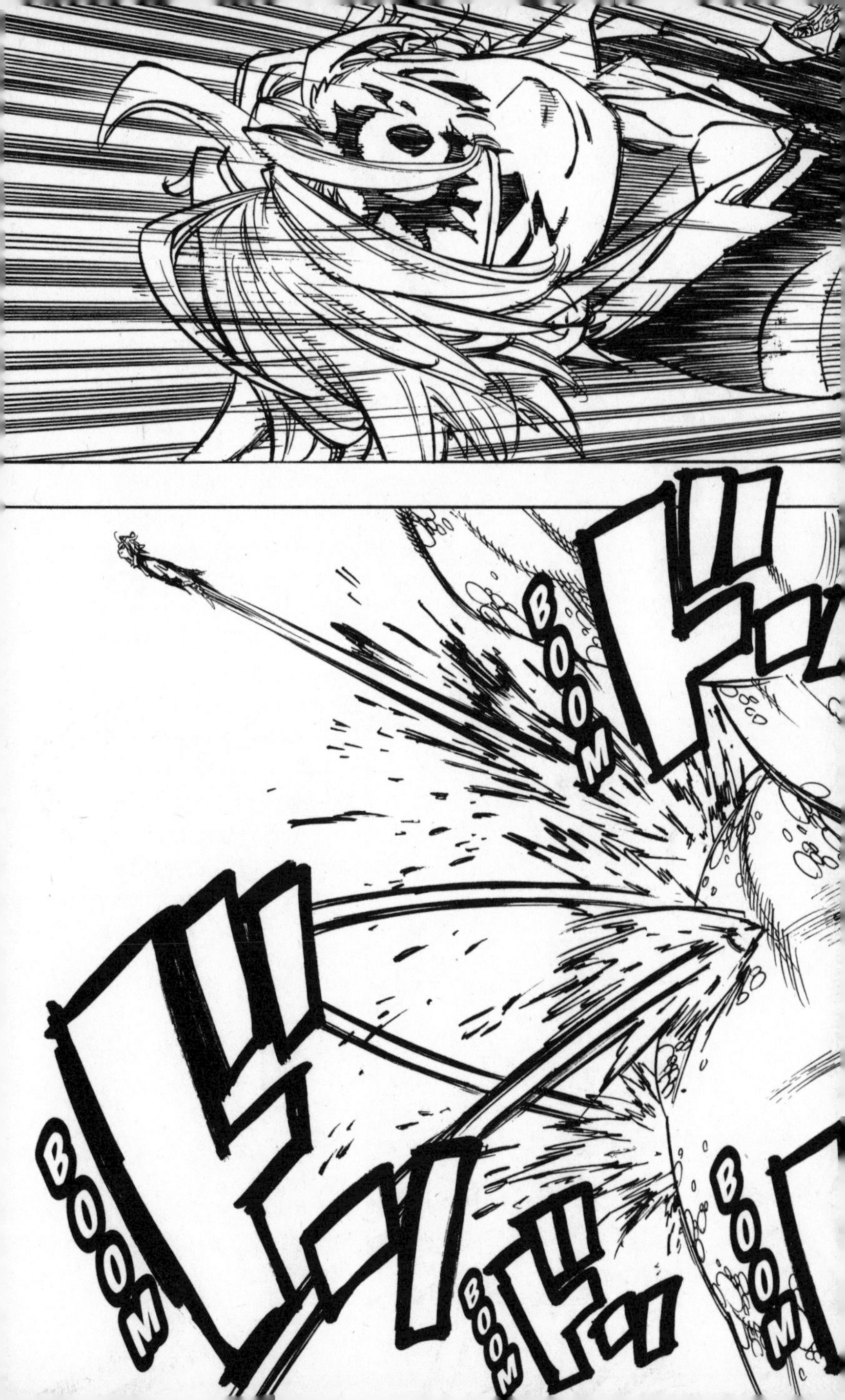
BOOM
BOOM
BOOM
BOOM

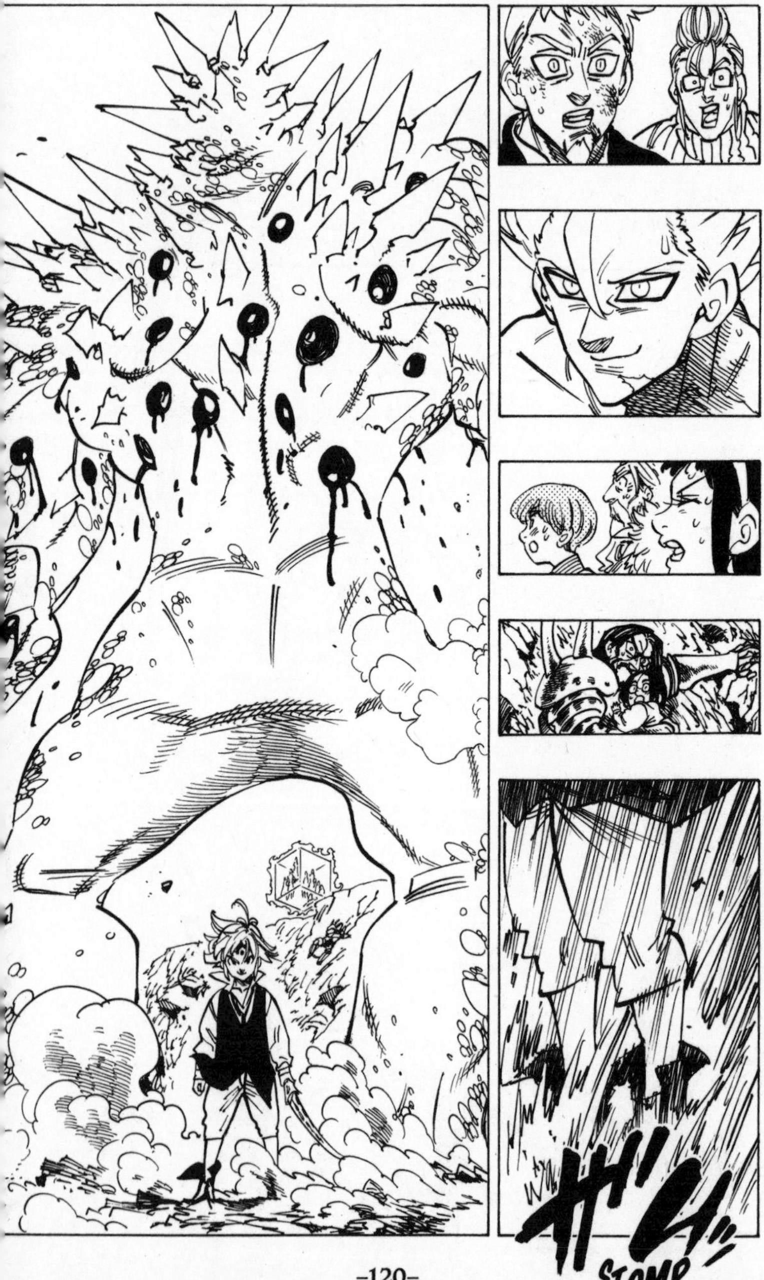

STOMP

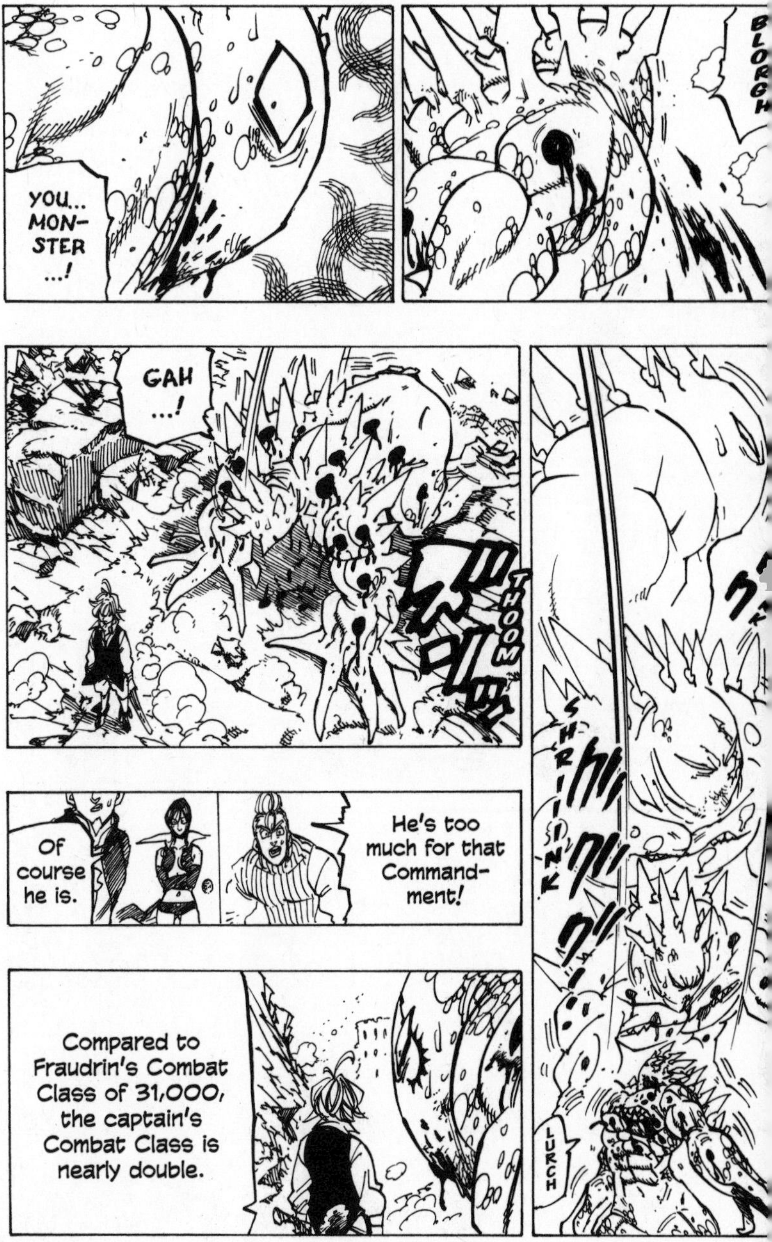
BLORGH
YOU... MONSTER ...!
SHRIIINK
LURCH
GAH ...!
THOOM
He's too much for that Command- ment!
Of course he is.
Compared to Fraudrin's Combat Class of 31,000, the captain's Combat Class is nearly double.

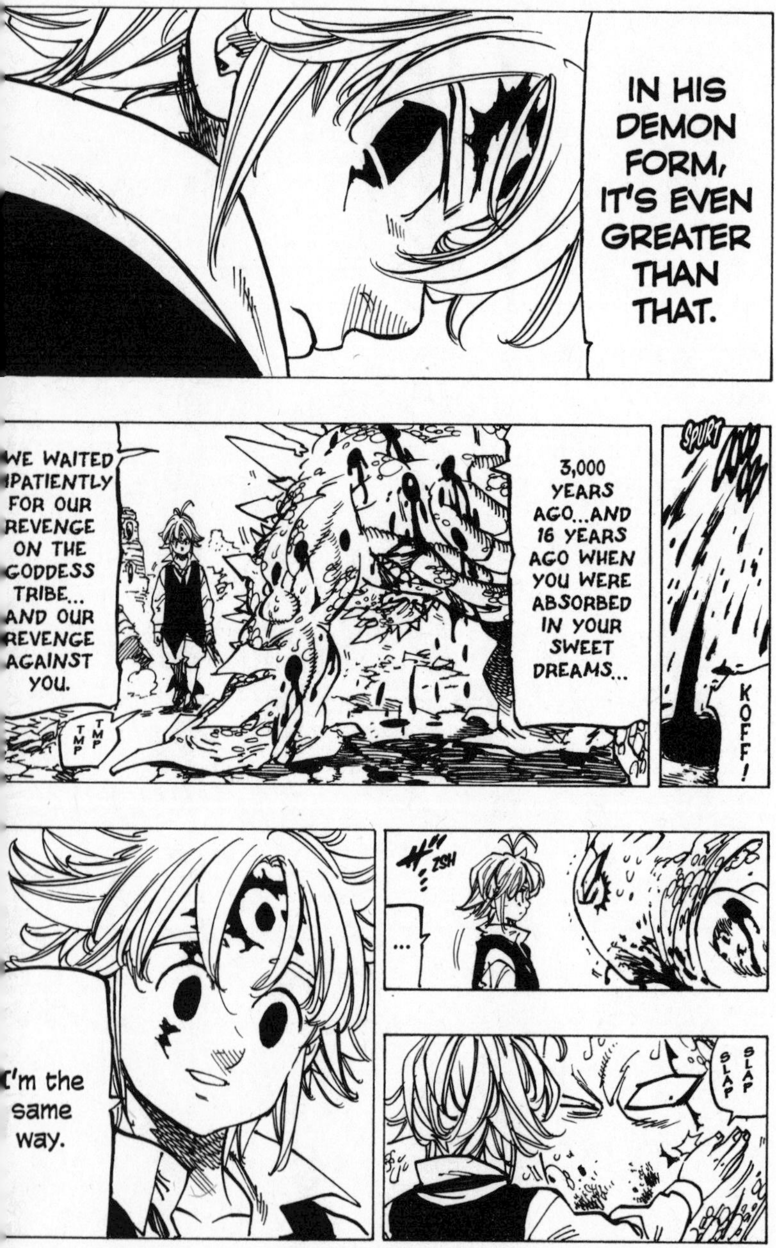
IN HIS DEMON FORM, IT'S EVEN GREATER THAN THAT.
SPURT
KOFF!
3,000 YEARS AGO...AND 16 YEARS AGO WHEN YOU WERE ABSORBED IN YOUR SWEET DREAMS...
WE WAITED PATIENTLY FOR OUR REVENGE ON THE GODDESS TRIBE... AND OUR REVENGE AGAINST YOU.
TMP TMP
ZSH
...
I'm the same way.
SLAP SLAP

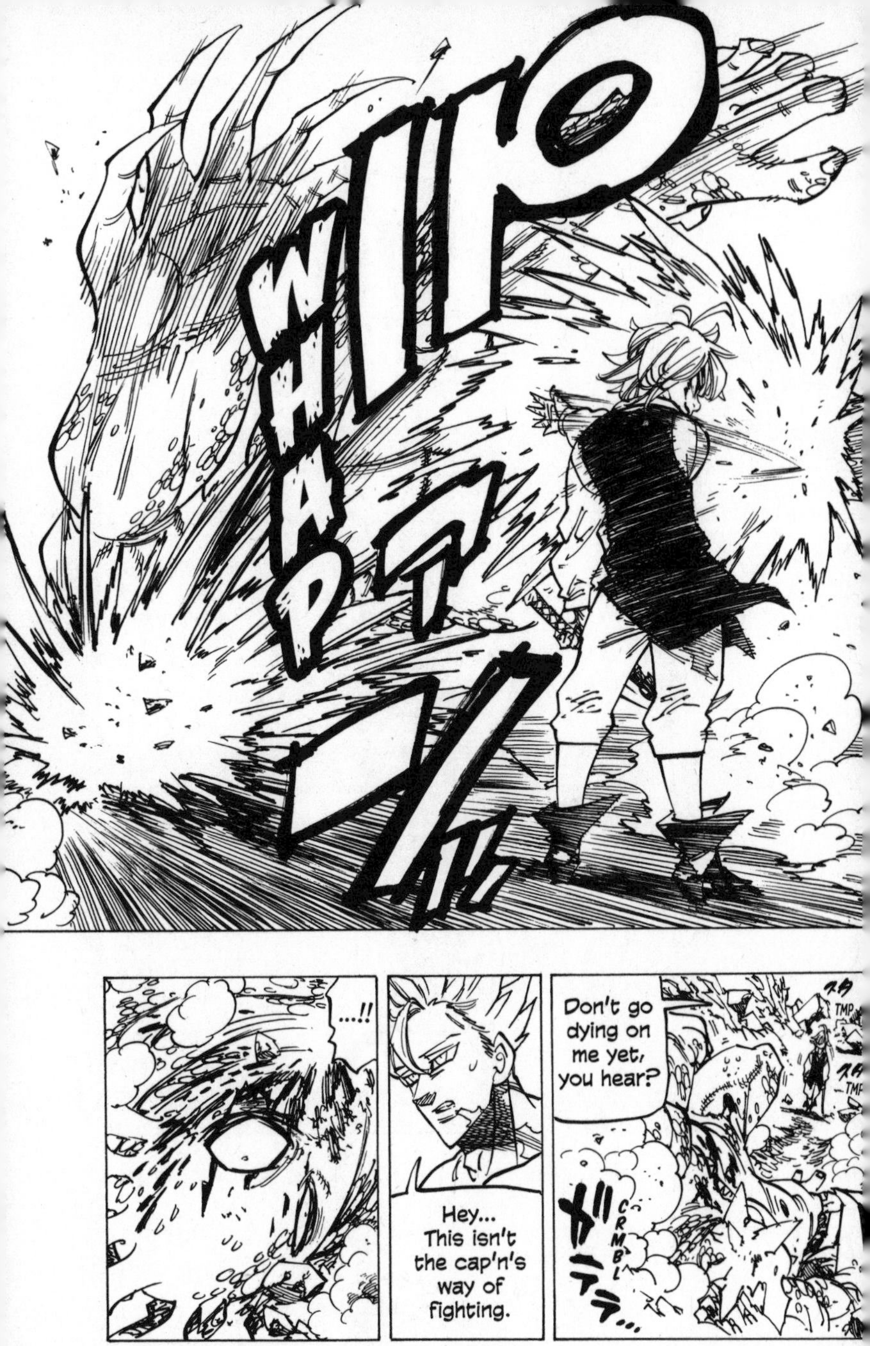
WHAP
Don't go dying on me yet, you hear?
TMP
TMP
CRMBL
Hey... This isn't the cap'n's way of fighting.
...!!

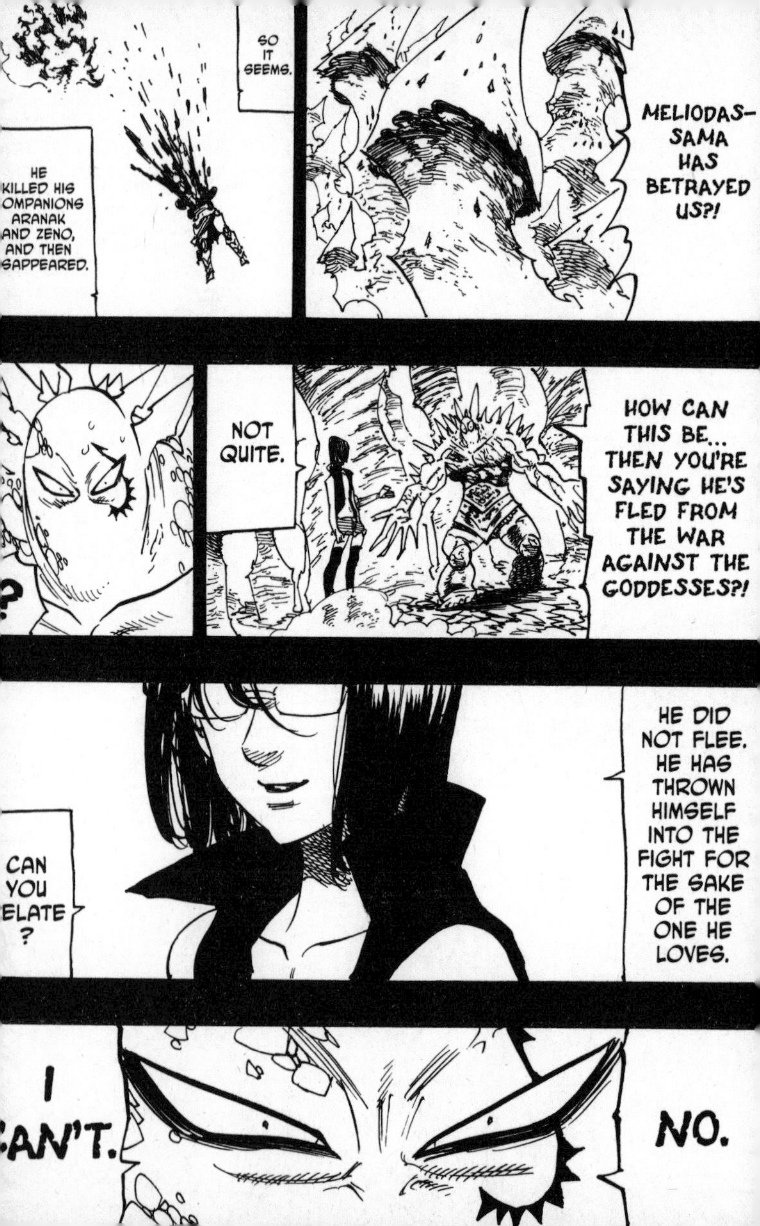
MELIODAS-SAMA HAS BETRAYED US?!
SO IT SEEMS.
HE KILLED HIS OMPANIONS ARANAK AND ZENO, AND THEN SAPPEARED.
HOW CAN THIS BE... THEN YOU'RE SAYING HE'S FLED FROM THE WAR AGAINST THE GODDESSES?!
NOT QUITE.
?
HE DID NOT FLEE. HE HAS THROWN HIMSELF INTO THE FIGHT FOR THE SAKE OF THE ONE HE LOVES.
CAN YOU ELATE ?
NO.
I AN'T.

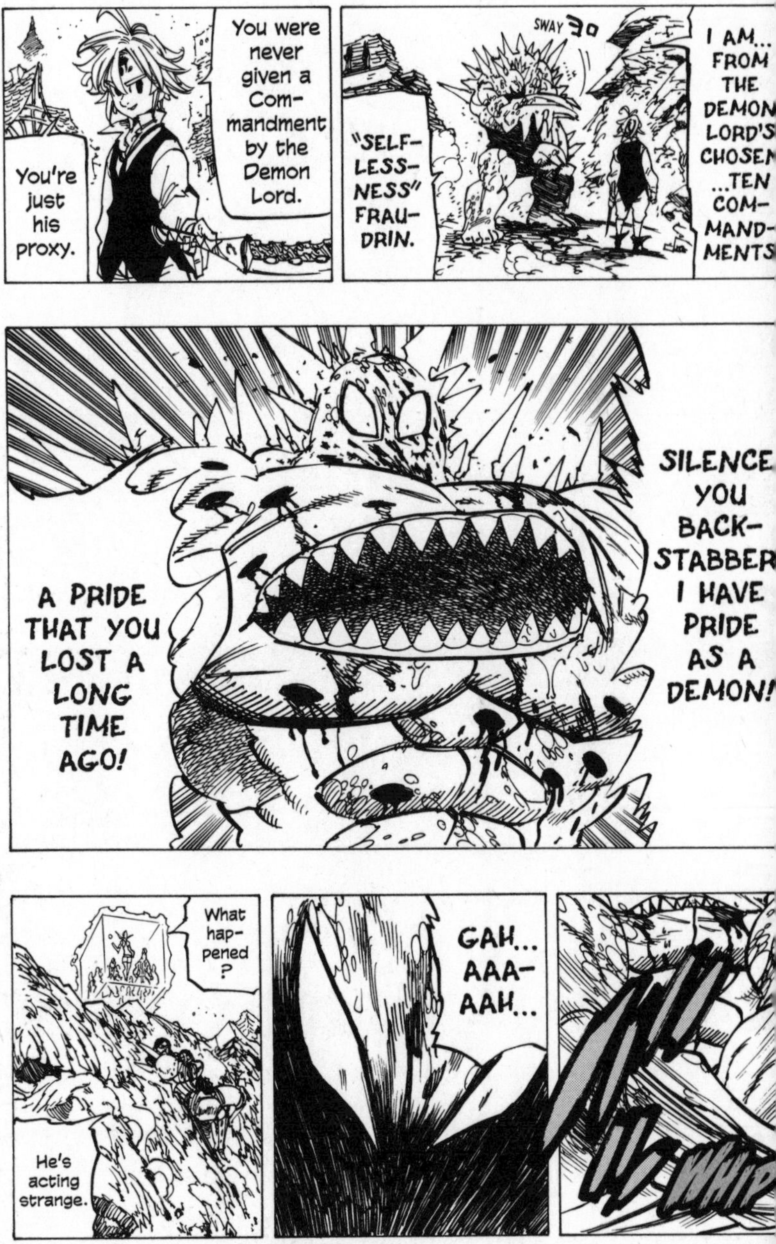
SWAY
I AM... FROM THE DEMON LORD'S CHOSEN ...TEN COMMANDMENTS
"SELFLESSNESS" FRAUDRIN.
You were never given a Commandment by the Demon Lord.
You're just his proxy.
SILENCE YOU BACKSTABBER I HAVE PRIDE AS A DEMON!
A PRIDE THAT YOU LOST A LONG TIME AGO!
WHIP
GAH... AAA-AAH...
What happened?
He's acting strange.

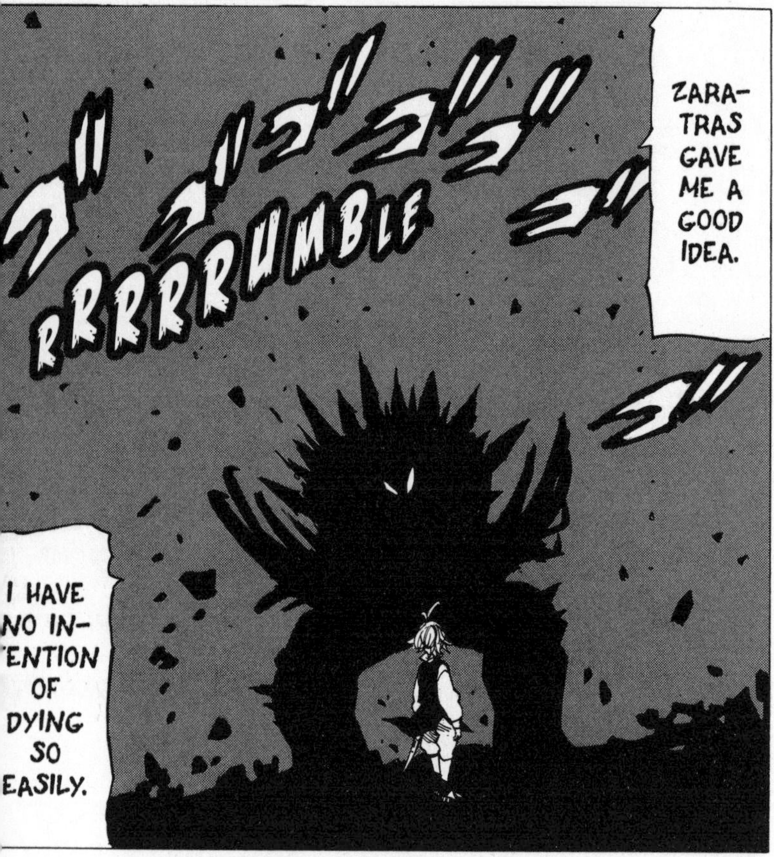
ZARA-TRAS GAVE ME A GOOD IDEA.
RRRRRUMBLE
I HAVE NO IN-TENTION OF DYING SO EASILY.

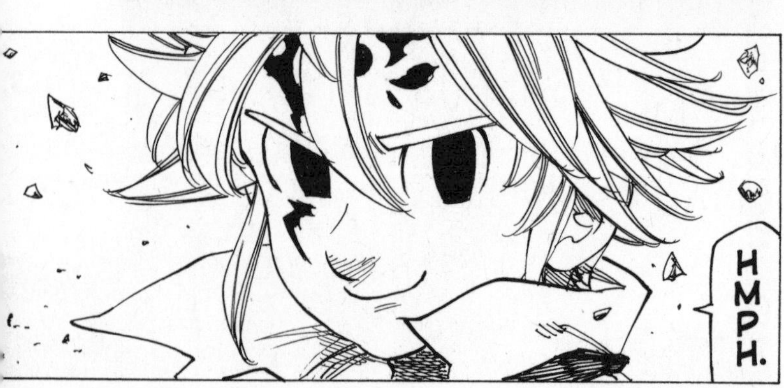
HMPH.

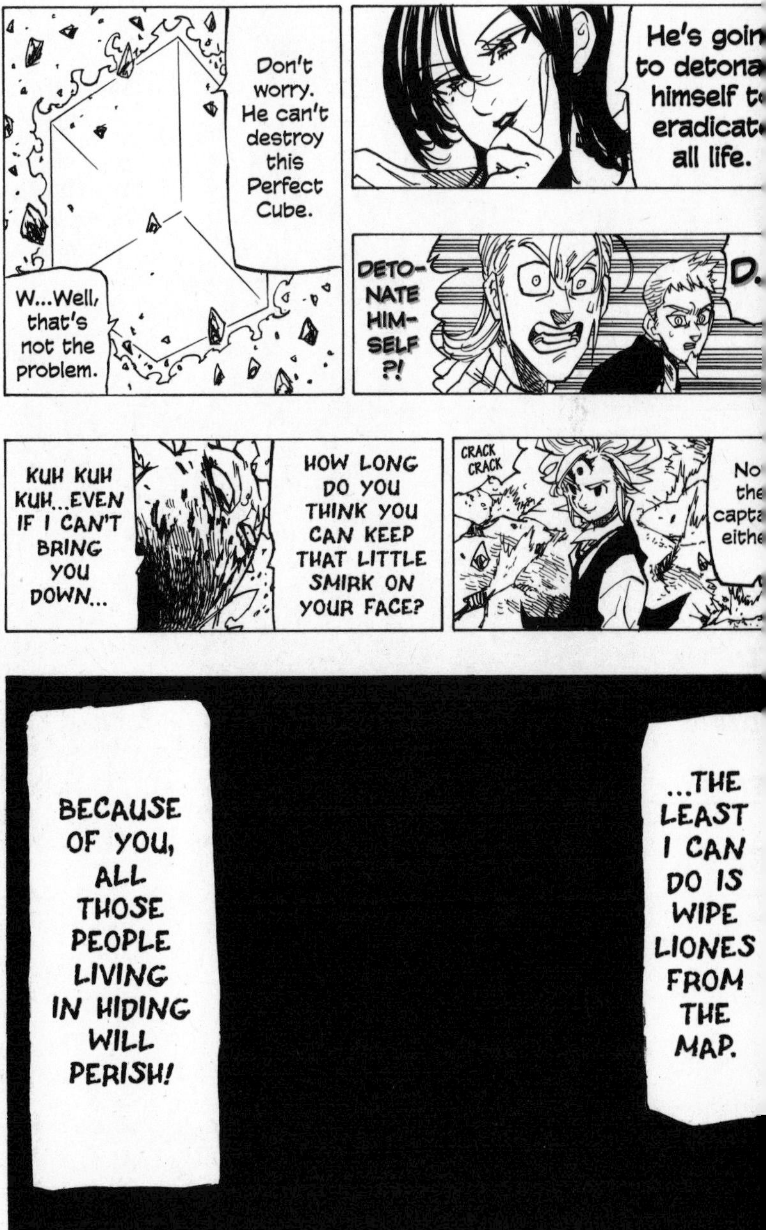
He's goin to detona himself t eradicat all life.
D.
DETO-NATE HIM-SELF ?!
Don't worry. He can't destroy this Perfect Cube.
W...Well, that's not the problem.
No the capta eithe
CRACK CRACK
HOW LONG DO YOU THINK YOU CAN KEEP THAT LITTLE SMIRK ON YOUR FACE?
KUH KUH KUH...EVEN IF I CAN'T BRING YOU DOWN...
...THE LEAST I CAN DO IS WIPE LIONES FROM THE MAP.
BECAUSE OF YOU, ALL THOSE PEOPLE LIVING IN HIDING WILL PERISH!

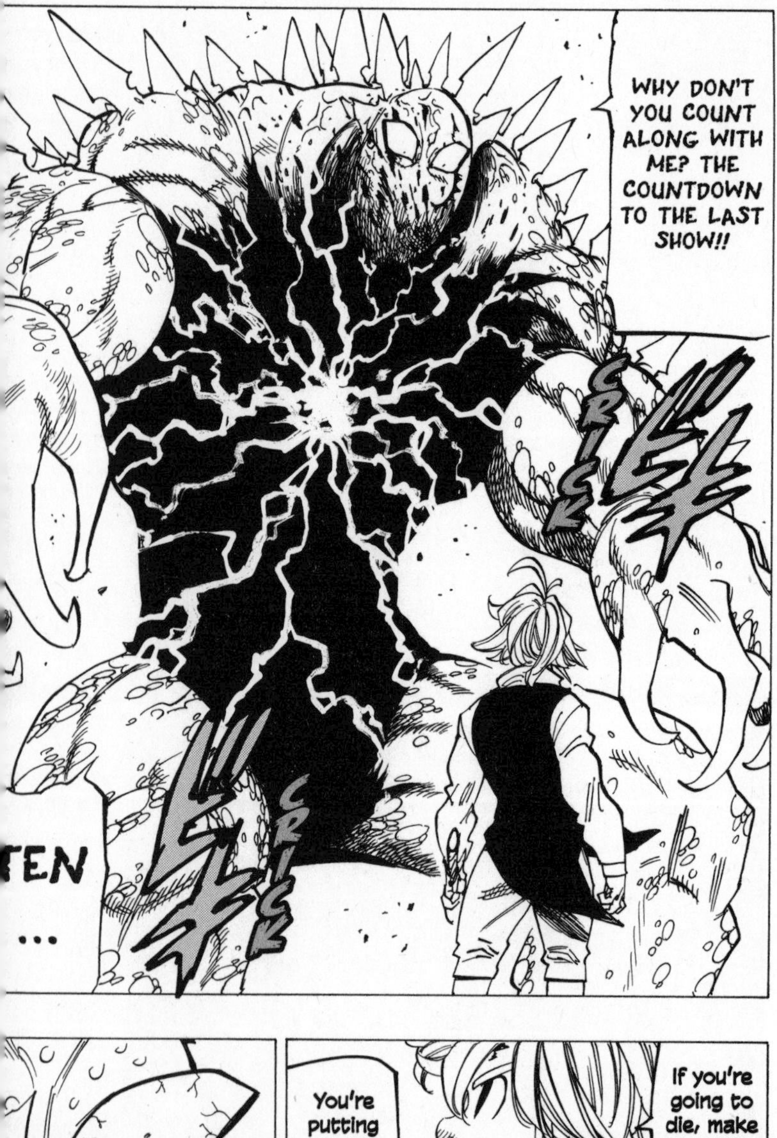
WHY DON'T YOU COUNT ALONG WITH ME? THE COUNTDOWN TO THE LAST SHOW!!
CRICK
CRICK
TEN ...
If you're going to die, make it quick.
You're putting me to sleep here.
!!

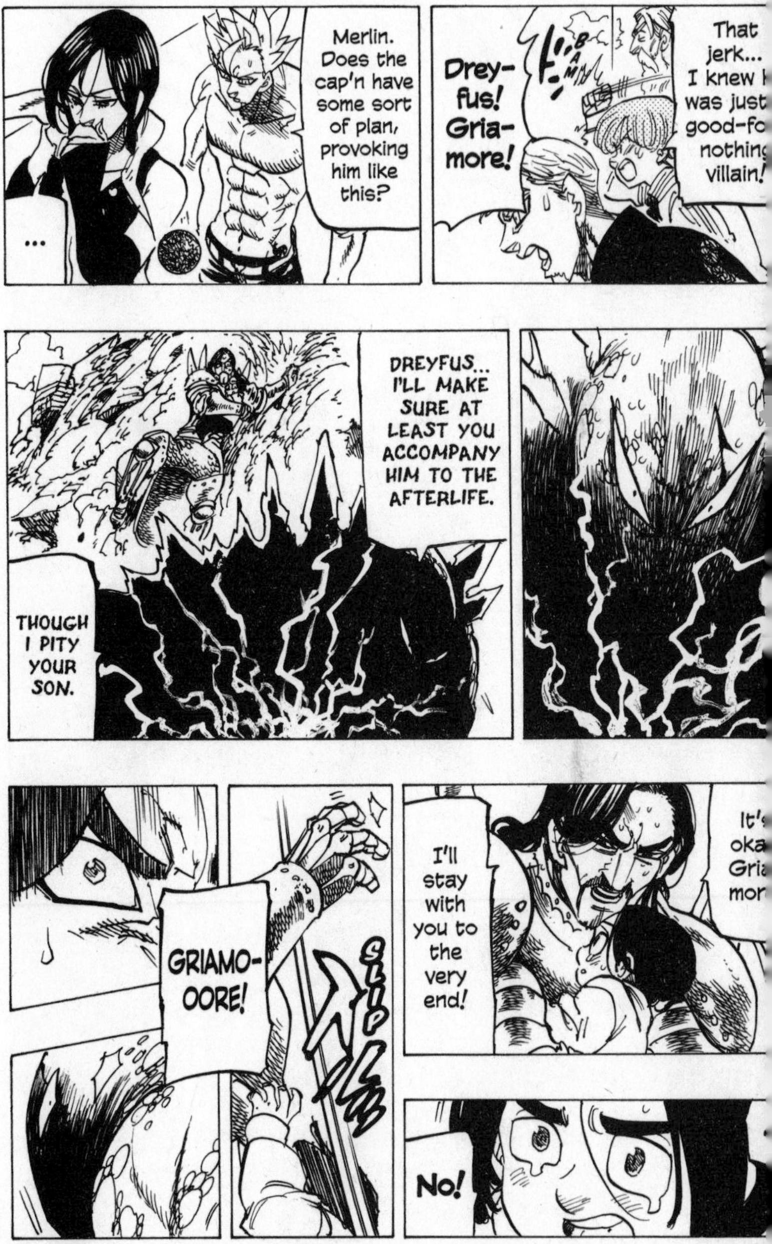
That jerk... I knew h
was just good-fo
nothing villain!
B-BAM
Dreyfus! Griamore!
Merlin. Does the cap'n have some sort of plan, provoking him like this?
...
DREYFUS... I'LL MAKE SURE AT LEAST YOU ACCOMPANY HIM TO THE AFTERLIFE.
THOUGH I PITY YOUR SON.
It' oka Gri mor
I'll stay with you to the very end!
No!
SLIP
GRIAMO-OORE!

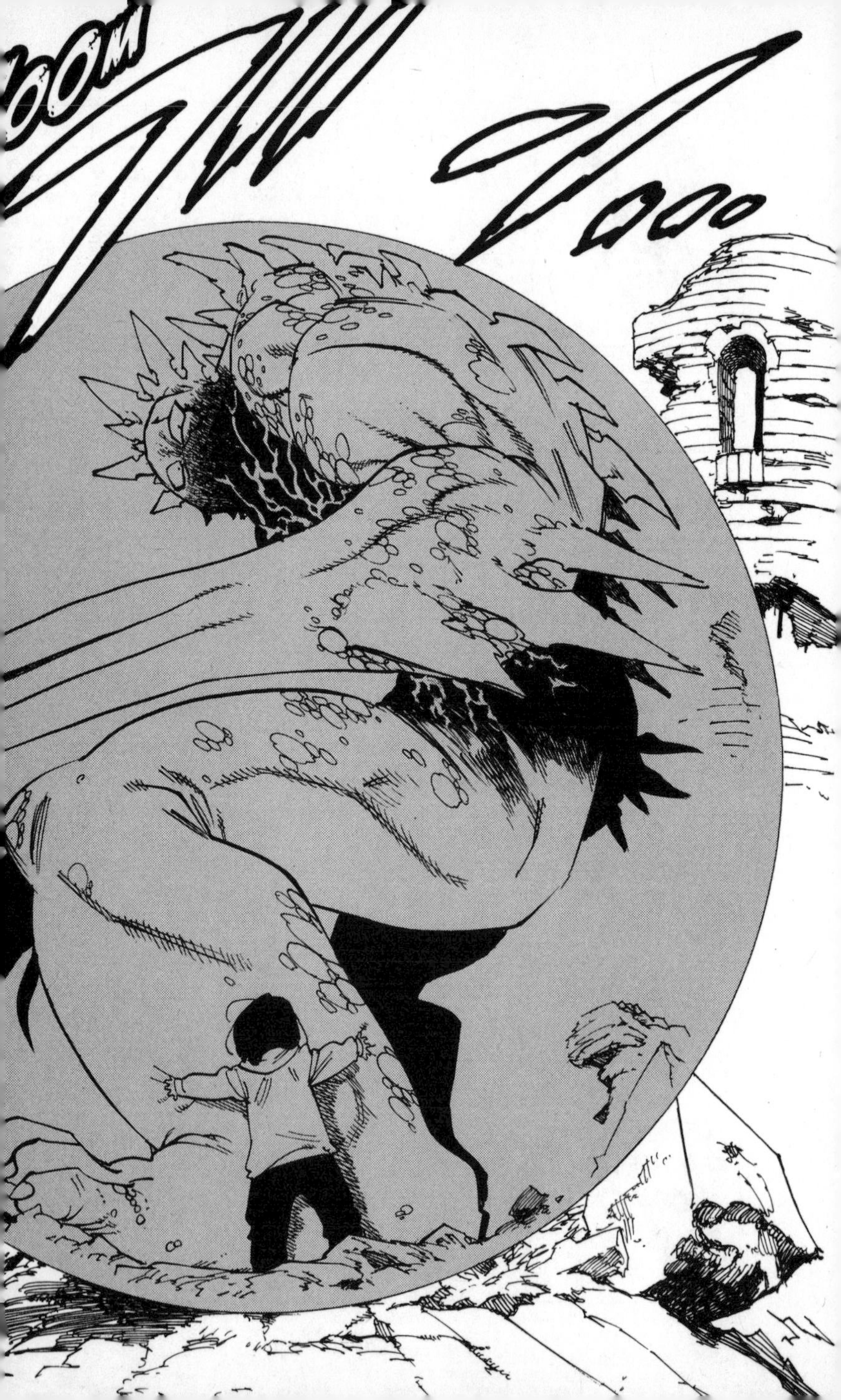

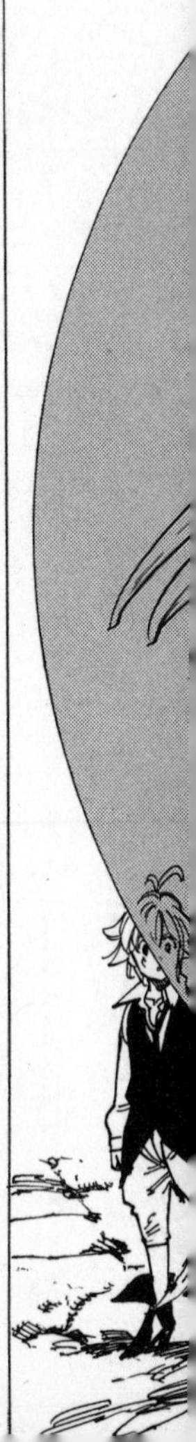

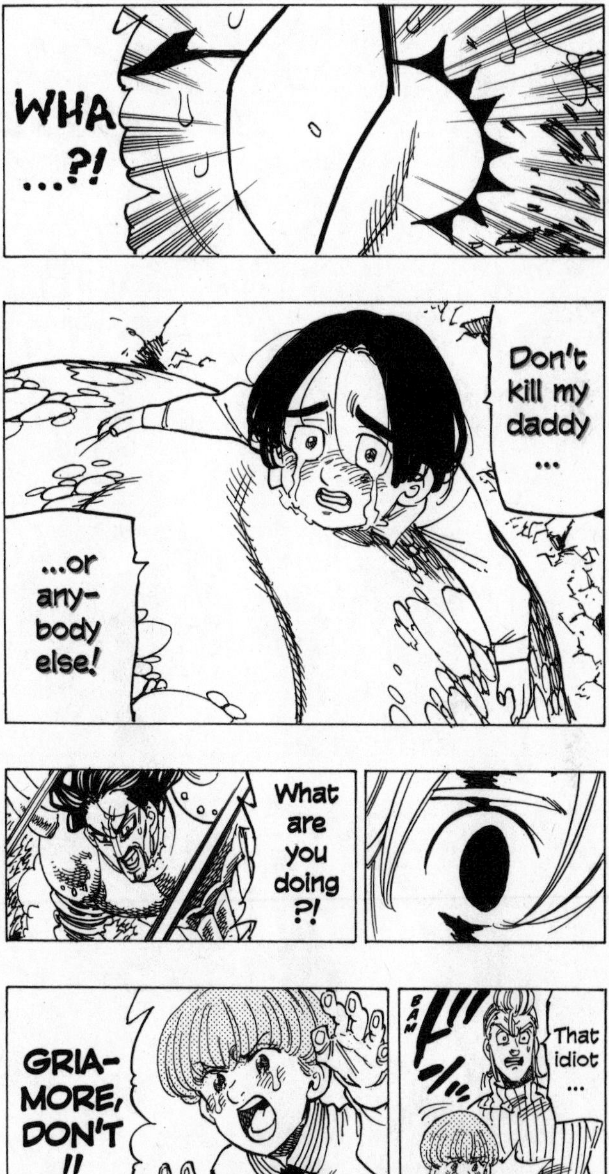
WHA ...?!
Don't kill my daddy ...
...or anybody else!
What are you doing ?!
BAM
That idiot ...
GRIAMORE, DON'T !!

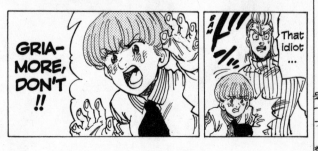

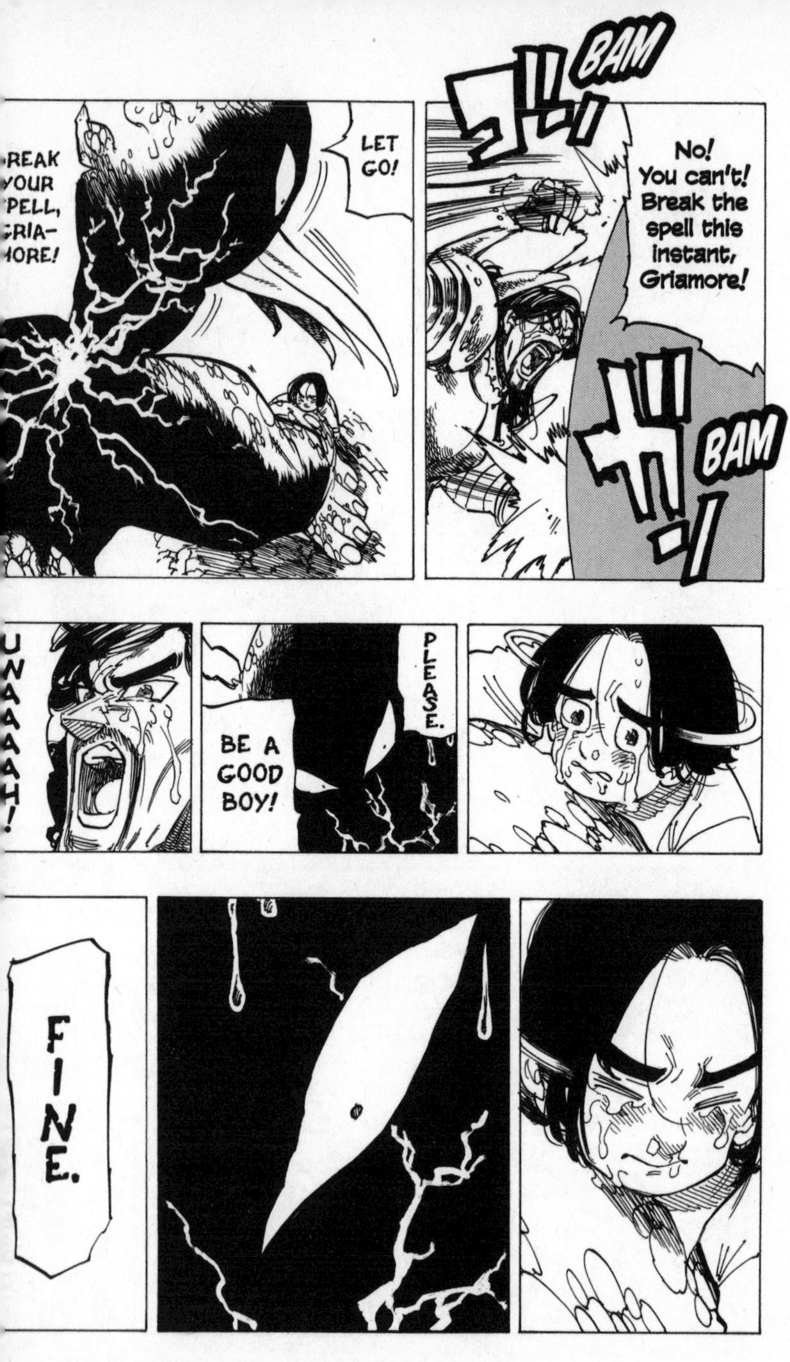
BAM
No! You can't! Break the spell this instant, Griamore!
BAM
LET GO!
REAK YOUR PELL, RIA- ORE!
PLEASE.
BE A GOOD BOY!
UNAAAAAH!
FINE.

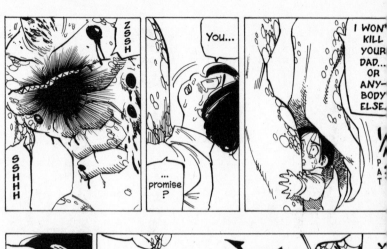

ZSSH

SSHHH

You...

...promise?

I WON'T KILL YOUR DAD... OR ANY-BODY ELSE.

PAT

RUB

SO LET DOWN THIS WALL... AND GO BACK TO YOUR DAD.

YEAH

SHWOOP

SHWOOP

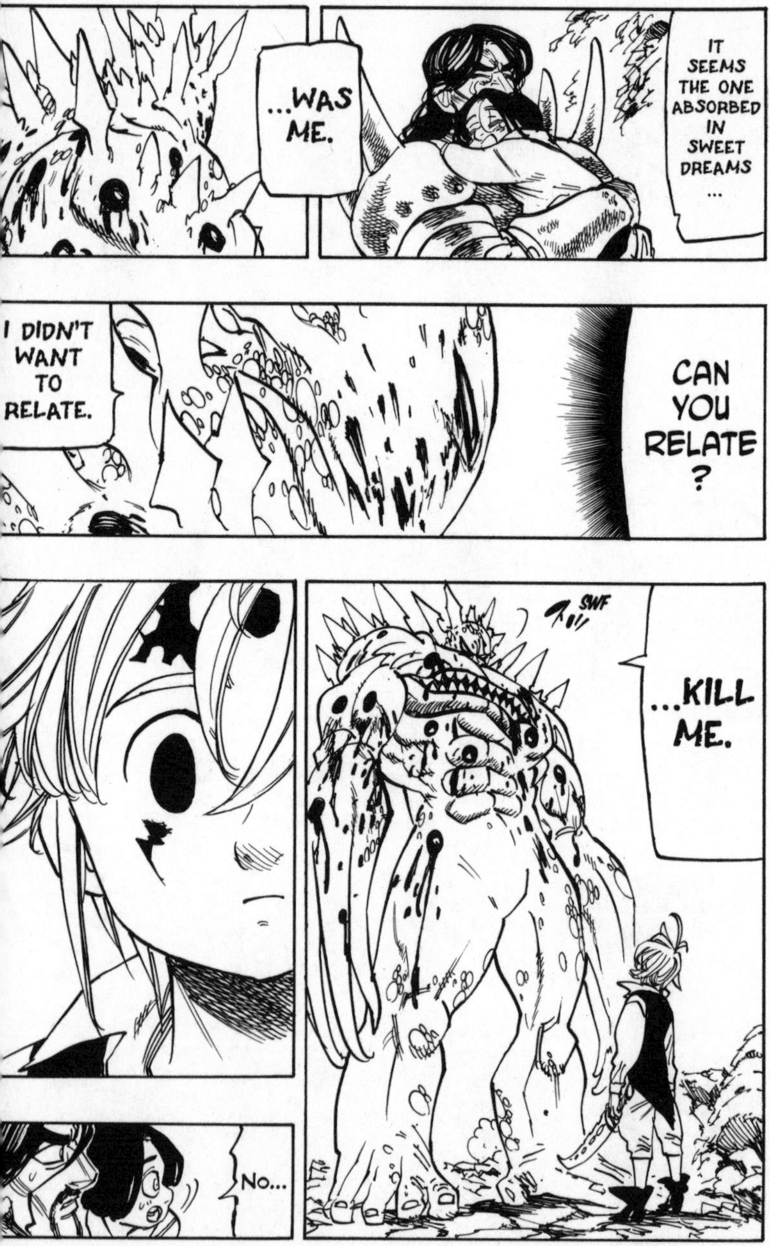
IT SEEMS THE ONE ABSORBED IN SWEET DREAMS ...
...WAS ME.
CAN YOU RELATE?
I DIDN'T WANT TO RELATE.
SWF
...KILL ME.
NO...

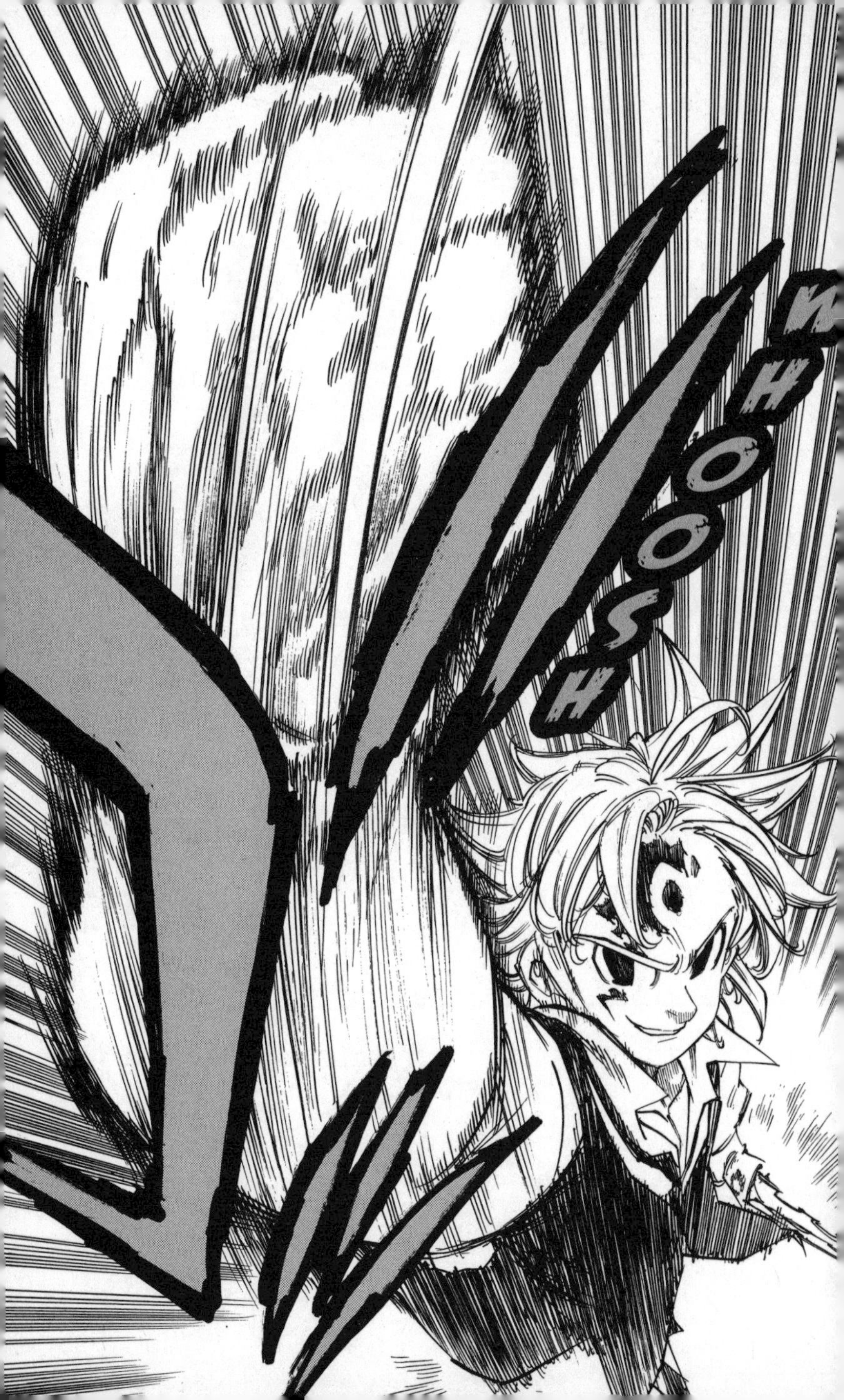
WHOOSH

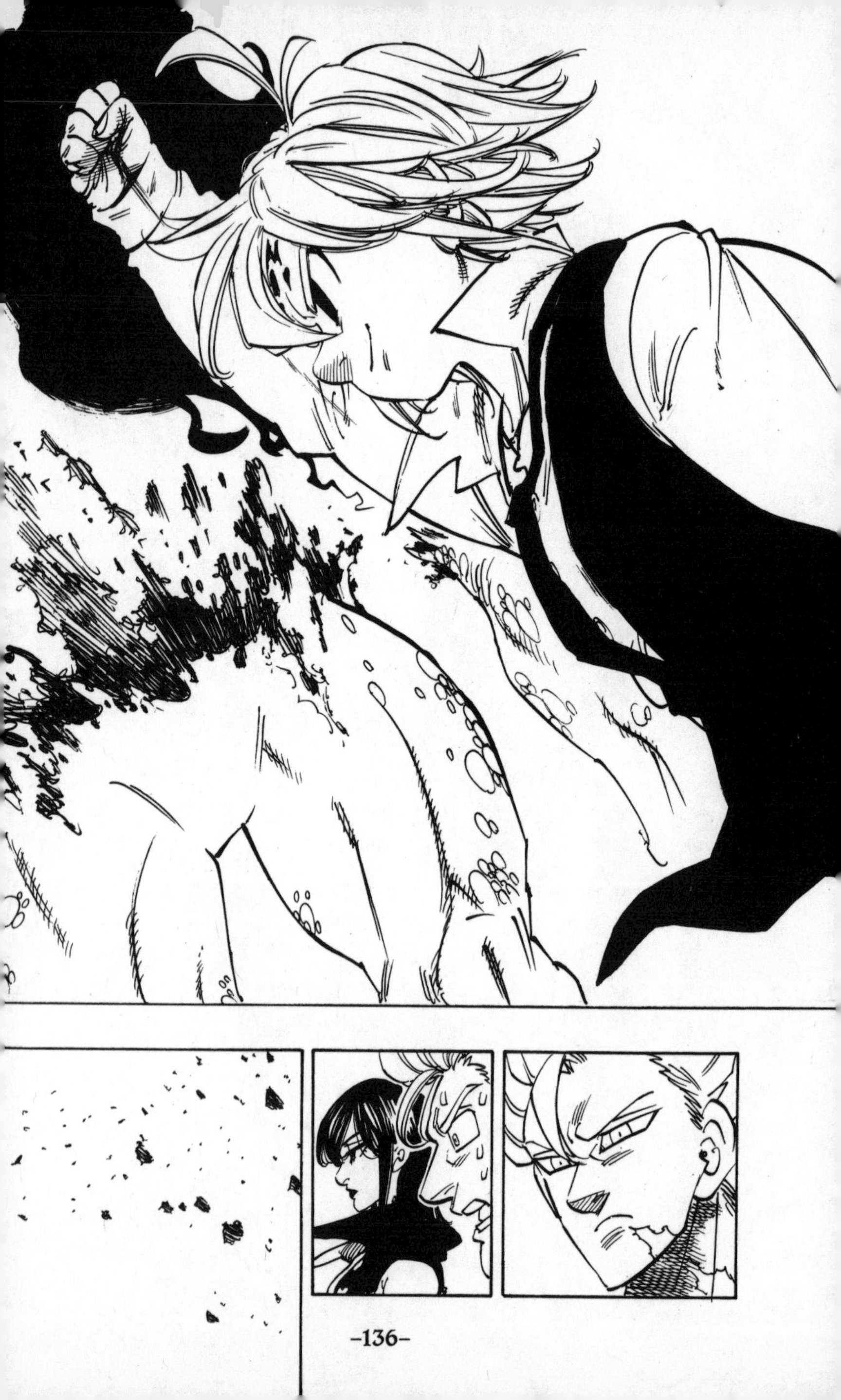

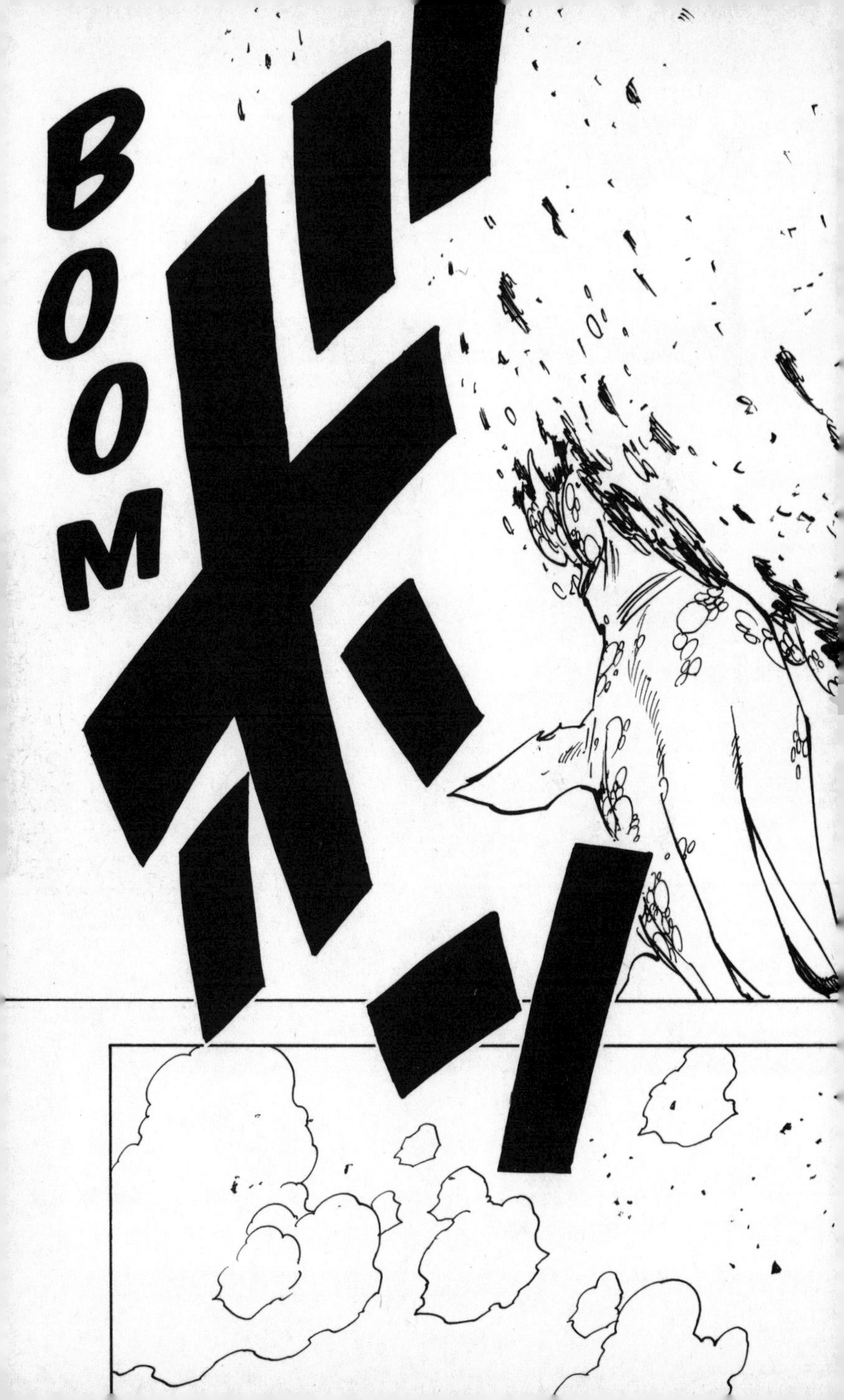
BOOM

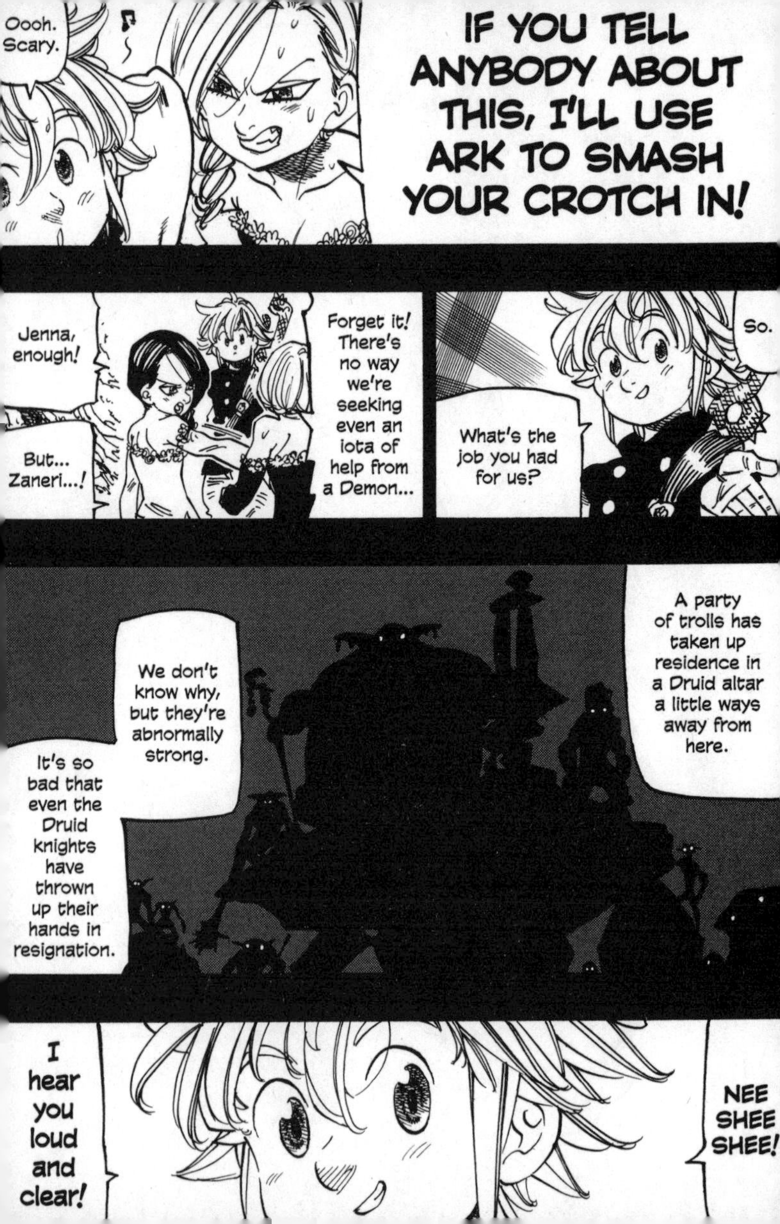
IF YOU TELL ANYBODY ABOUT THIS, I'LL USE ARK TO SMASH YOUR CROTCH IN!
Oooh. Scary.
So.
What's the job you had for us?
Forget it! There's no way we're seeking even an iota of help from a Demon...
Jenna, enough!
But... Zaneri...!
A party of trolls has taken up residence in a Druid altar a little ways away from here.
We don't know why, but they're abnormally strong.
It's so bad that even the Druid knights have thrown up their hands in resignation.
NEE SHEE SHEE!
I hear you loud and clear!

Chapter 196 - So Long As You're Here

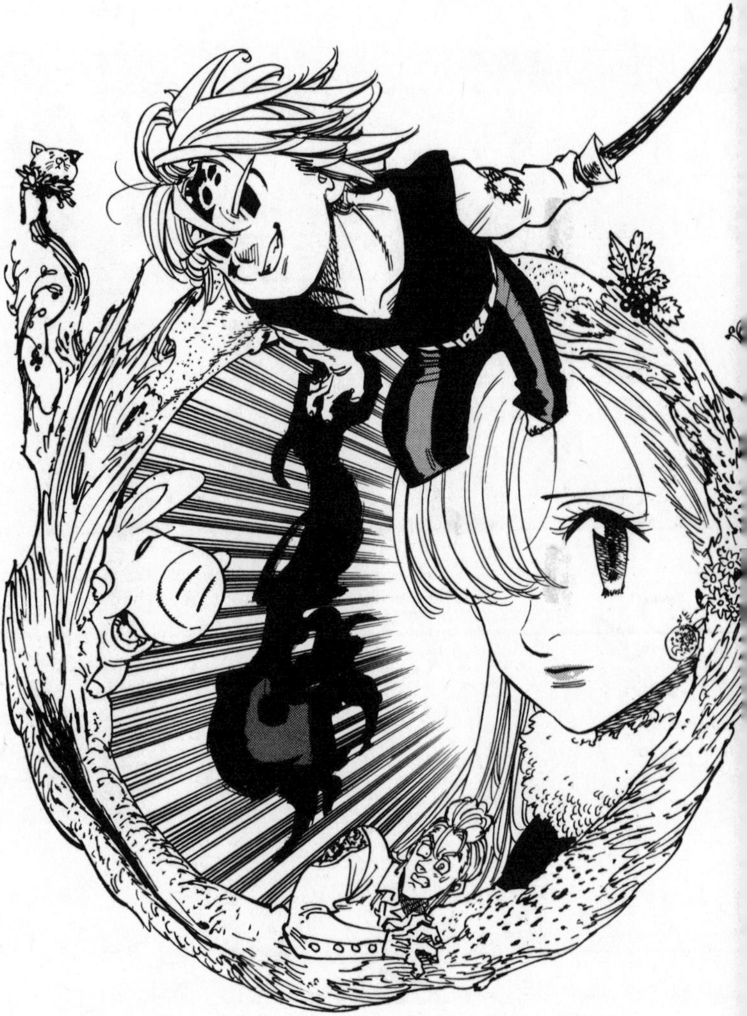

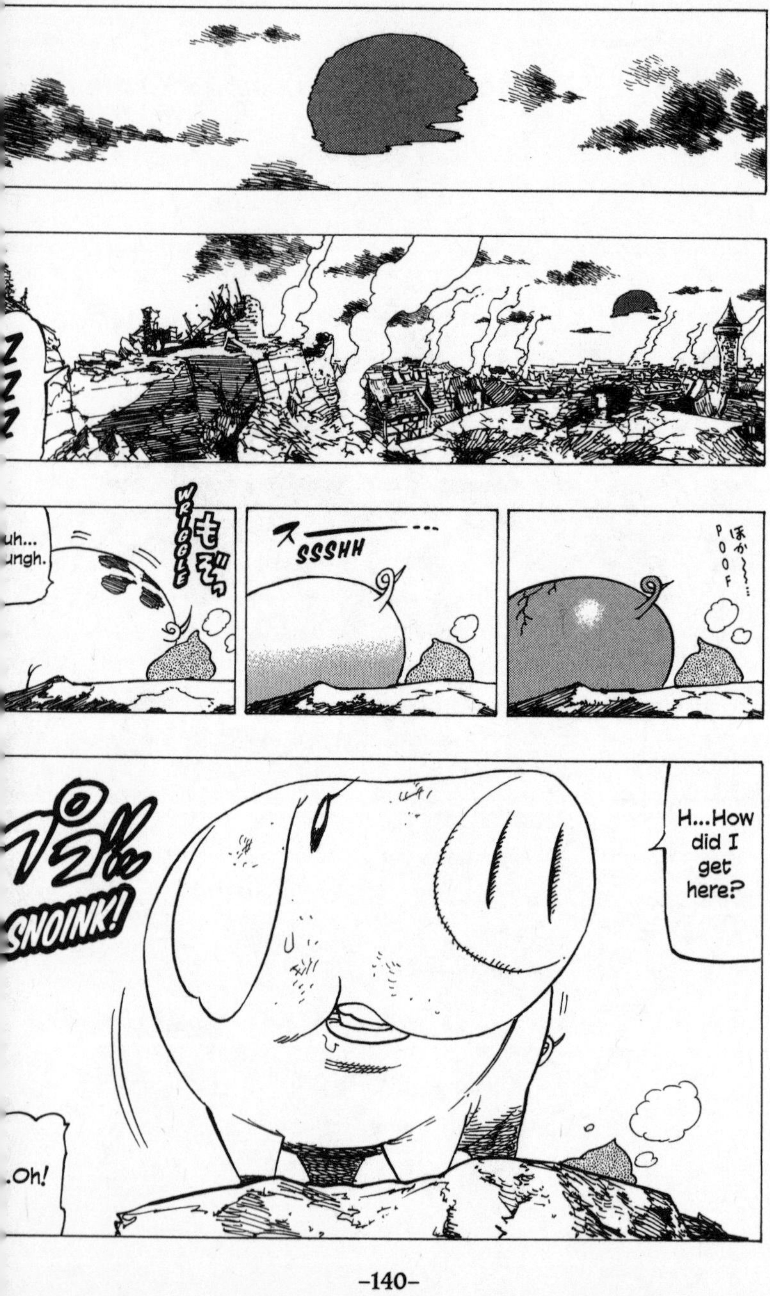

ZZZ
ほか~~... POOF
ス SSSHH
もぞっ WRIGGLE
uh... ungh.
H...How did I get here?
SNOINK!
.Oh!

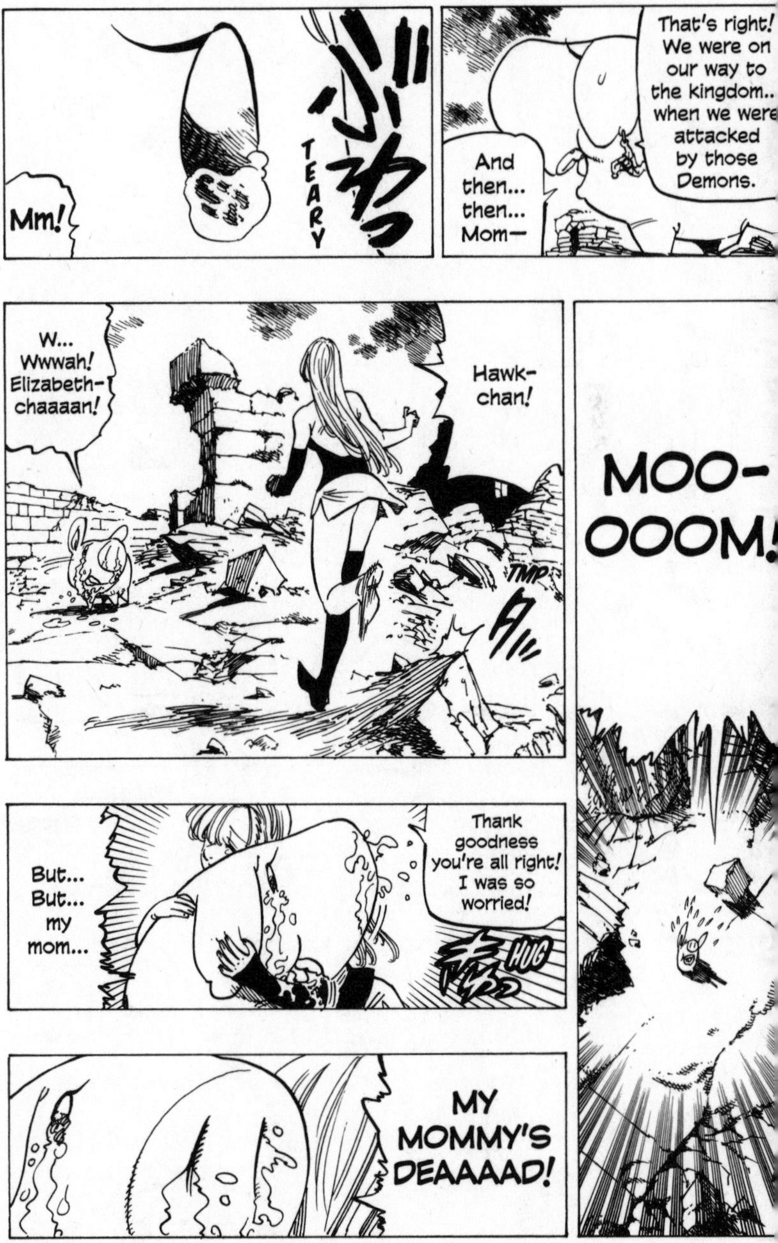
That's right! We were on our way to the kingdom.. when we were attacked by those Demons.
And then... then... Mom—
TEARY
Mm!
MOO-OOOM!
Hawk-chan!
W... Wwwah! Elizabeth-chaaaan!
TMP
Thank goodness you're all right! I was so worried!
HUG
But... But... my mom...
MY MOMMY'S DEAAAAD!

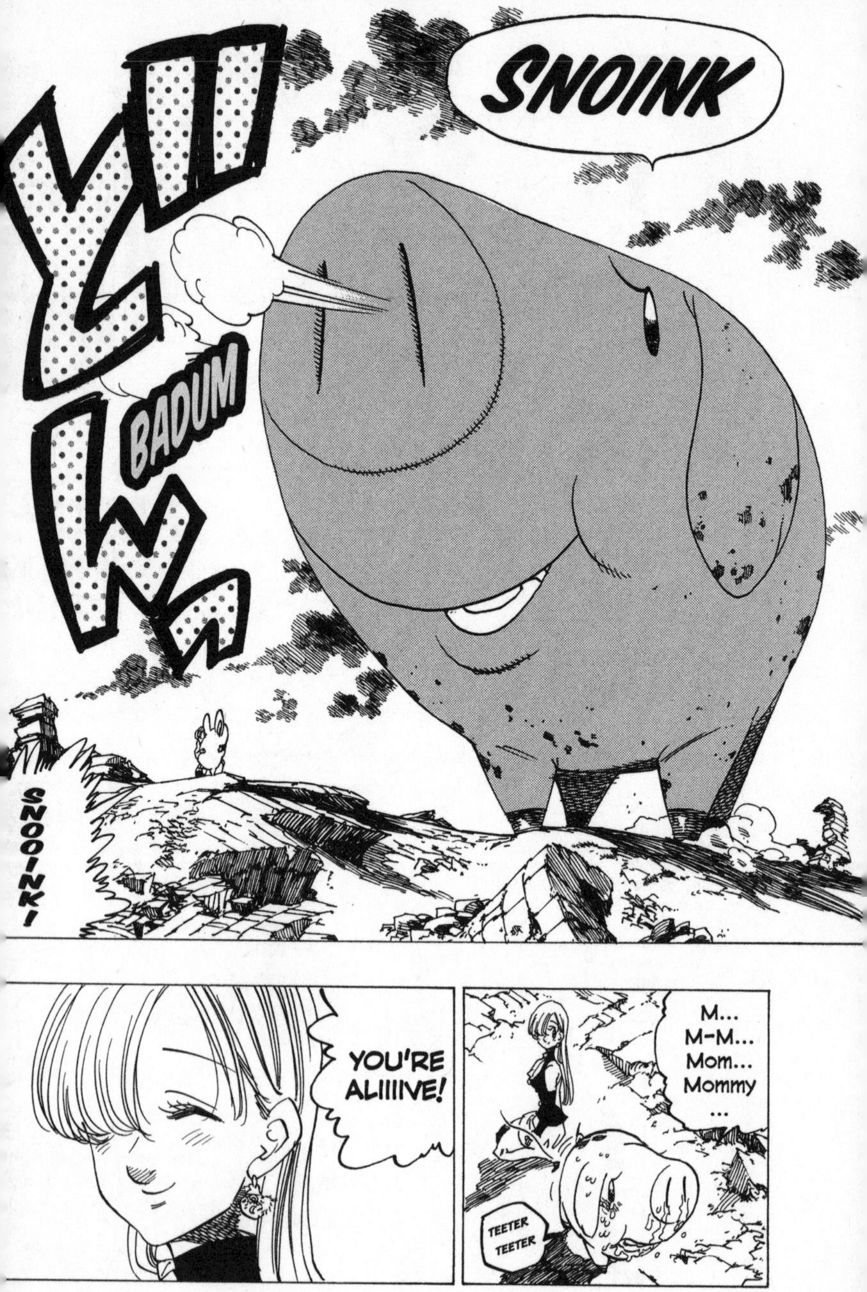
SNOINK
BADUM
SNOOINK!
M... M-M... Mom... Mommy ...
TEETER TEETER
YOU'RE ALIIIIVE!

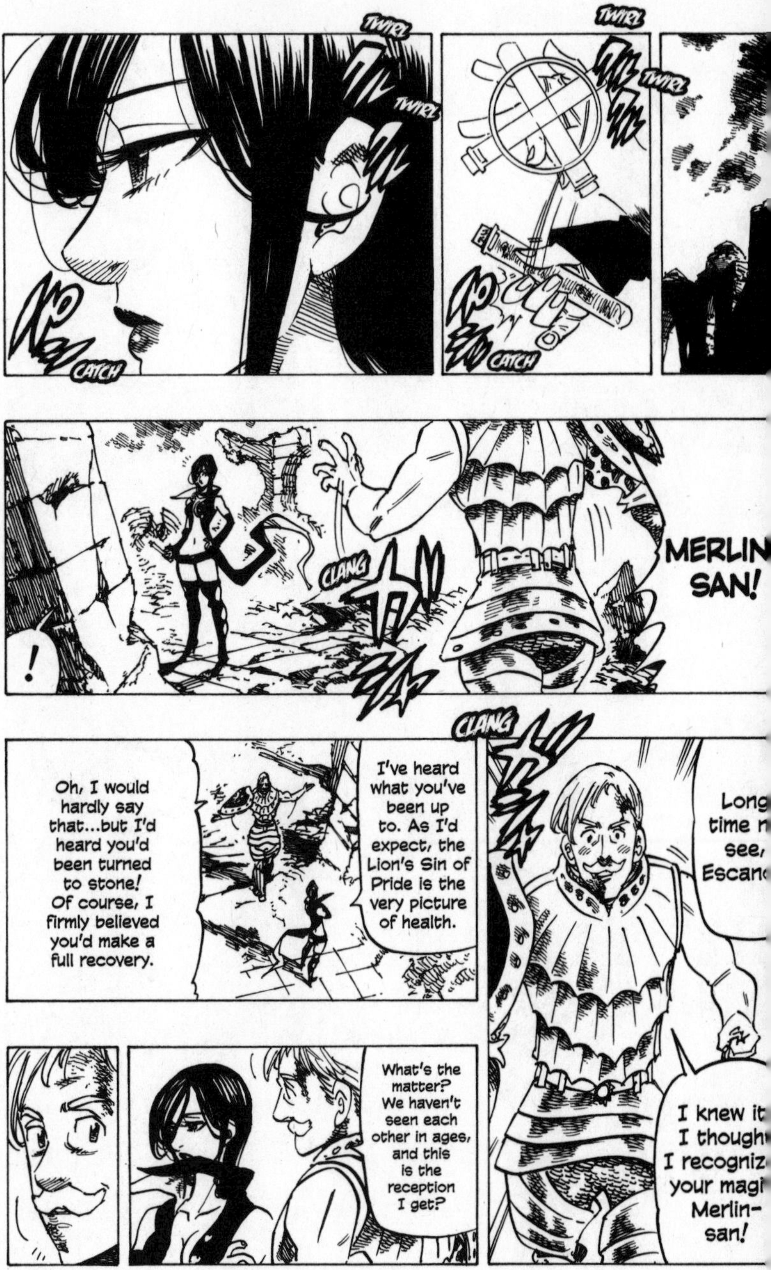
TWIRL
TWIRL
CATCH
TWIRL
TWIRL
CATCH
MERLIN SAN!
CLANG
!
CLANG
Long time n see, Escan
I've heard what you've been up to. As I'd expect, the Lion's Sin of Pride is the very picture of health.
Oh, I would hardly say that...but I'd heard you'd been turned to stone! Of course, I firmly believed you'd make a full recovery.
I knew it I though I recogniz your magi Merlin-san!
What's the matter? We haven't seen each other in ages, and this is the reception I get?

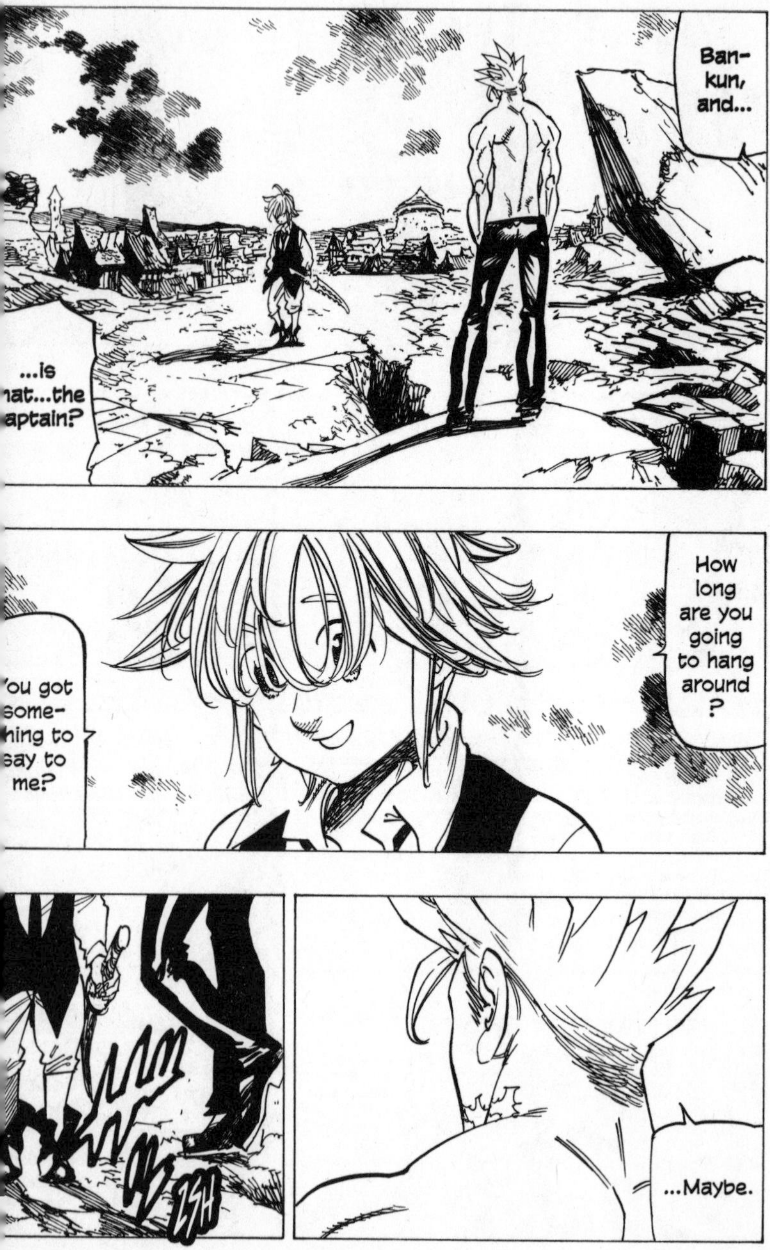
Ban-kun, and...
...is nat...the aptain?
How long are you going to hang around?
'ou got some-hing to say to me?
...Maybe.
ZSH

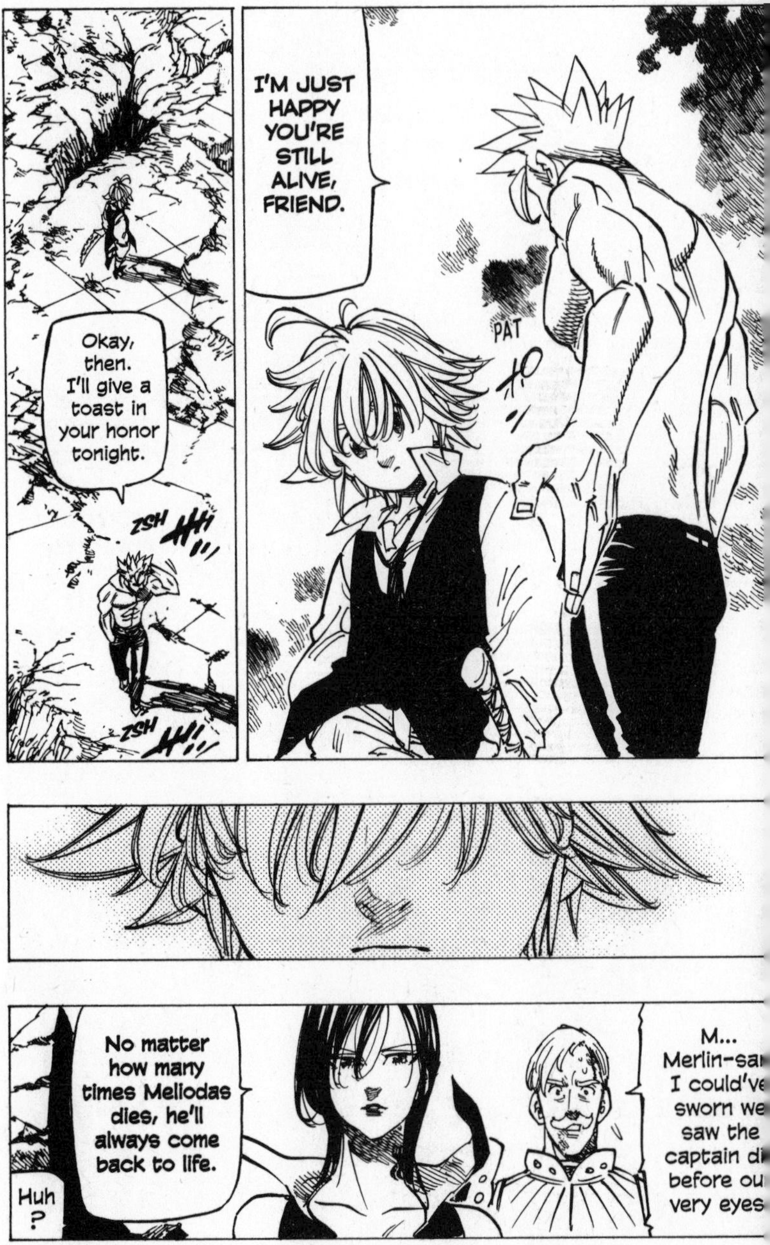

I'M JUST HAPPY YOU'RE STILL ALIVE, FRIEND.
PAT
Okay, then. I'll give a toast in your honor tonight.
ZSH
ZSH
M... Merlin-sa I could've sworn we saw the captain di before ou very eyes
No matter how many times Meliodas dies, he'll always come back to life.
Huh?

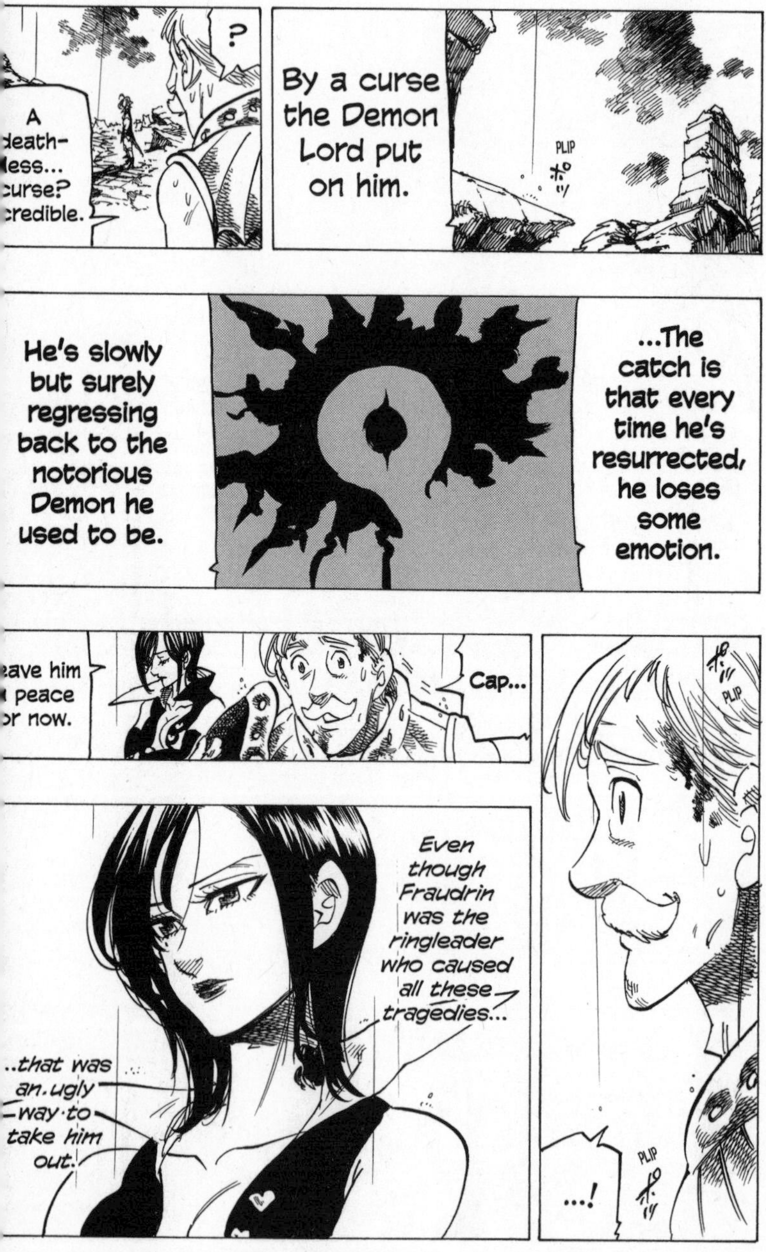
By a curse the Demon Lord put on him.
PLIP
?
A death-less... curse? credible.
...The catch is that every time he's resurrected, he loses some emotion.
He's slowly but surely regressing back to the notorious Demon he used to be.
PLIP
PLIP
...!
Cap...
eave him peace or now.
Even though Fraudrin was the ringleader who caused all these tragedies...
..that was an ugly way to take him out.

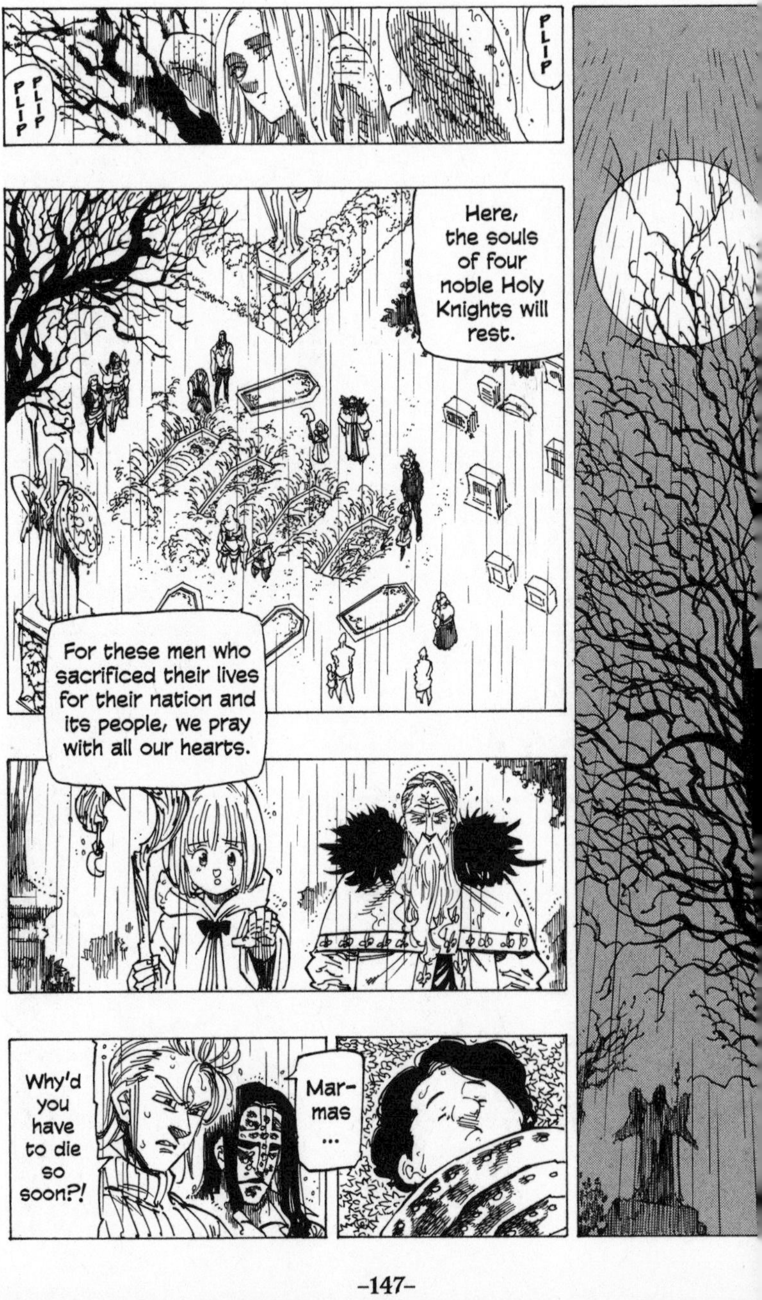
PLIP
PLIP PLIP
Here, the souls of four noble Holy Knights will rest.
For these men who sacrificed their lives for their nation and its people, we pray with all our hearts.
Mar-mas...
Why'd you have to die so soon?!

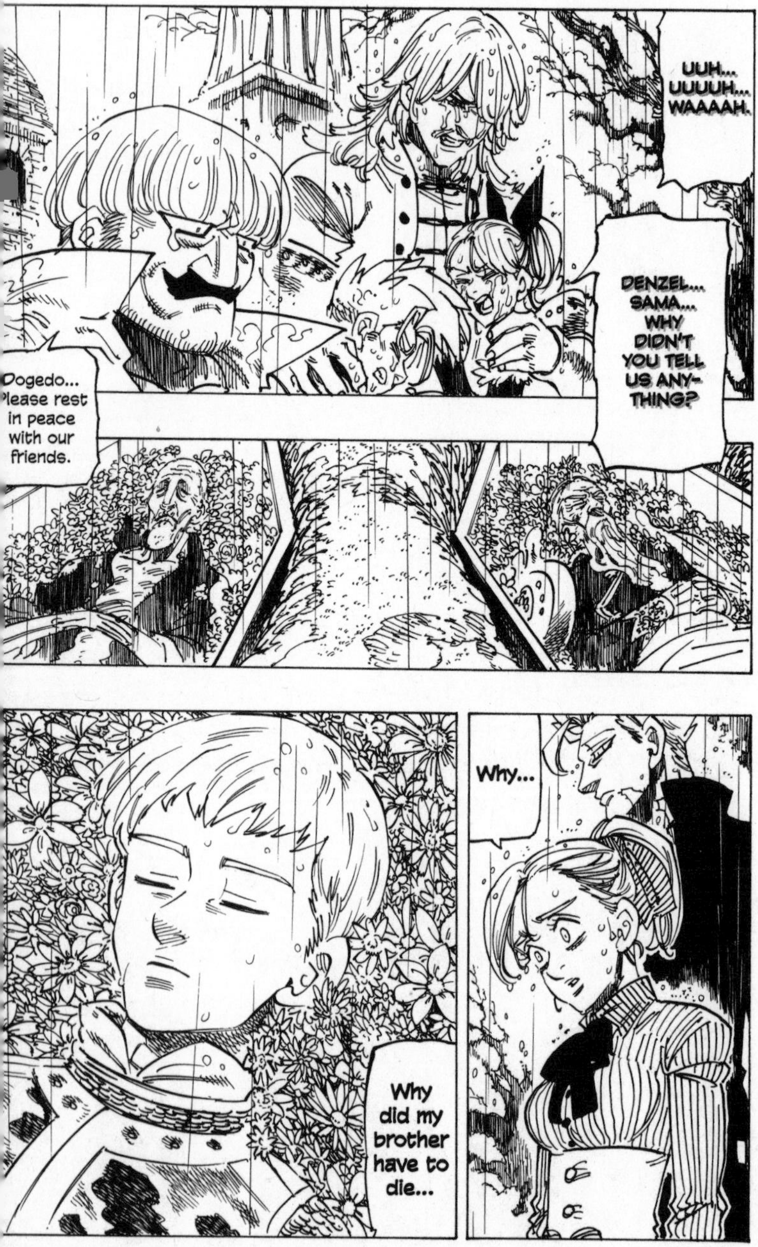
UUH... UUUUH... WAAAAH.
DENZEL... SAMA... WHY DIDN'T YOU TELL US ANYTHING?
Dogedo... Please rest in peace with our friends.
Why...
Why did my brother have to die...

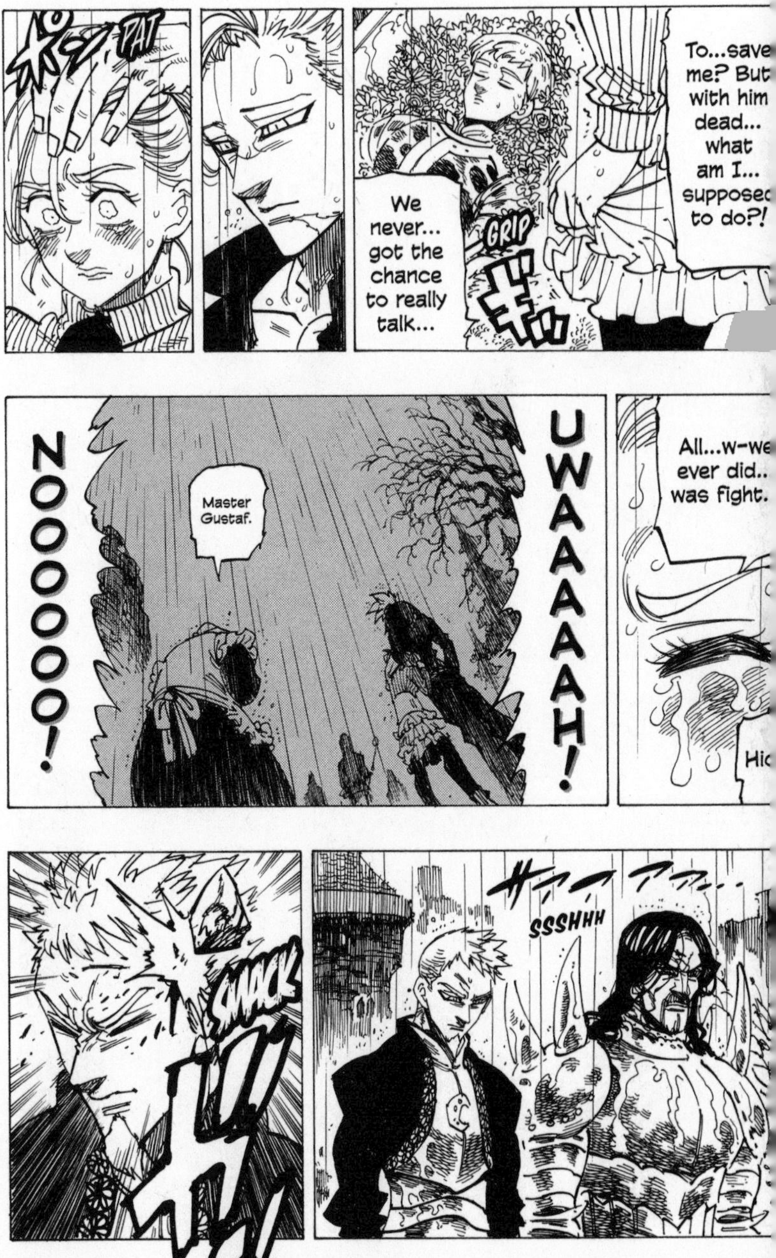
To...save me? But with him dead... what am I... supposed to do?!
We never... got the chance to really talk...
GRIP
PAT
All...w-we ever did... was fight.
Hic
UWAAAAAH!
Master Gustaf.
NOOOOOOO!
SSSHHH
SMACK

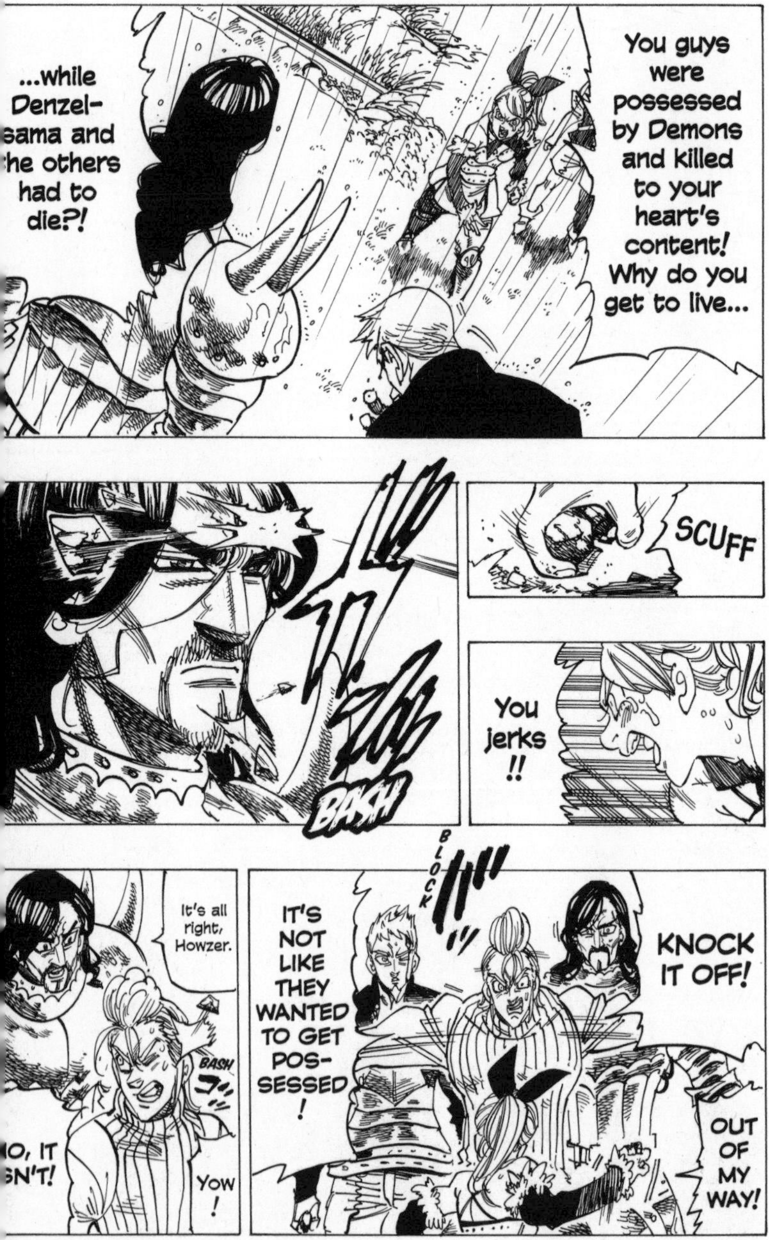

You guys were possessed by Demons and killed to your heart's content! Why do you get to live...
...while Denzel-sama and he others had to die?!
SCUFF
You jerks!!
BASH
KNOCK IT OFF!
IT'S NOT LIKE THEY WANTED TO GET POS-SESSED!
BLOCK
OUT OF MY WAY!
It's all right, Howzer.
BASH
O, IT SN'T!
YOW!

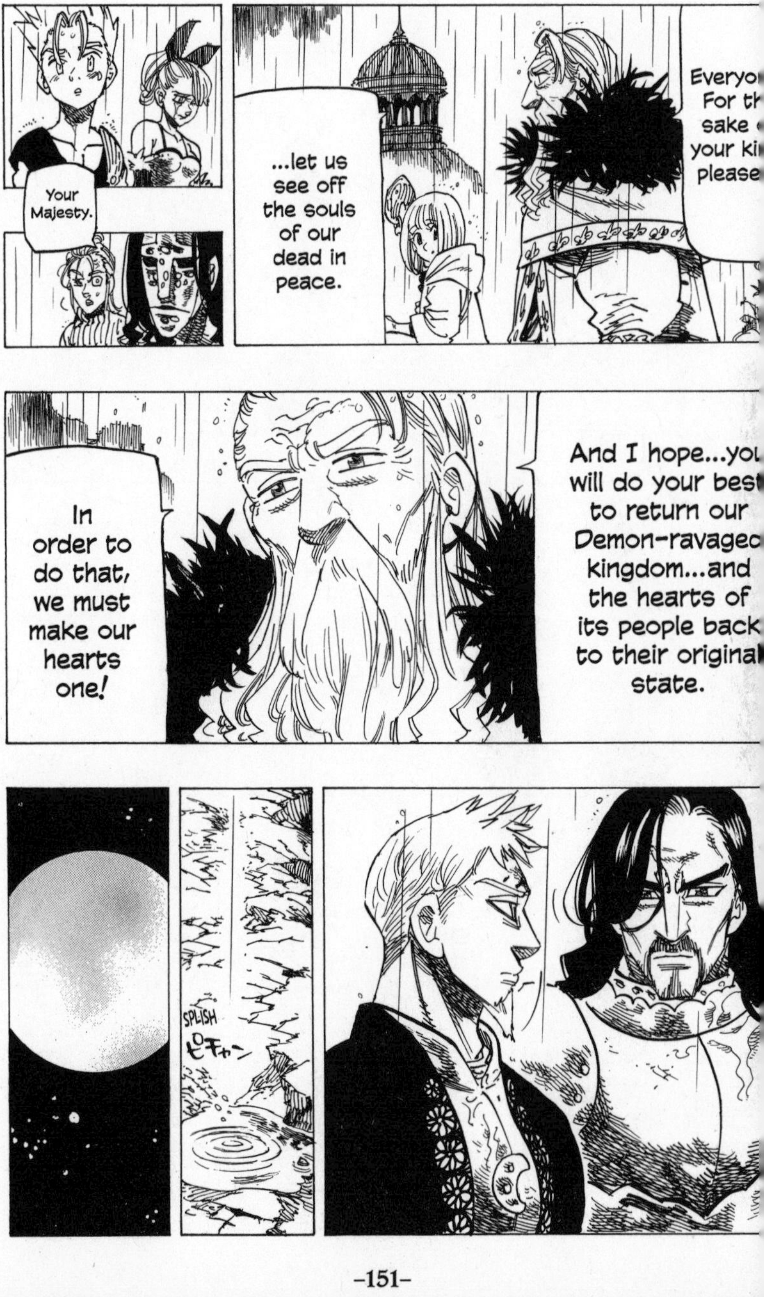
Everyo For th sake your ki please
...let us see off the souls of our dead in peace.
Your Majesty.
And I hope...yo will do your bes to return our Demon-ravage kingdom...and the hearts of its people back to their origina state.
In order to do that, we must make our hearts one!
SPLISH
ピチャン

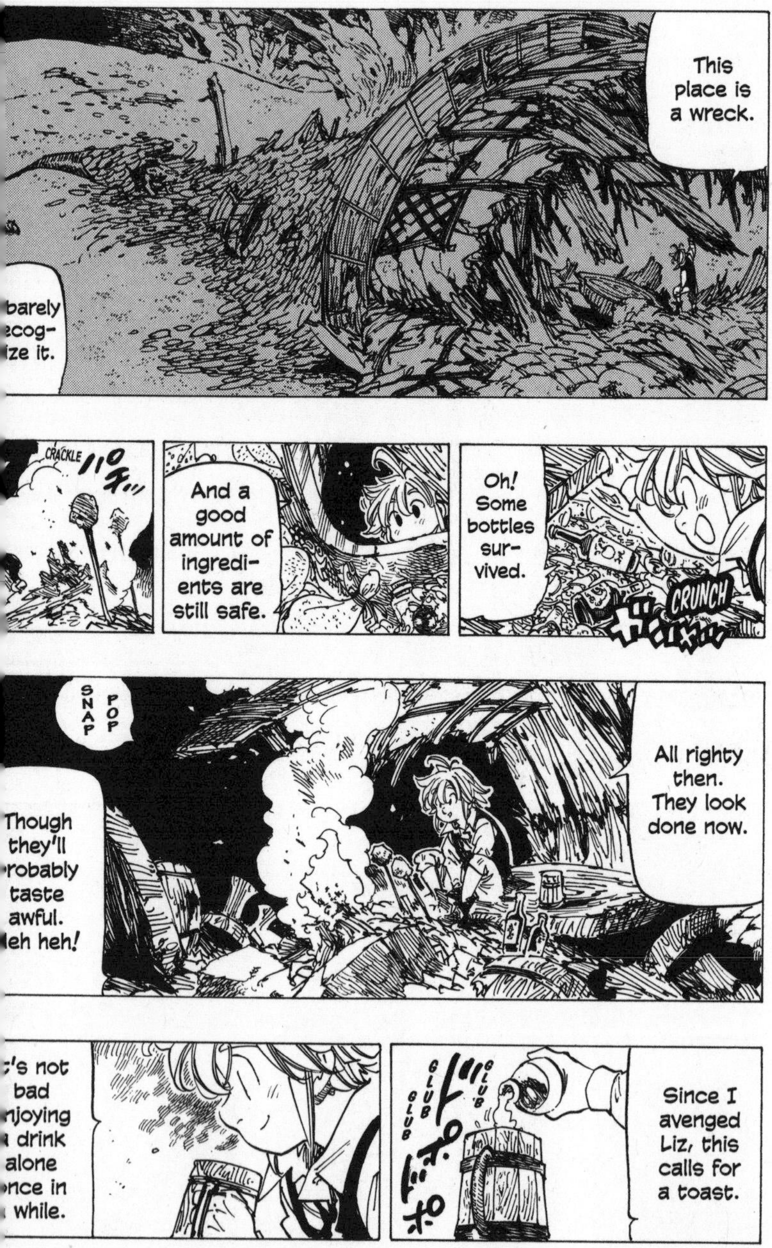
This place is a wreck.
barely ecog- ize it.
Oh! Some bottles sur- vived.
CRUNCH
And a good amount of ingredi- ents are still safe.
CRACKLE
All righty then. They look done now.
SNAP POP
Though they'll robably taste awful. eh heh!
Since I avenged Liz, this calls for a toast.
GLUB GLUB GLUB
's not bad njoying drink alone nce in while.

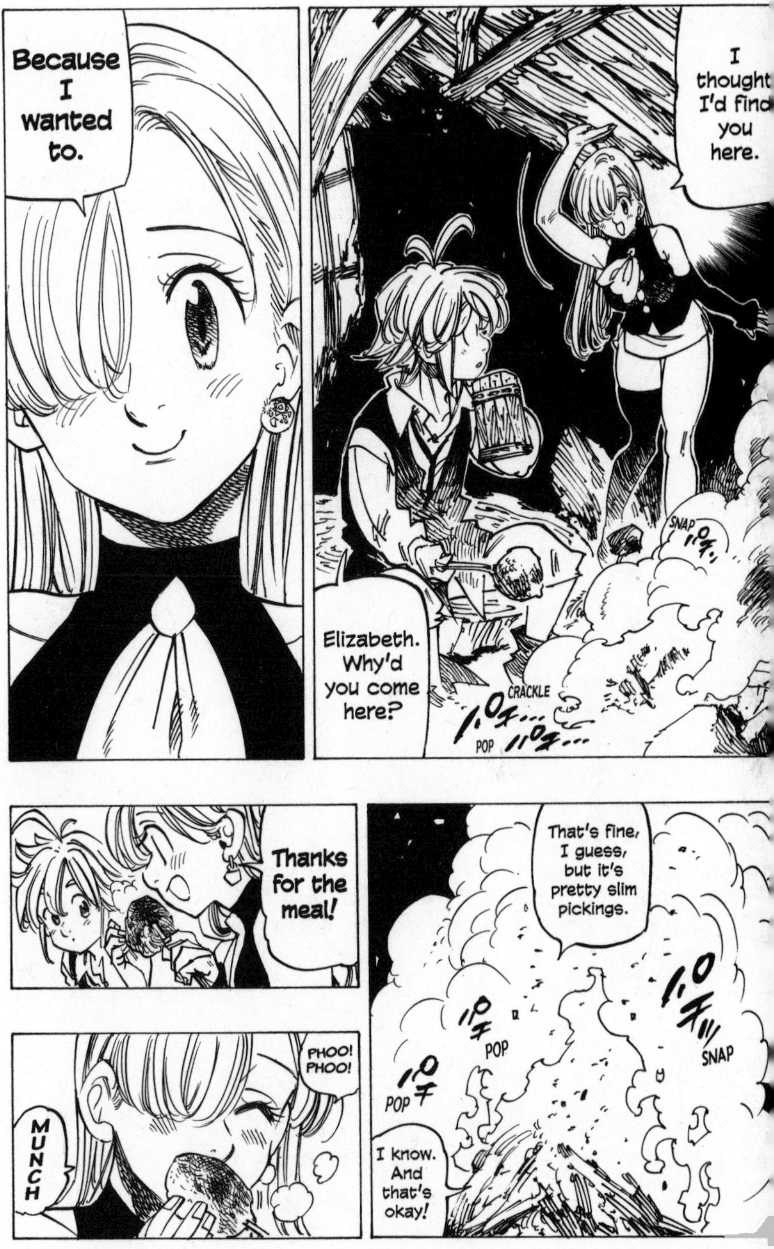
I thought I'd find you here.
SNAP
Elizabeth. Why'd you come here?
CRACKLE
POP
Because I wanted to.
That's fine, I guess, but it's pretty slim pickings.
POP
SNAP
POP
I know. And that's okay!
Thanks for the meal!
PHOO! PHOO!
MUNCH

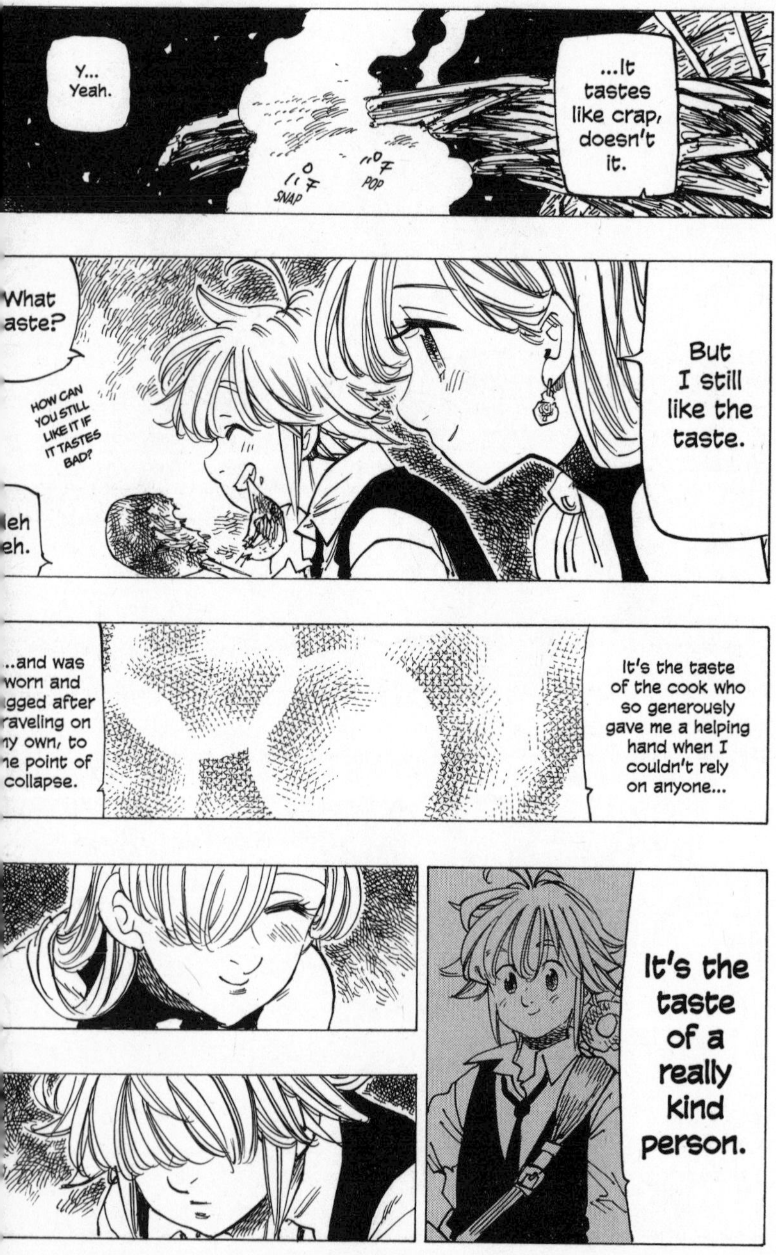
...It tastes like crap, doesn't it.
POP
SNAP
Y... Yeah.
But I still like the taste.
What aste?
HOW CAN YOU STILL LIKE IT IF IT TASTES BAD?
eh eh.
It's the taste of the cook who so generously gave me a helping hand when I couldn't rely on anyone...
...and was worn and gged after raveling on y own, to e point of collapse.
It's the taste of a really kind person.

I wonder what Ban's expression was when he looked at me earlier.

I give up.

I can't even look my best friend in the face.

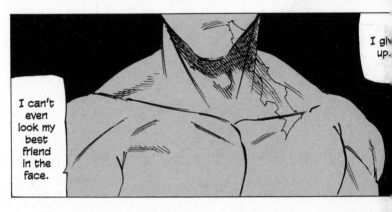

Melio-das...

I felt incredible when I killed Fraudrin.

In fact, I still feel a high over it!

RUSTLE

I don't get it.

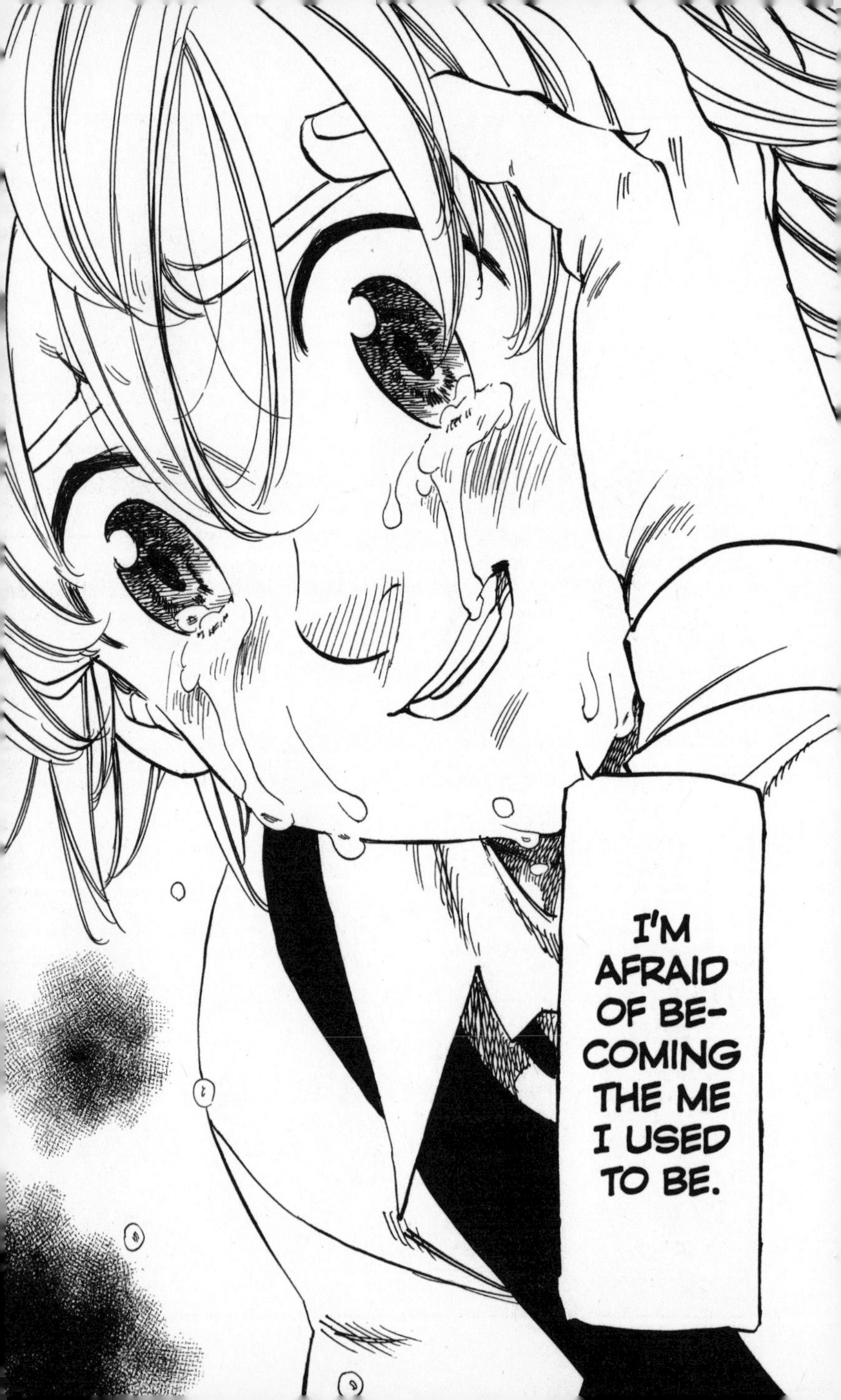
I'M AFRAID OF BE- COMING THE ME I USED TO BE.

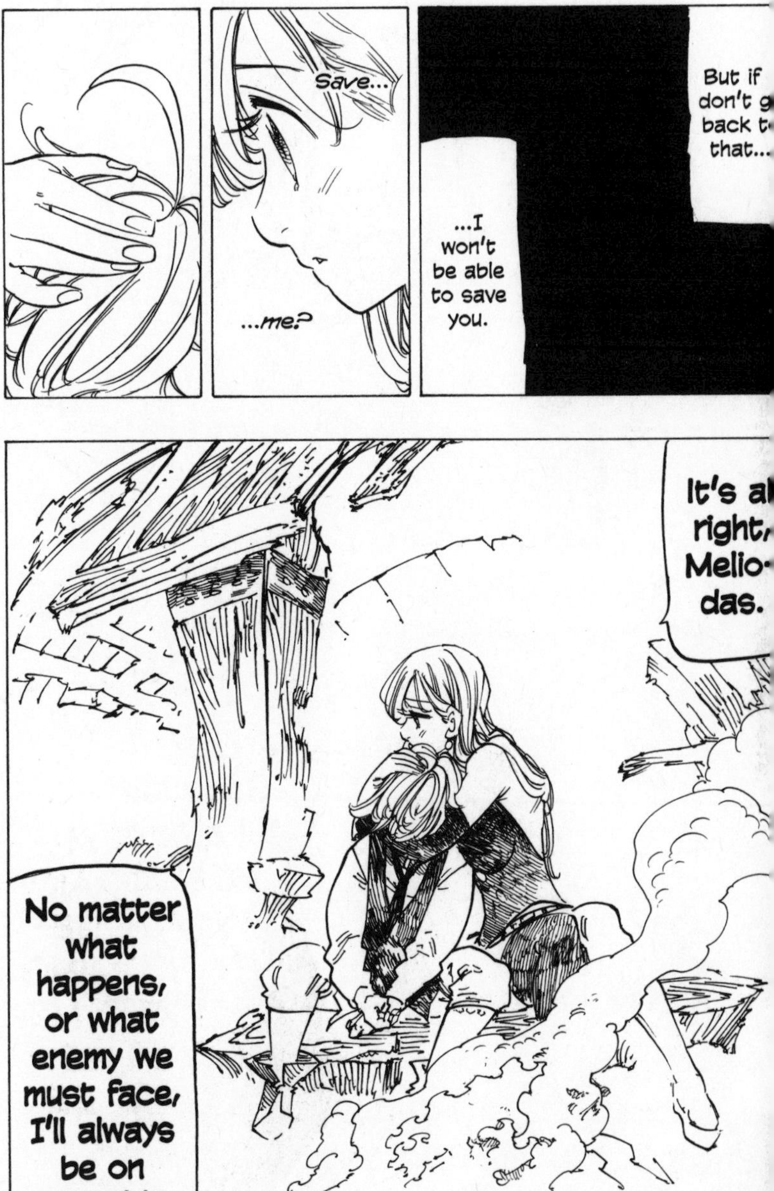
But if don't g back t that...
...I won't be able to save you.
Save...
...me?
It's al right, Melio-das.
No matter what happens, or what enemy we must face, I'll always be on your side.

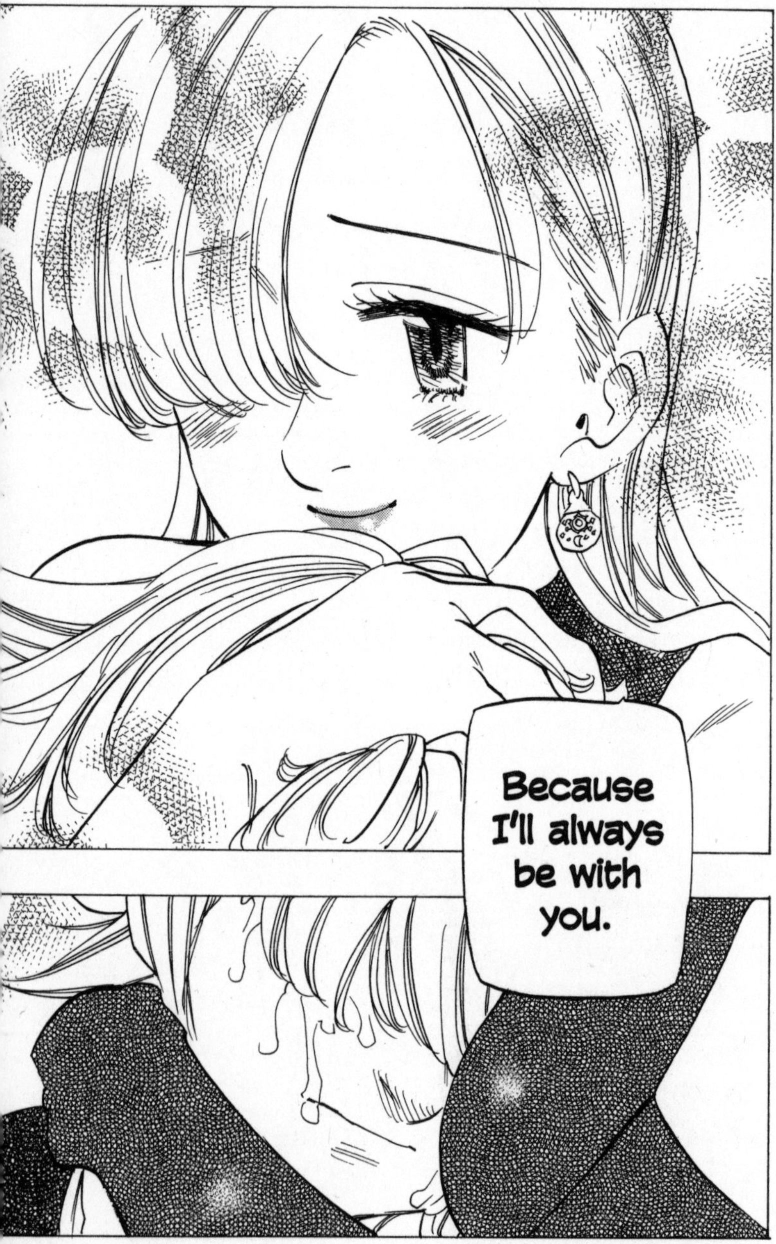
Because I'll always be with you.

Chapter 197 – To Each His Own Answe

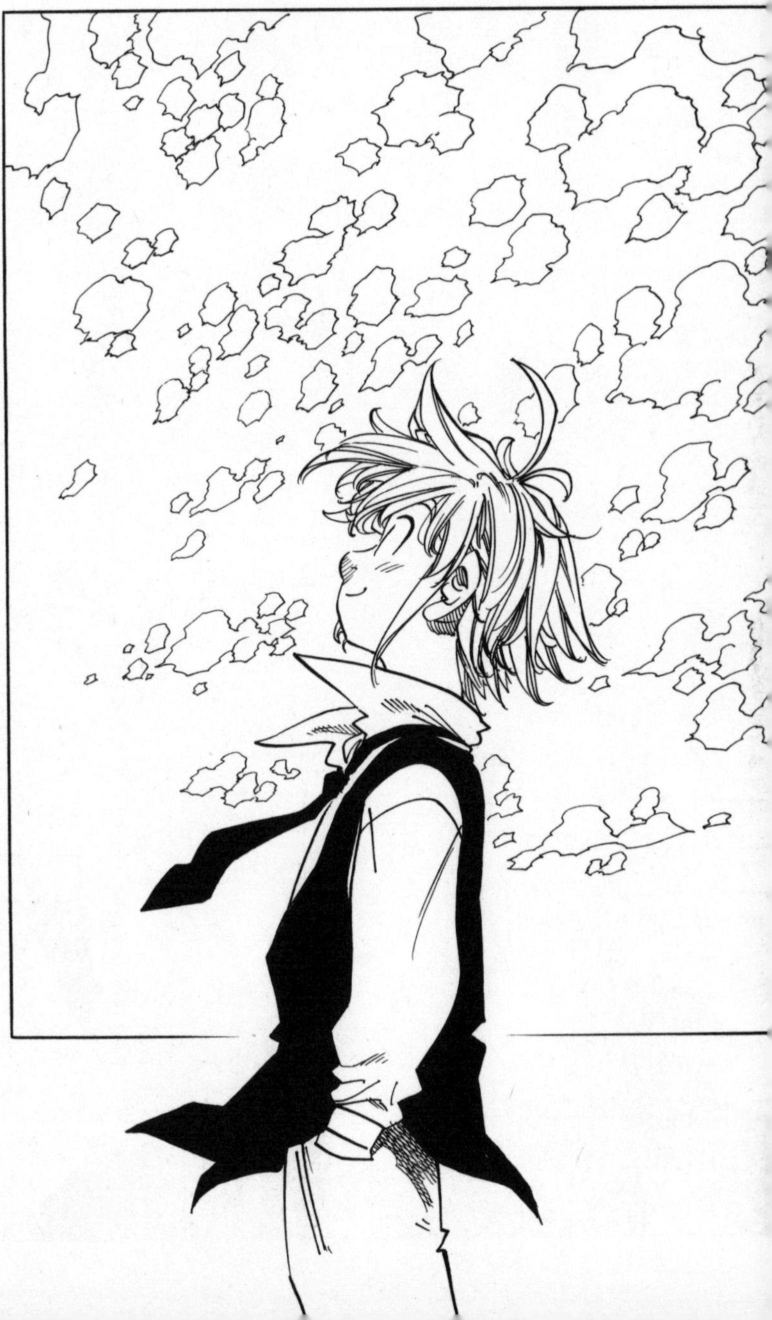

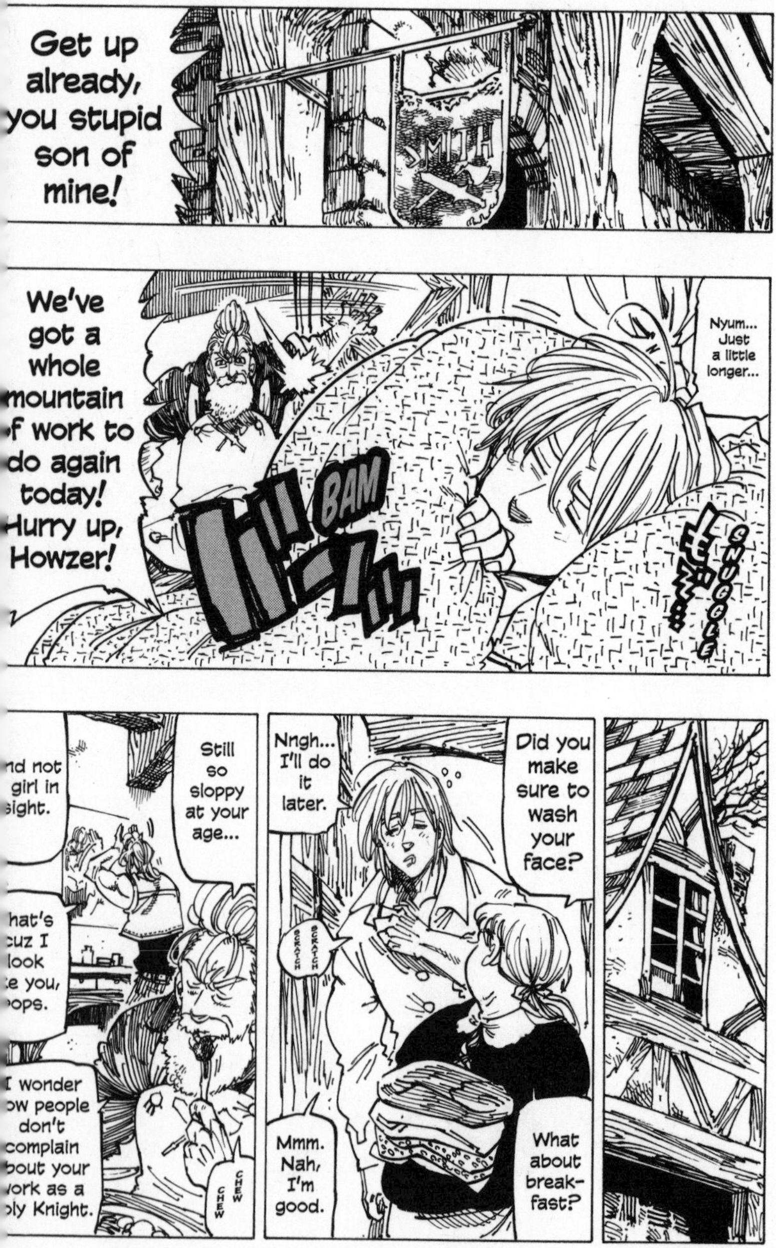
Get up already, you stupid son of mine!
SMITH
Nyum... Just a little longer...
SNUGGLE
We've got a whole mountain of work to do again today! Hurry up, Howzer!
BAM
Did you make sure to wash your face?
Nngh... I'll do it later.
SCRATCH SCRATCH
What about breakfast?
Mmm. Nah, I'm good.
Still so sloppy at your age...
nd not girl in sight.
hat's cuz I look e you, ops.
CHEW CHEW
I wonder ow people don't complain bout your ork as a oly Knight.

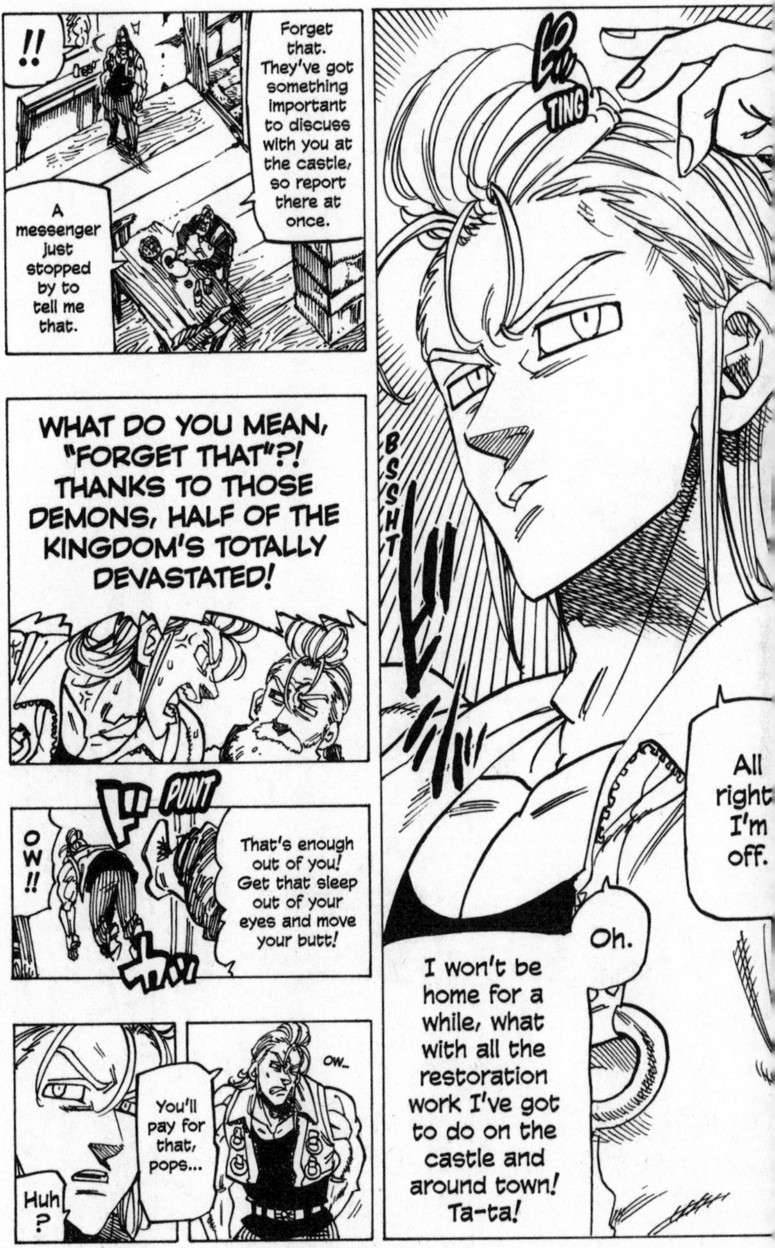
TING
BSSHT
All right I'm off.
Oh.
I won't be home for a while, what with all the restoration work I've got to do on the castle and around town! Ta-ta!
Forget that. They've got something important to discuss with you at the castle, so report there at once.
!!
A messenger just stopped by to tell me that.
WHAT DO YOU MEAN, "FORGET THAT"?! THANKS TO THOSE DEMONS, HALF OF THE KINGDOM'S TOTALLY DEVASTATED!
PUNT
That's enough out of you! Get that sleep out of your eyes and move your butt!
OW!!
OW...
You'll pay for that, pops...
Huh?

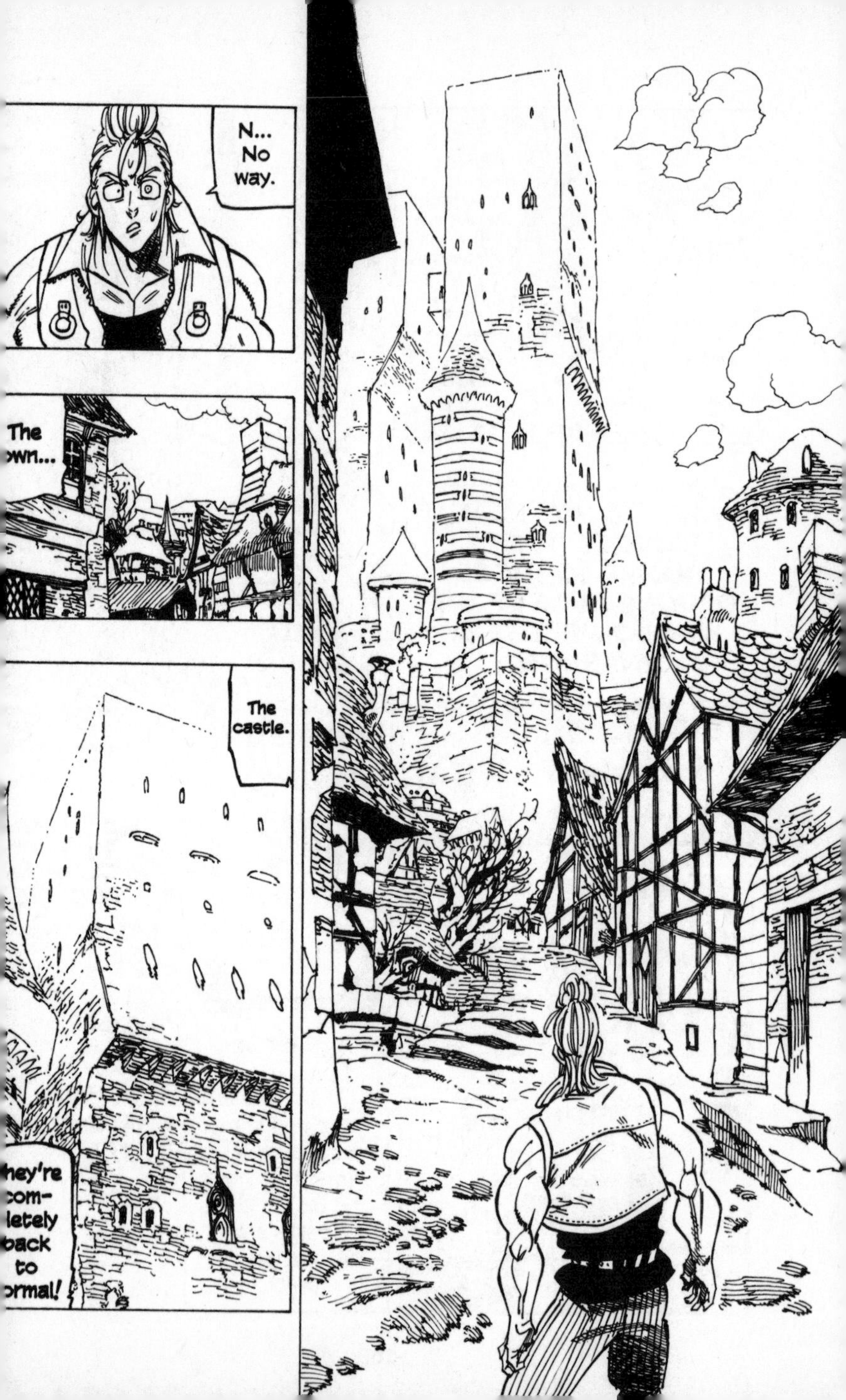
N... No way.
The own...
The castle.
hey're com-letely back to ormal!

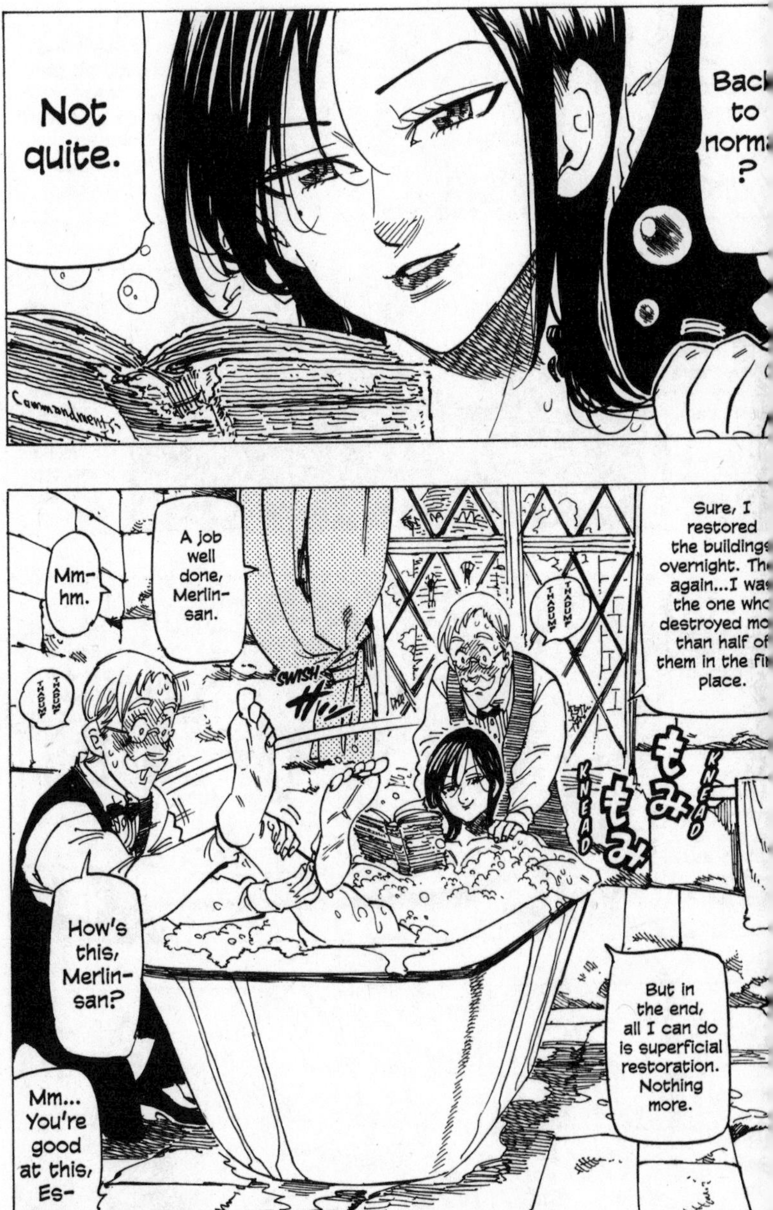
Back to norm ?
Not quite.
Commandments
Sure, I restored the buildings overnight. Th again...I was the one who destroyed mo than half of them in the fi place.
THADUMP THADUMP
A job well done, Merlin-san.
Mm-hm.
SWISH
THADUMP THADUMP
もみ KNEAD
もみ KNEAD
But in the end, all I can do is superficial restoration. Nothing more.
How's this, Merlin-san?
Mm... You're good at this, Es-canor.

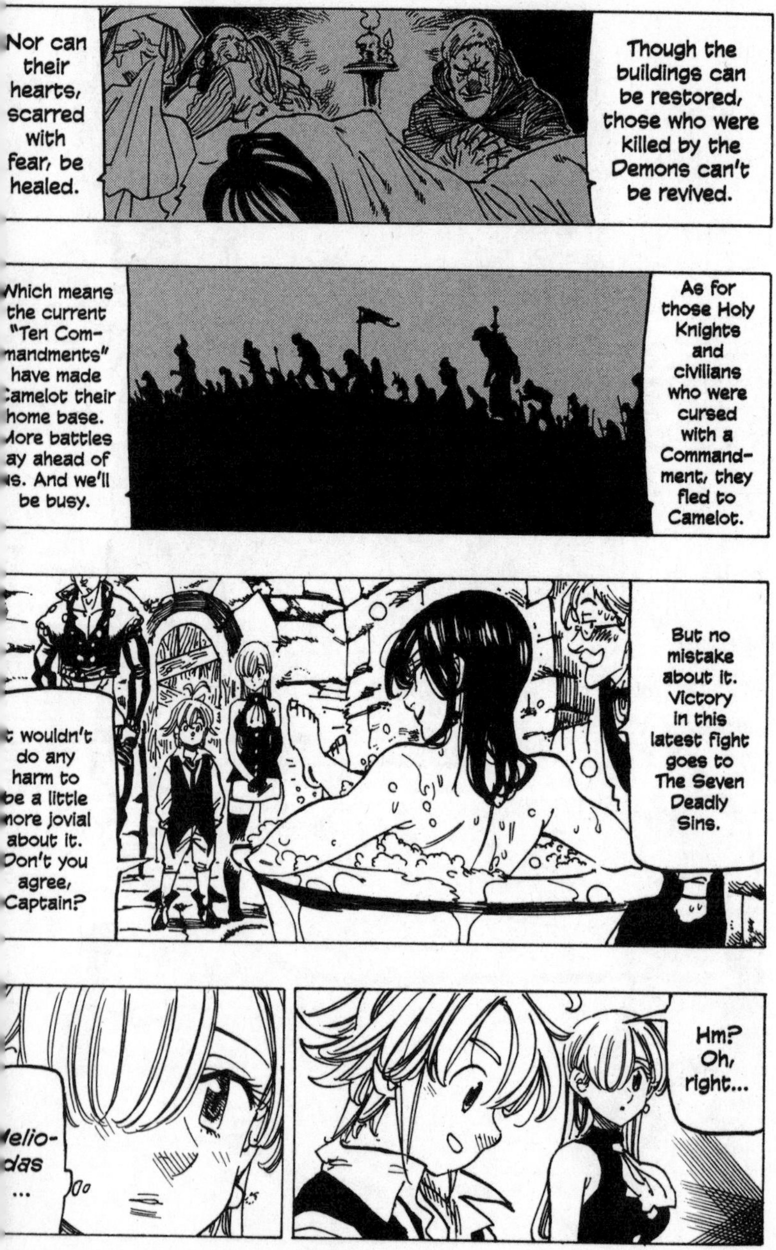
Though the buildings can be restored, those who were killed by the Demons can't be revived.
Nor can their hearts, scarred with fear, be healed.
As for those Holy Knights and civilians who were cursed with a Command-ment, they fled to Camelot.
Which means the current "Ten Com-mandments" have made Camelot their home base. More battles lay ahead of us. And we'll be busy.
But no mistake about it. Victory in this latest fight goes to The Seven Deadly Sins.
It wouldn't do any harm to be a little more jovial about it. Don't you agree, Captain?
Hm? Oh, right...
Melio-das...

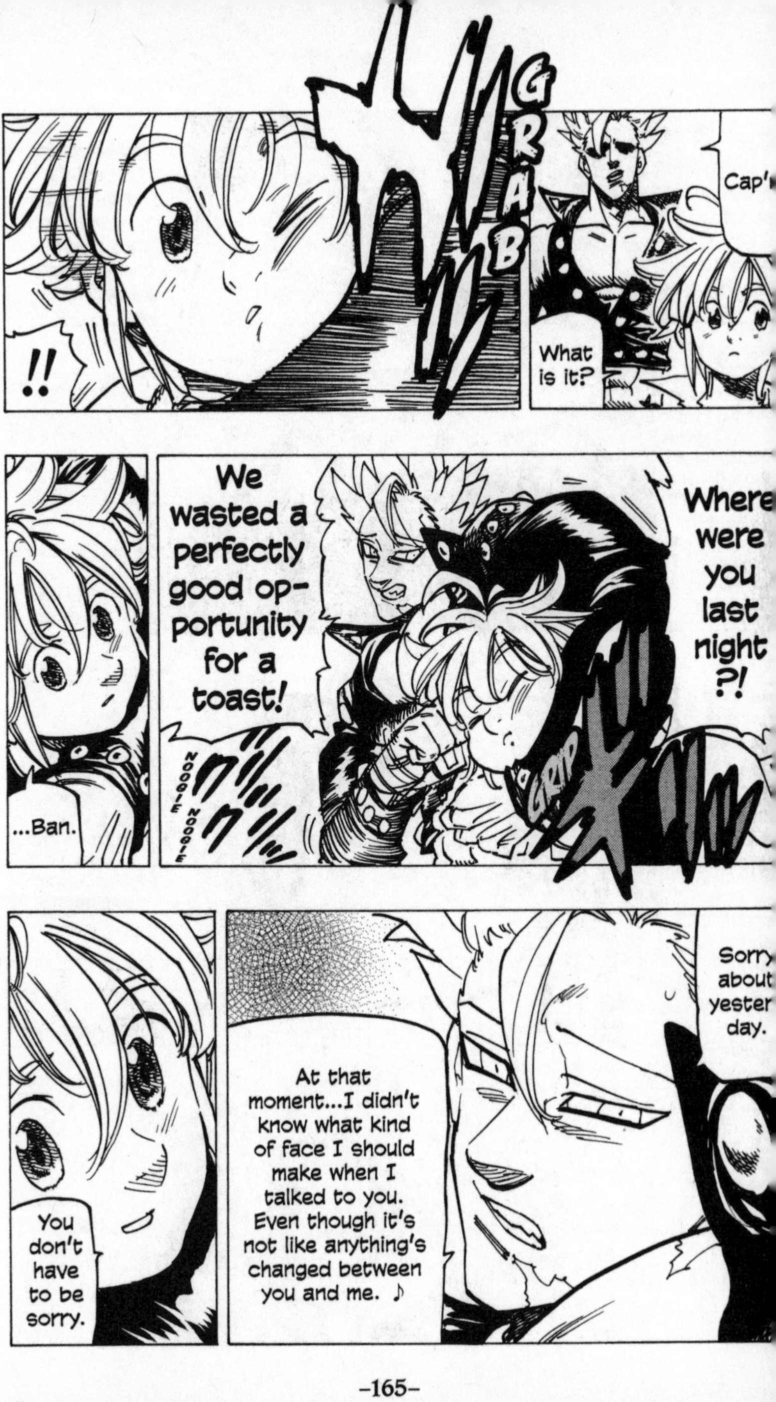
Cap'
What is it?
GRAB
!!
Where were you last night?!
We wasted a perfectly good opportunity for a toast!
NOOGIE NOOGIE
GRIP
...Ban.
Sorry about yester day.
At that moment...I didn't know what kind of face I should make when I talked to you. Even though it's not like anything's changed between you and me. ♪
You don't have to be sorry.

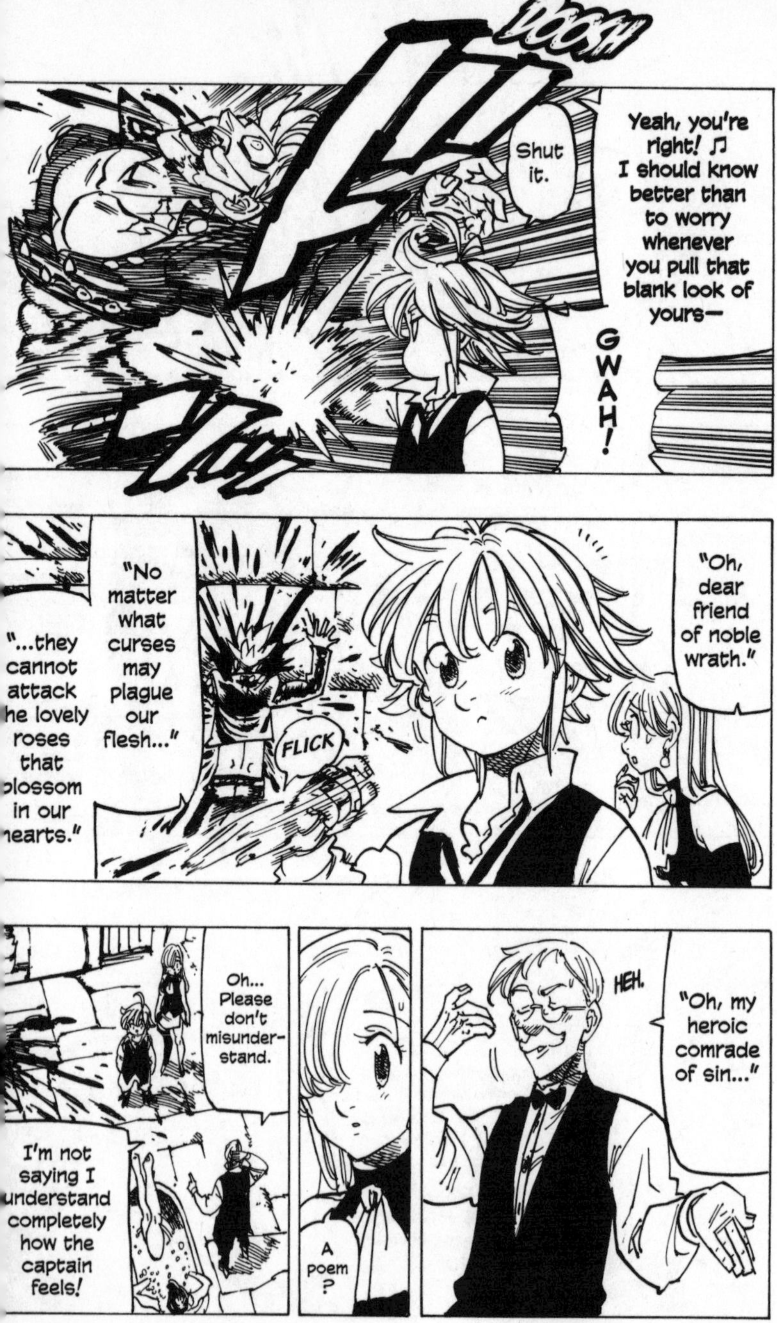

Yeah, you're right! ♫ I should know better than to worry whenever you pull that blank look of yours—
Shut it.
DOOSH
GWAH!
"Oh, dear friend of noble wrath."
"No matter what curses may plague our flesh..."
FLICK
"...they cannot attack he lovely roses that blossom in our hearts."
HEH.
"Oh, my heroic comrade of sin..."
A poem?
Oh... Please don't misunderstand.
I'm not saying I understand completely how the captain feels!

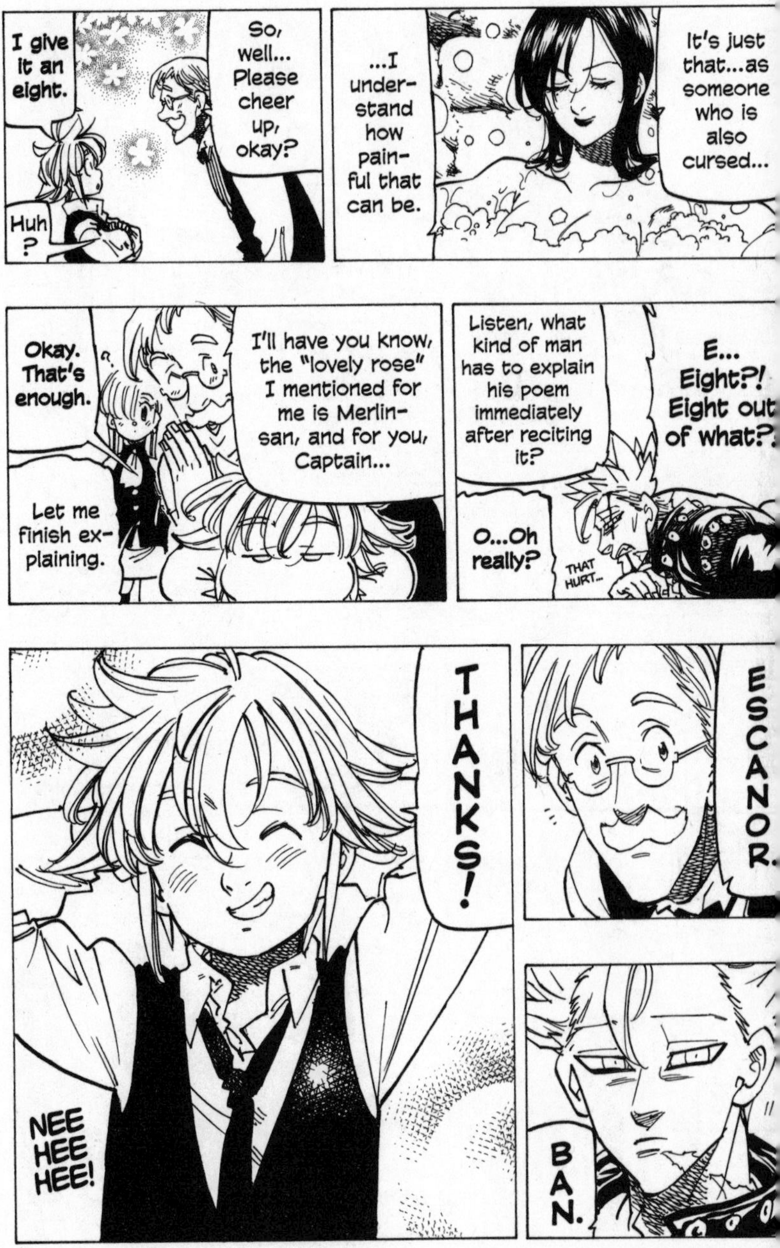
It's just that...as someone who is also cursed...
...I understand how painful that can be.
So, well... Please cheer up, okay?
I give it an eight.
Huh?
E... Eight?! Eight out of what?!
Listen, what kind of man has to explain his poem immediately after reciting it?
O...Oh really?
THAT HURT...
I'll have you know, the "lovely rose" I mentioned for me is Merlin-san, and for you, Captain...
Okay. That's enough.
Let me finish explaining.
ESCANOR.
BAN.
THANKS!
NEE HEE HEE!

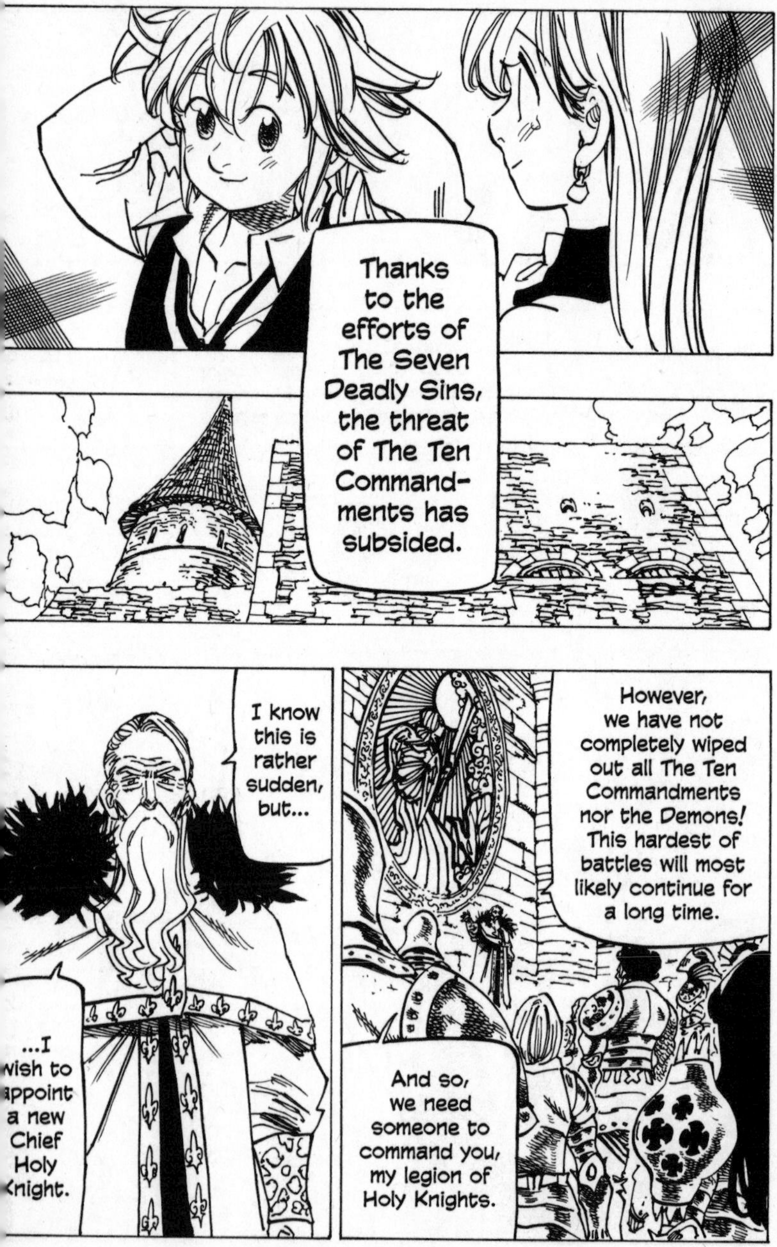
Thanks to the efforts of The Seven Deadly Sins, the threat of The Ten Command-ments has subsided.
However, we have not completely wiped out all The Ten Commandments nor the Demons! This hardest of battles will most likely continue for a long time.
And so, we need someone to command you, my legion of Holy Knights.
I know this is rather sudden, but...
...I wish to appoint a new Chief Holy Knight.

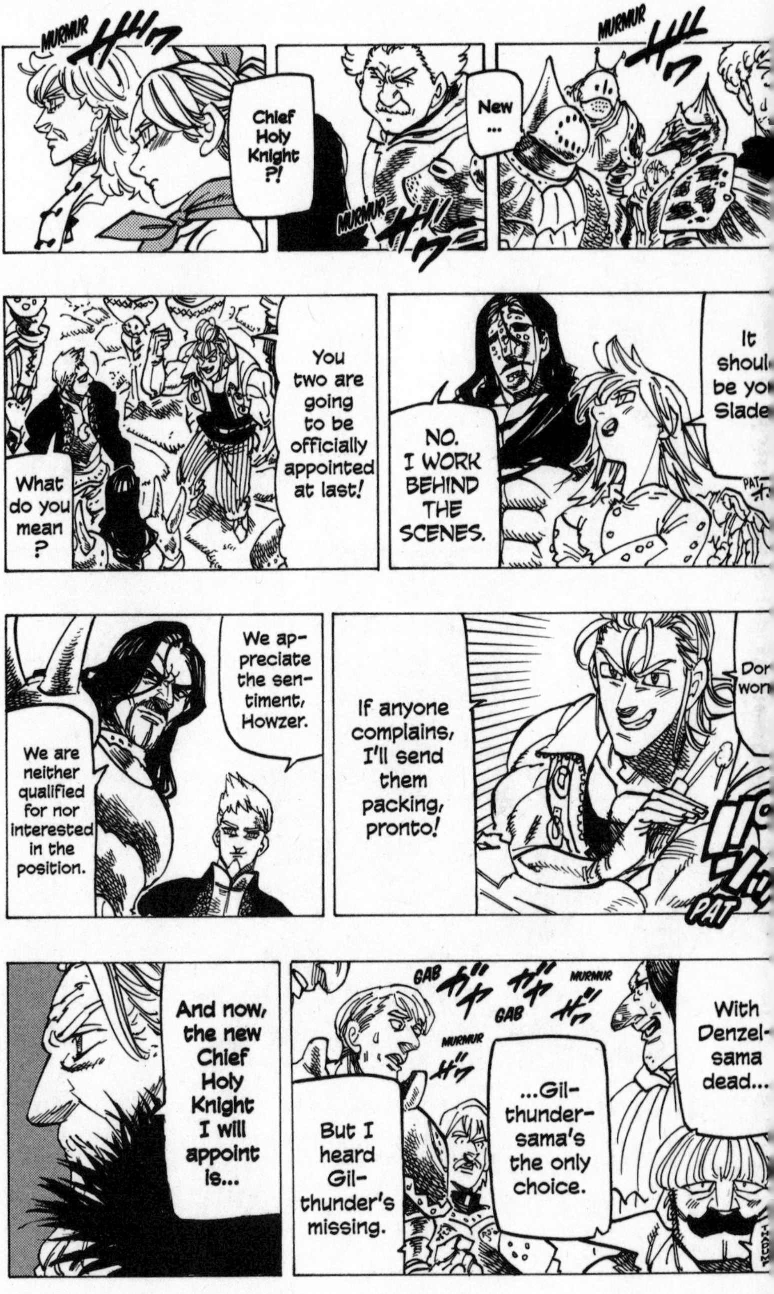
MURMUR
New ...
MURMUR
Chief Holy Knight ?!
MURMUR
It shoul be yo Slade
PAT
NO. I WORK BEHIND THE SCENES.
You two are going to be officially appointed at last!
What do you mean ?
Dor wor
PAT
If anyone complains, I'll send them packing, pronto!
We appreciate the sentiment, Howzer.
We are neither qualified for nor interested in the position.
With Denzel-sama dead...
MURMUR
GAB
GAB
MURMUR
...Gil-thunder-sama's the only choice.
But I heard Gil-thunder's missing.
And now, the new Chief Holy Knight I will appoint is...

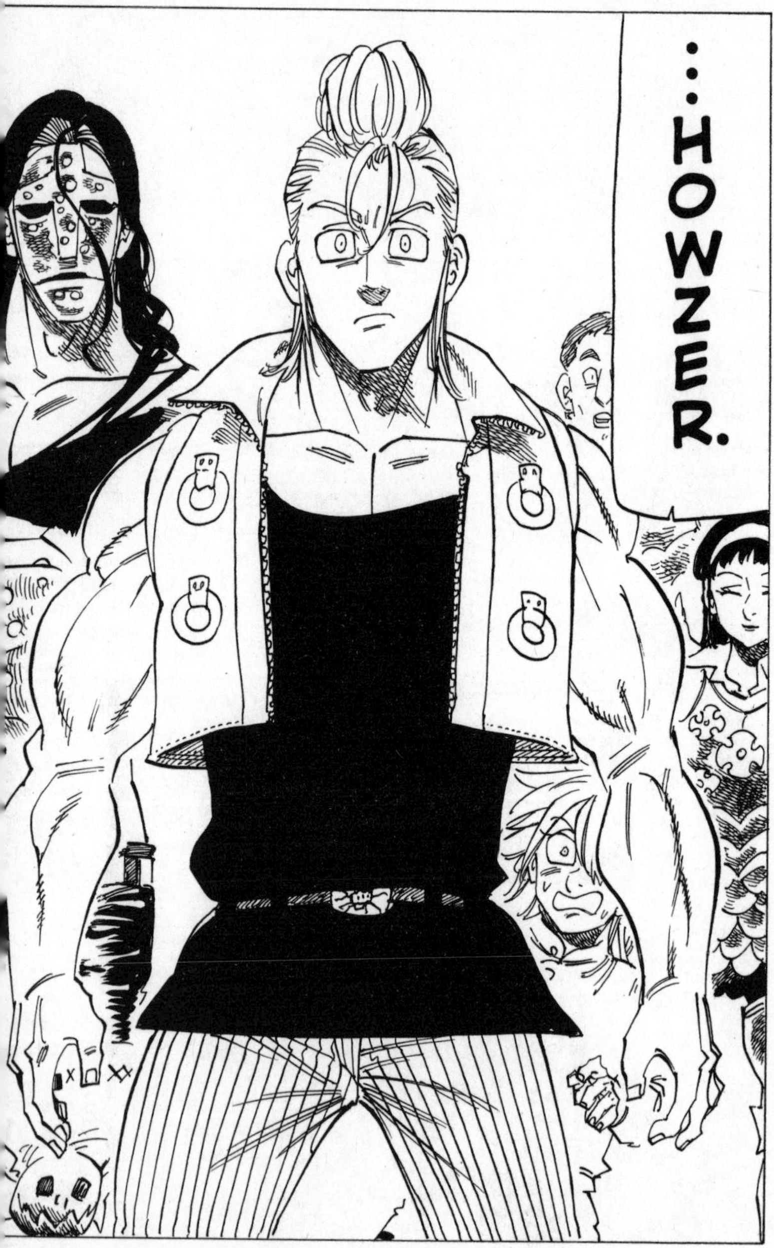
...HOWZER.

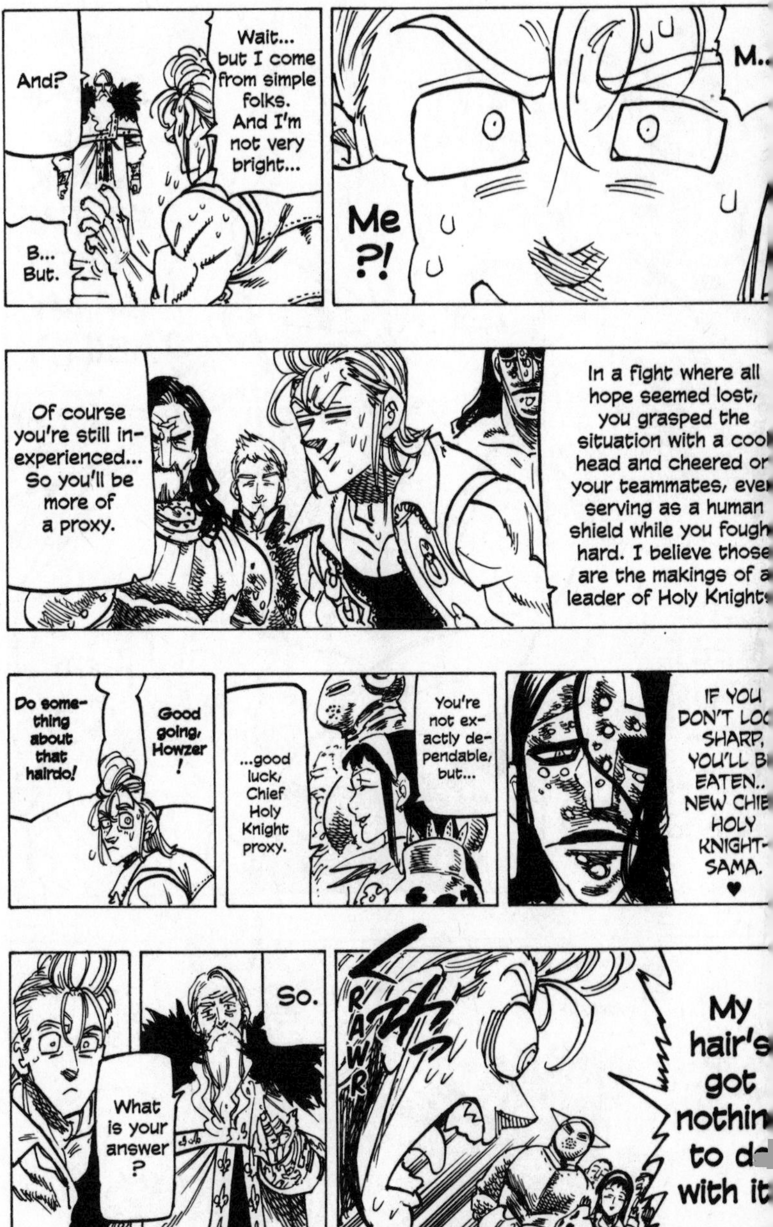
M...
Me ?!
Wait... but I come from simple folks. And I'm not very bright...
And?
B... But.
In a fight where all hope seemed lost, you grasped the situation with a coo head and cheered or your teammates, eve serving as a human shield while you fough hard. I believe those are the makings of a leader of Holy Knight
Of course you're still in-experienced... So you'll be more of a proxy.
IF YOU DON'T LOO SHARP, YOU'LL B EATEN.. NEW CHIE HOLY KNIGHT-SAMA. ♥
You're not ex-actly de-pendable, but...
...good luck, Chief Holy Knight proxy.
Good going, Howzer !
Do some-thing about that hairdo!
My hair's got nothin to d with it
RAWR
So.
What is your answer ?

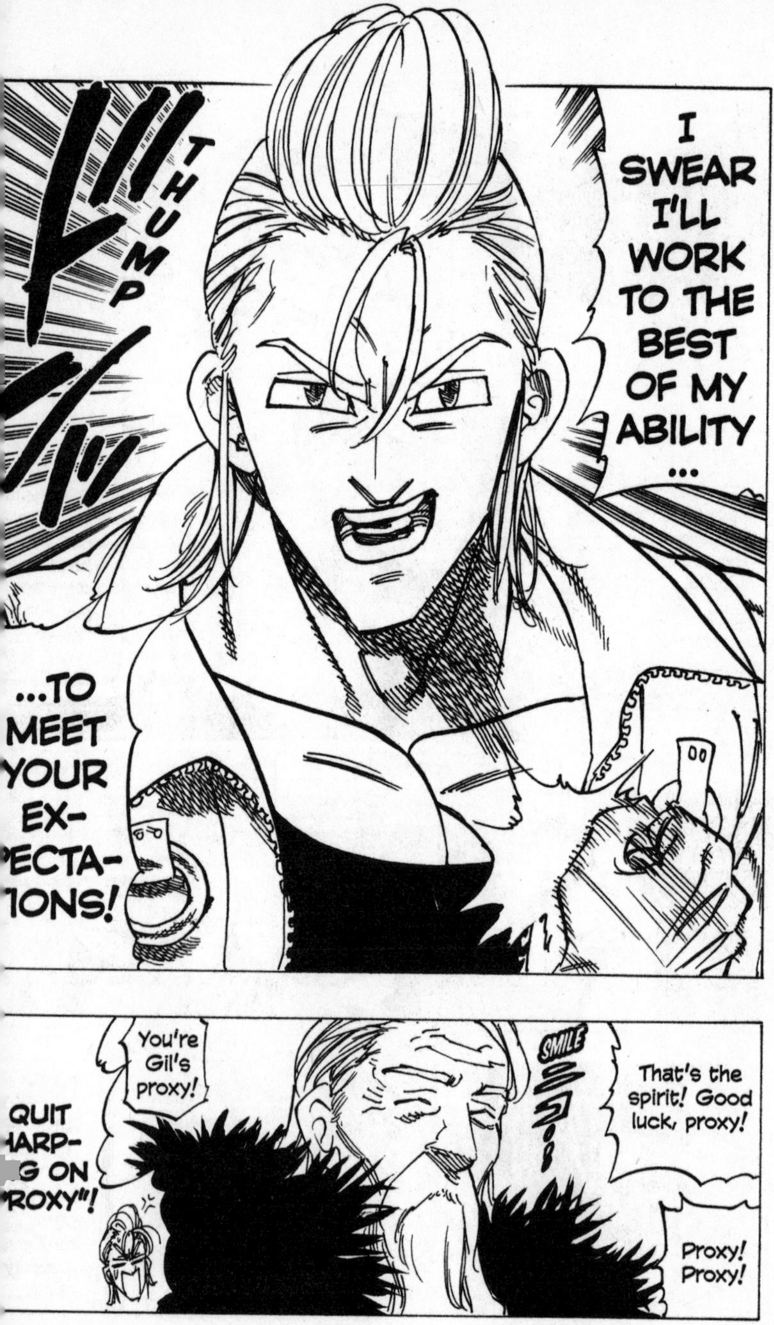

I SWEAR I'LL WORK TO THE BEST OF MY ABILITY ...
THUMP
...TO MEET YOUR EX- ECTA- IONS!
That's the spirit! Good luck, proxy!
SMILE
Proxy! Proxy!
You're Gil's proxy!
QUIT ARP- G ON ROXY"!

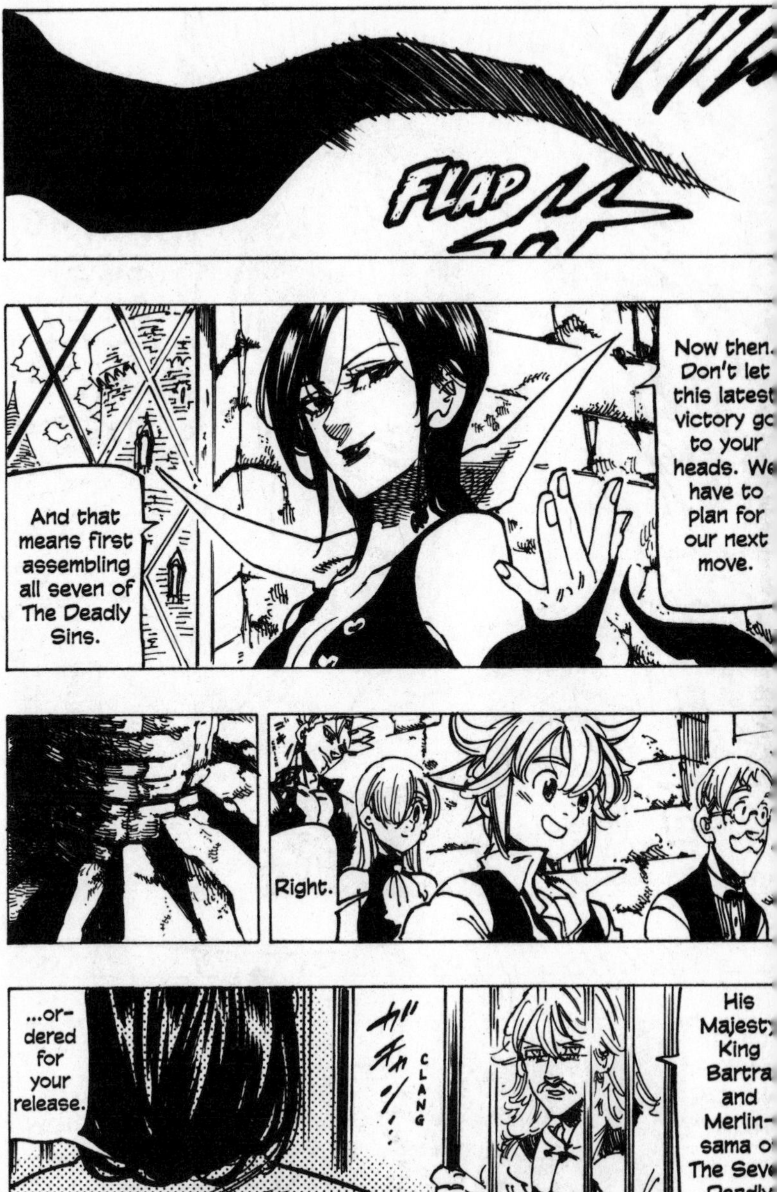
FLAP
Now then. Don't let this latest victory go to your heads. We have to plan for our next move.
And that means first assembling all seven of The Deadly Sins.
Right.
His Majesty King Bartra and Merlin-sama of The Seve Deadly Sins...
CLANG
...or-dered for your release.

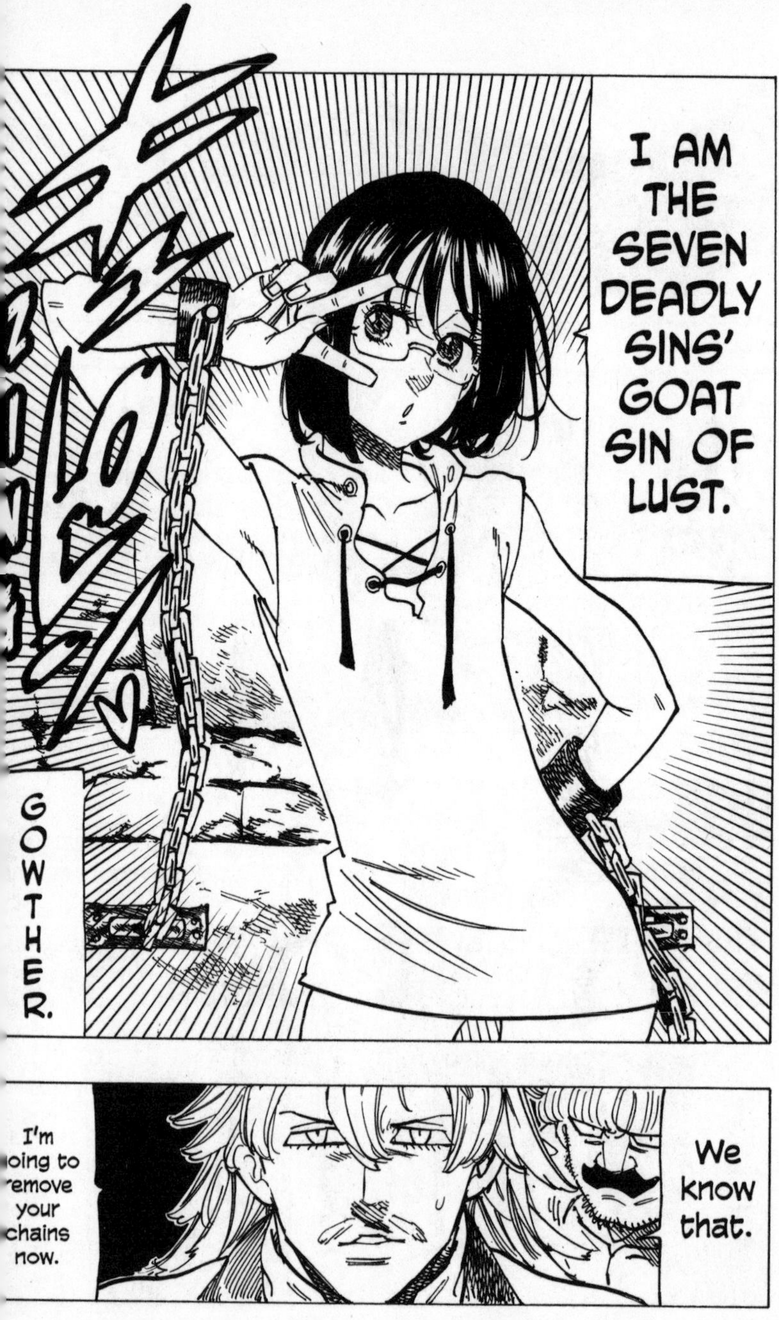

I AM THE SEVEN DEADLY SINS' GOAT SIN OF LUST.
GOWTHER.
We know that.
I'm oing to emove your chains now.

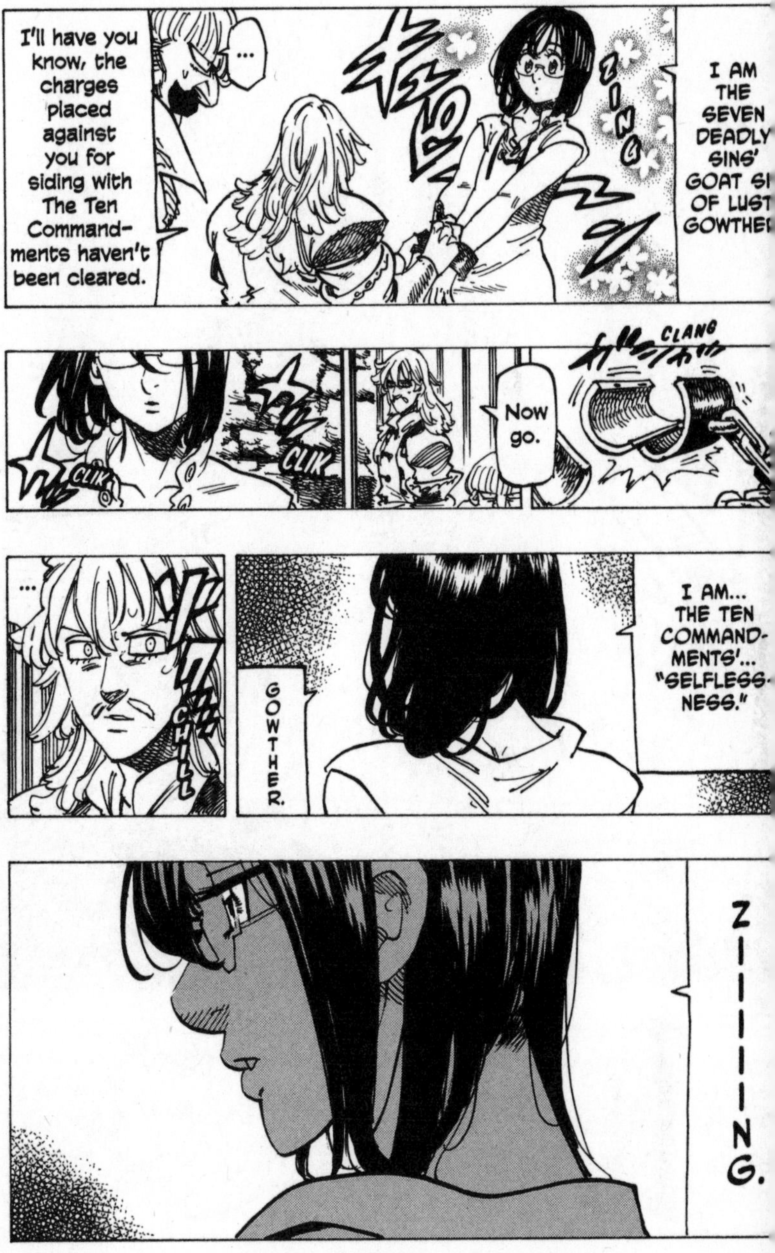

I AM THE SEVEN DEADLY SINS' GOAT SI OF LUST GOWTHE
ZING
...
I'll have you know, the charges placed against you for siding with The Ten Commandments haven't been cleared.
CLANG
Now go.
CLIK
CLIK
I AM... THE TEN COMMANDMENTS'... "SELFLESSNESS."
GOWTHER.
...
CHILL
ZIIIIING.

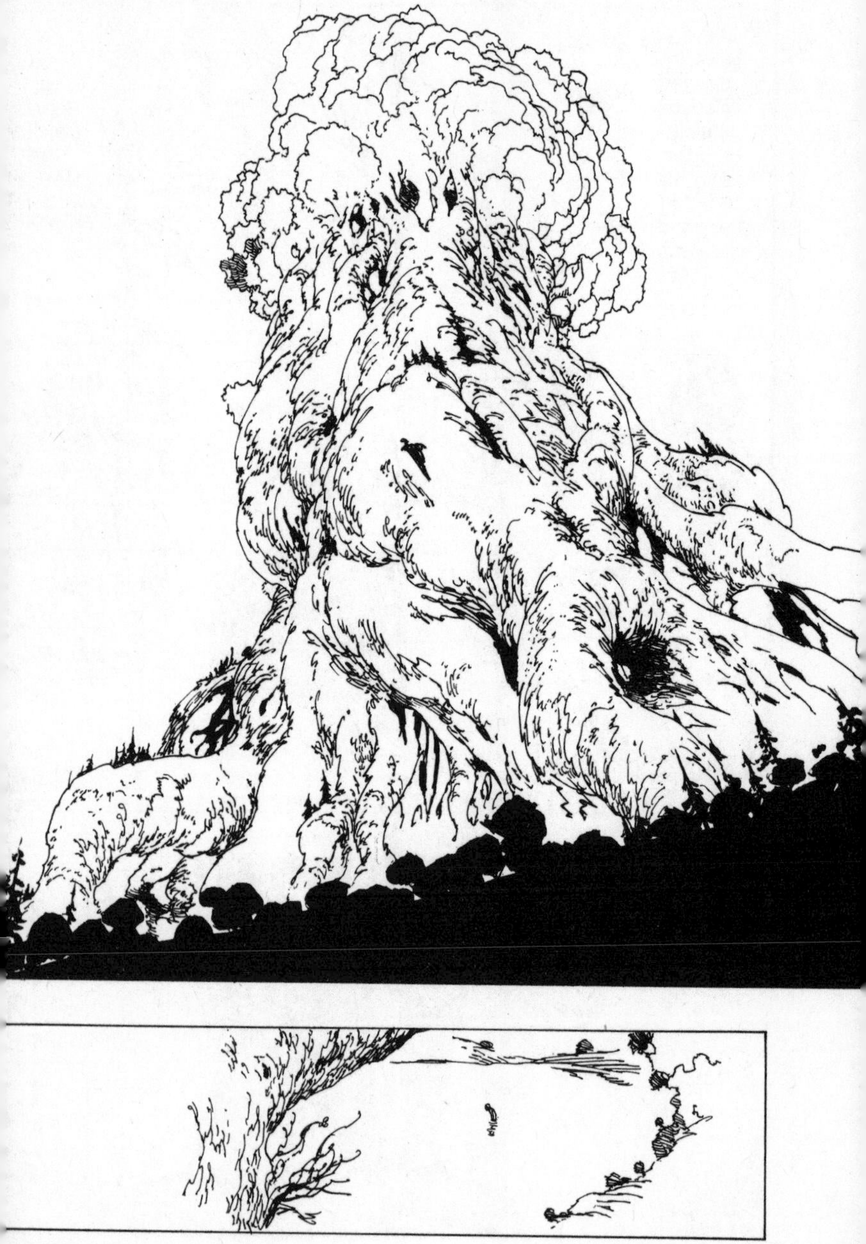

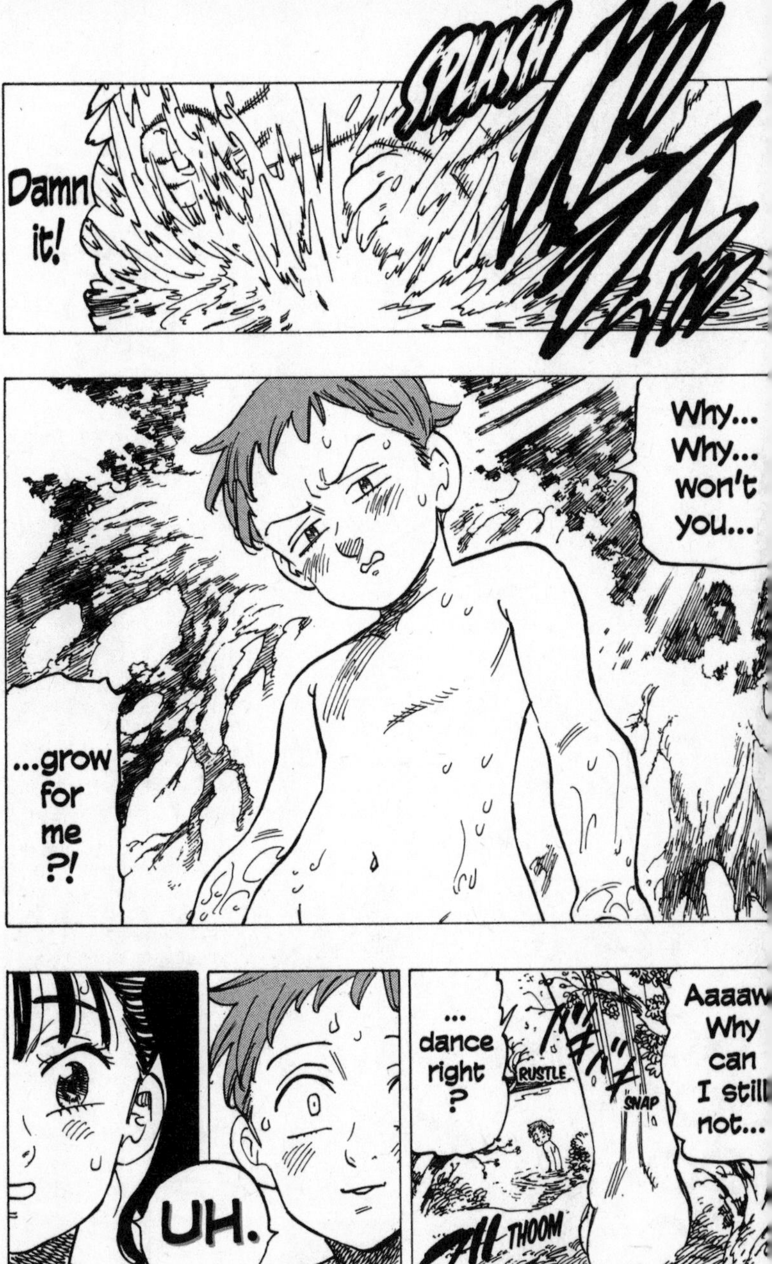
SPLASH
Damn it!
Why... Why... won't you...
...grow for me?!
Aaaaw Why can I still not...
... dance right?
RUSTLE
SNAP
THOOM
UH.

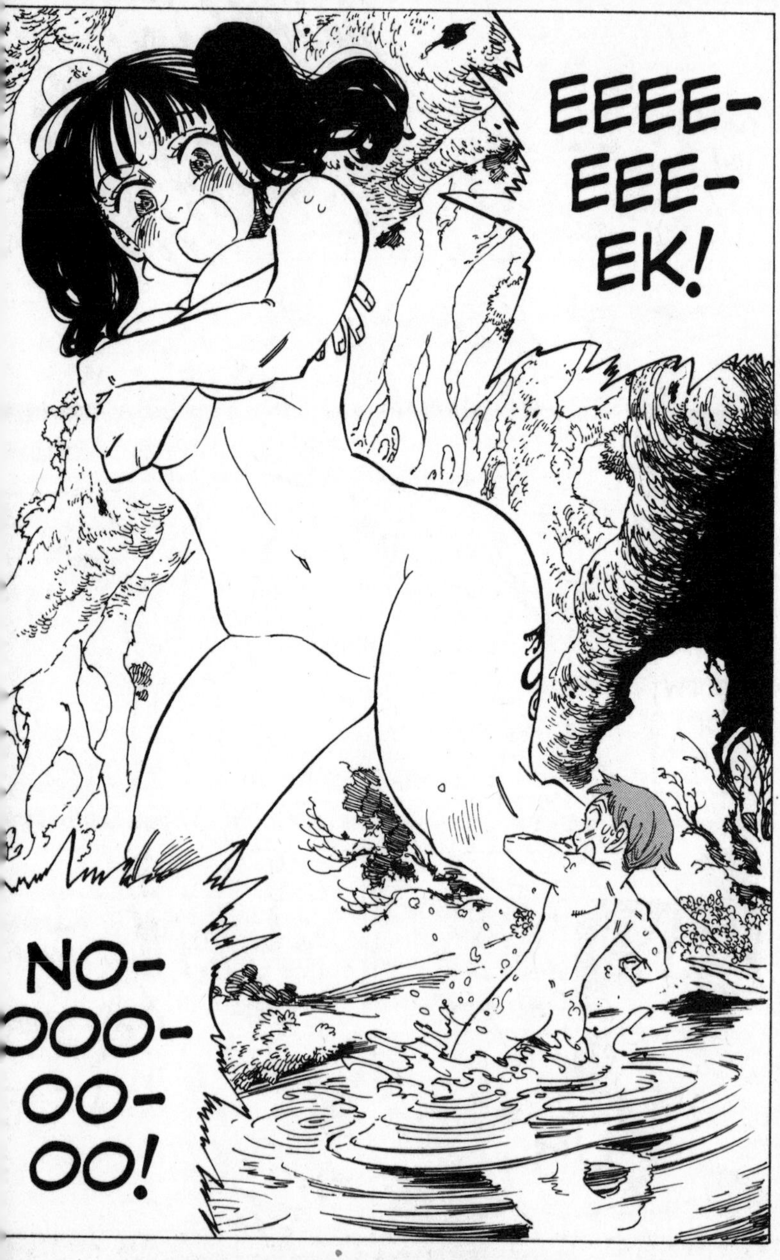
EEEE-EEE-EK!
NO-OOO-OO-OO!

To Be Continued in Volume 25...

TYRANT DRAGON VERSION

Magic 80

Strength 520 **Combat Class 610**

Vigor 10

The first instance of his transformation that should go down in history. His ears-turned-wings and the flames he shoots from his nose are not very useful, but he's still actually very strong.

Sand Crawler Version

Magic 80

Strength 100 **Combat Class 190**

Vigor 10

He's able to move through deserts and soil, but has never applied this newfound ability. Slippery to the touch.

RED DEMON VERSION

Magic 450

Strength 480 **Combat Class 1030**

Vigor 100

Unable to speak, he still has his usual emotions and intellect. The smell of leftovers on his breath is powerful enough to make Fraudrin recoil. Has a double chin.

Bonus Story – A Deadly Sins Vacation

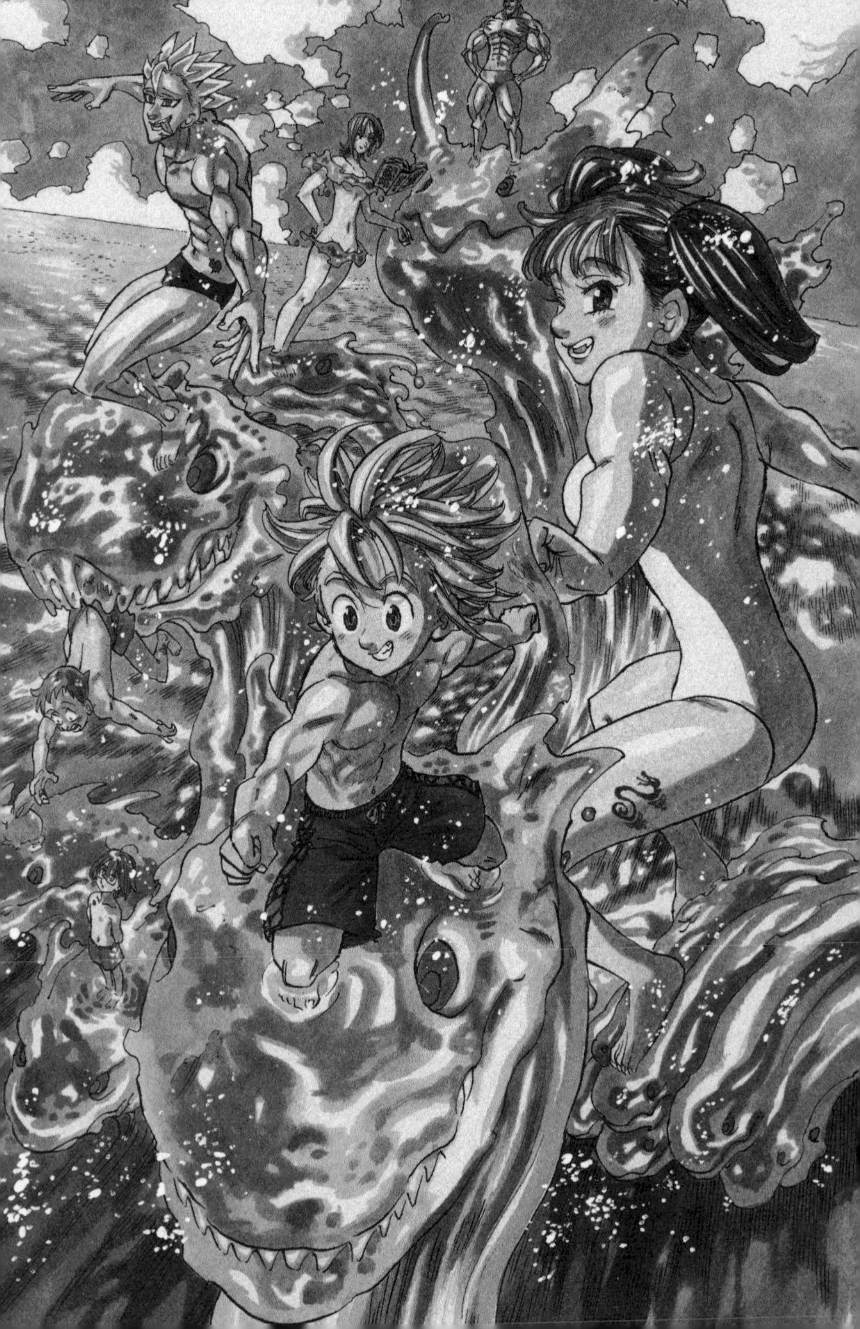

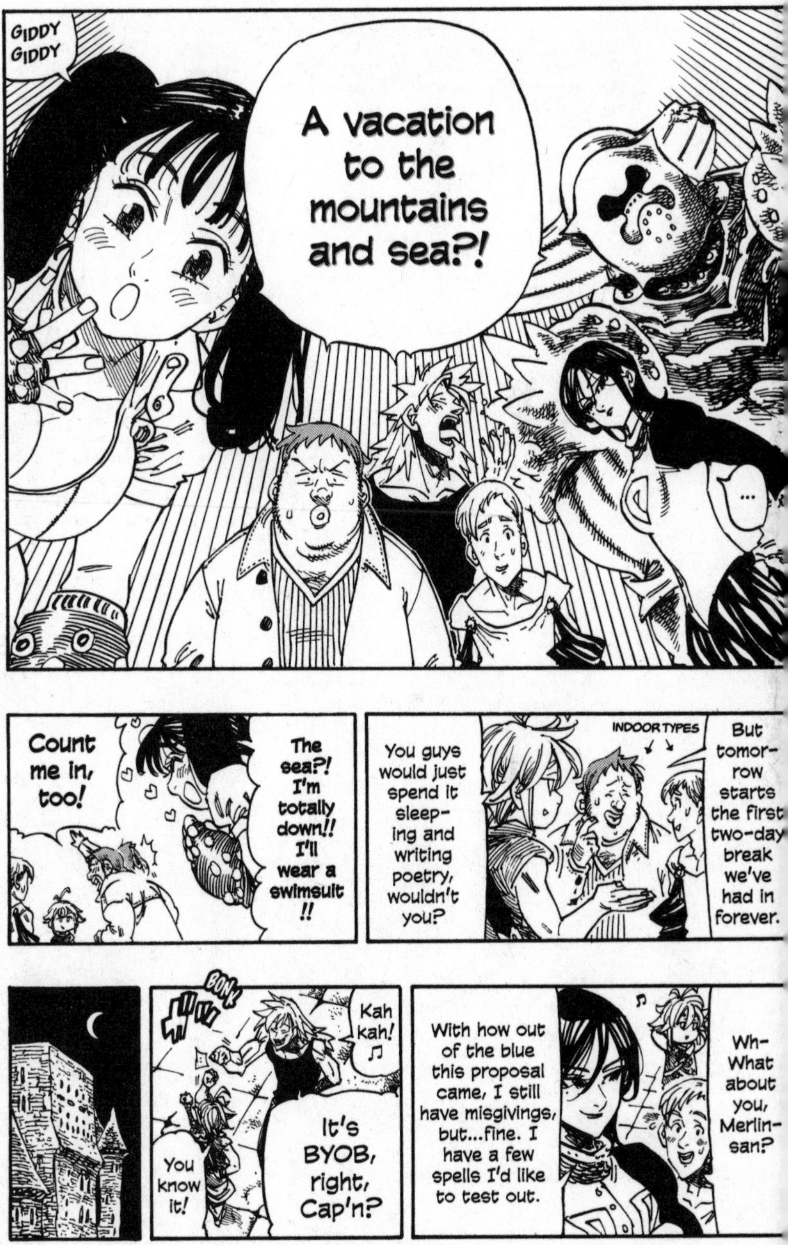
A vacation to the mountains and sea?!
...
GIDDY GIDDY
But tomorrow starts the first two-day break we've had in forever.
INDOOR TYPES
You guys would just spend it sleeping and writing poetry, wouldn't you?
The sea?! I'm totally down!! I'll wear a swimsuit!!
Count me in, too!
Wh- What about you, Merlin-san?
With how out of the blue this proposal came, I still have misgivings, but...fine. I have a few spells I'd like to test out.
Kah kah! ♫
BONK
It's BYOB, right, Cap'n?
You know it!

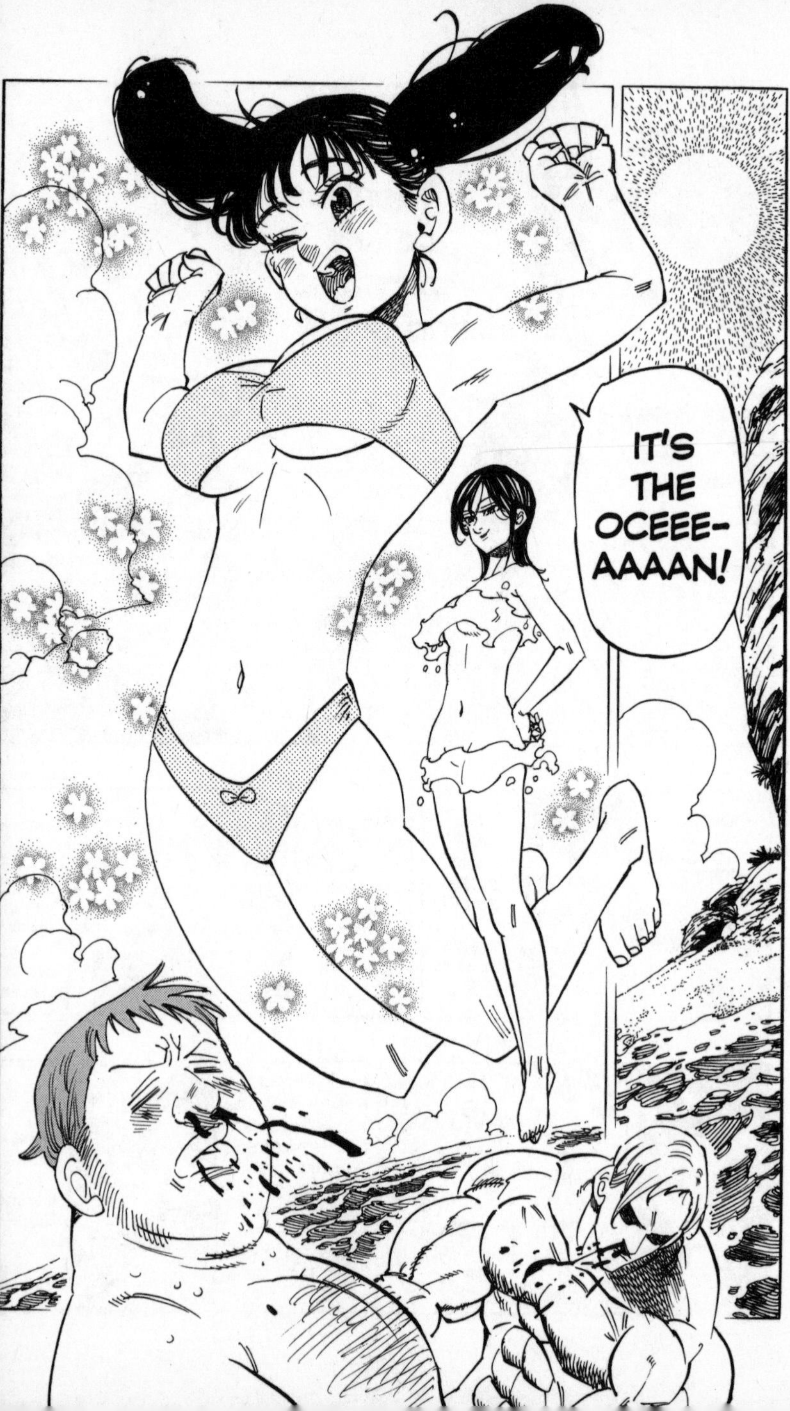
IT'S THE OCEEE-AAAAN!

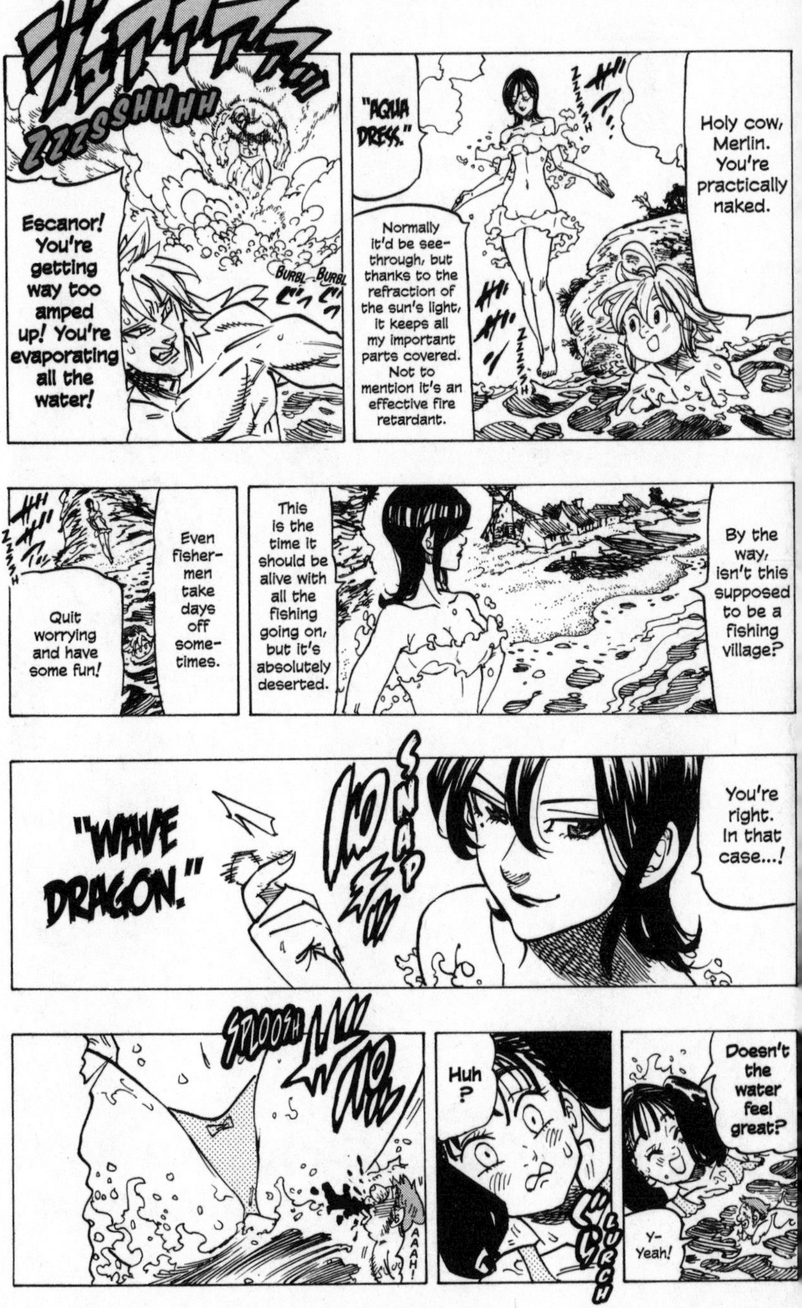
Holy cow, Merlin. You're practically naked.
ZZZZSSSH
"AQUA DRESS."
Normally it'd be see-through, but thanks to the refraction of the sun's light, it keeps all my important parts covered. Not to mention it's an effective fire retardant.
ZZZZSSSH
ZZZSSHHHH
BURBL BURBL
Escanor! You're getting way too amped up! You're evaporating all the water!
By the way, isn't this supposed to be a fishing village?
This is the time it should be alive with all the fishing going on, but it's absolutely deserted.
Even fisher-men take days off some-times.
ZZZSSH
Quit worrying and have some fun!
You're right. In that case...!
SNAP
"WAVE DRAGON."
Doesn't the water feel great?
Y-Yeah!
Huh?
LURCH
SPLOOSH
AAAAH!

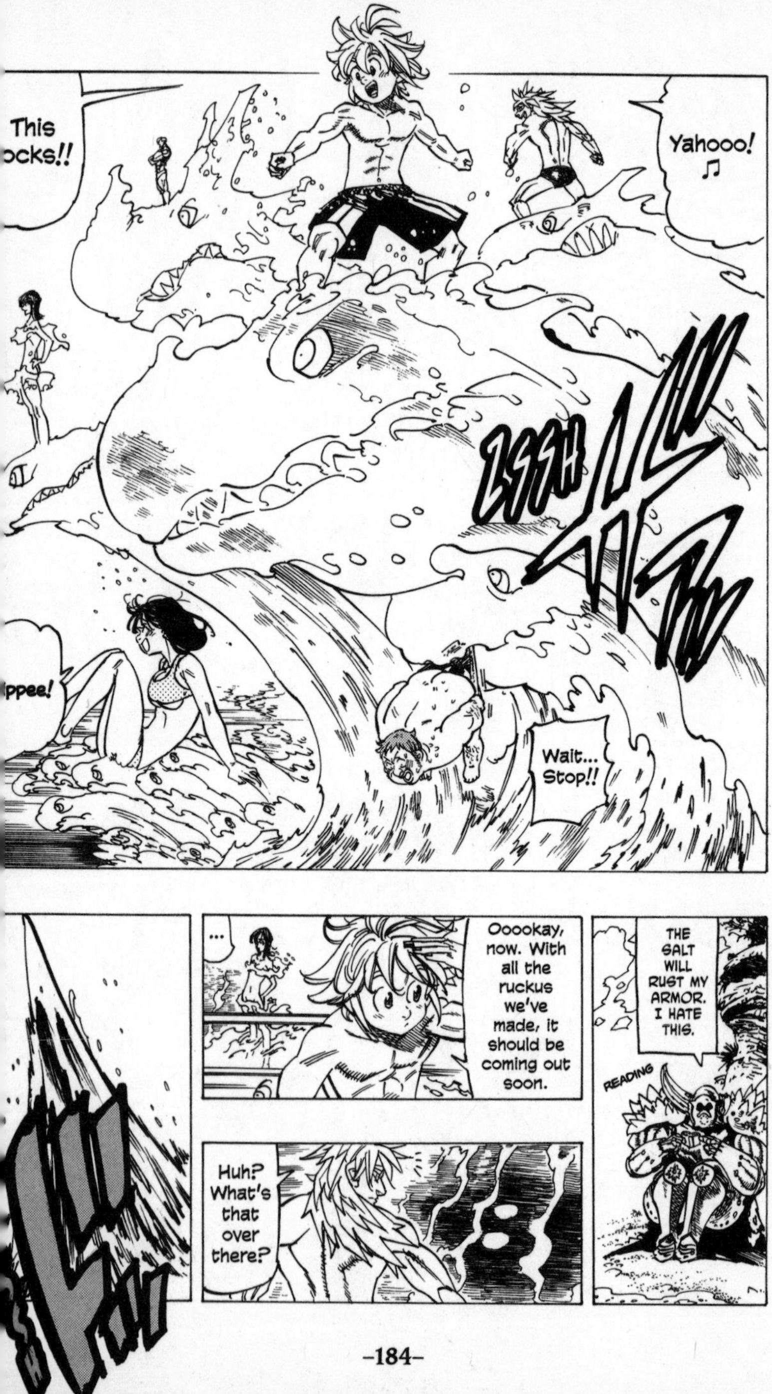
Yahooo! ♫
ZSSH
Wait... Stop!!
This
ocks!!
ppee!
THE SALT WILL RUST MY ARMOR. I HATE THIS.
READING
Ooookay, now. With all the ruckus we've made, it should be coming out soon.
...
Huh? What's that over there?

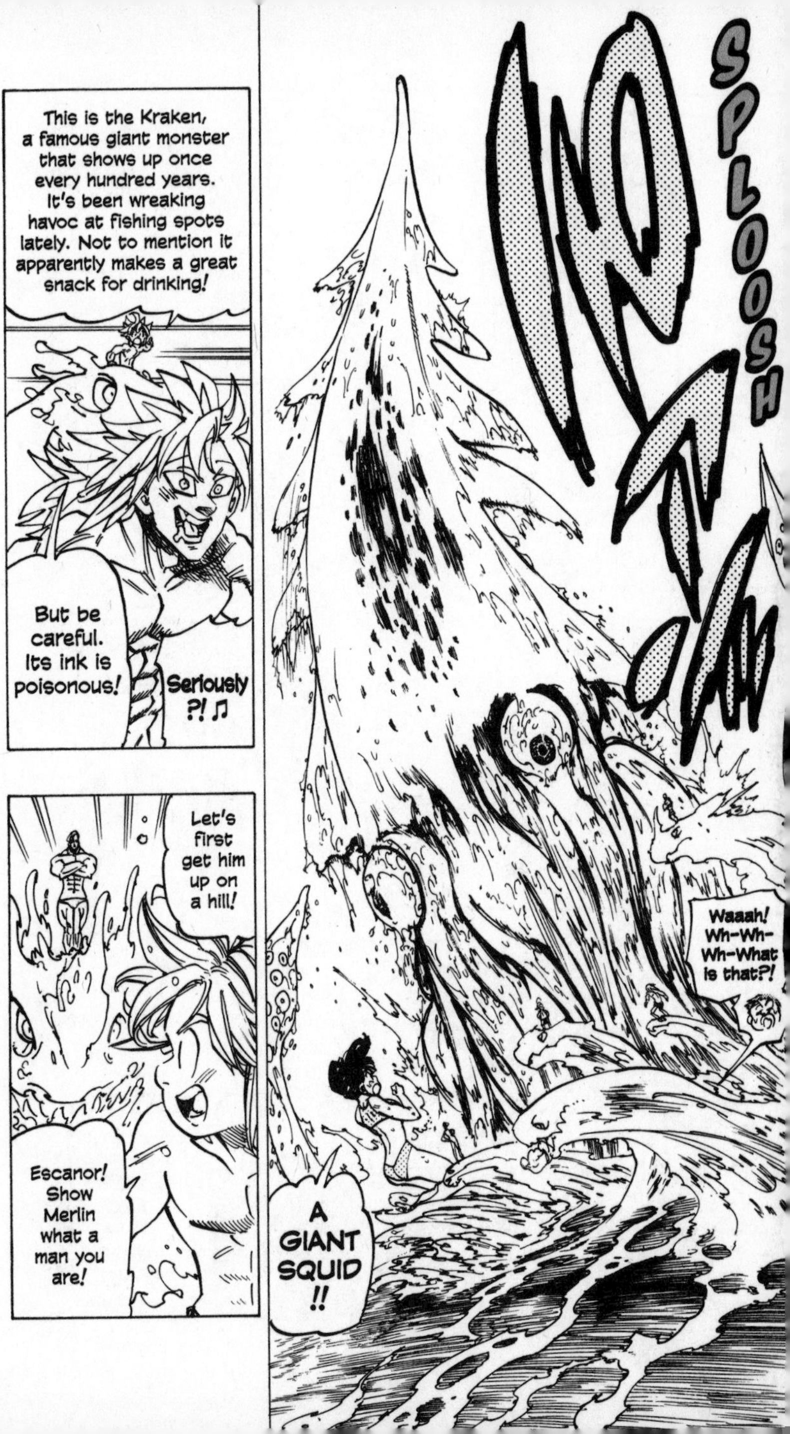
SPLOOSH
Waaah! Wh-Wh-Wh-What is that?!
A GIANT SQUID!!
This is the Kraken, a famous giant monster that shows up once every hundred years. It's been wreaking havoc at fishing spots lately. Not to mention it apparently makes a great snack for drinking!
But be careful. Its ink is poisonous!
Seriously?! ♫
Let's first get him up on a hill!
Escanor! Show Merlin what a man you are!

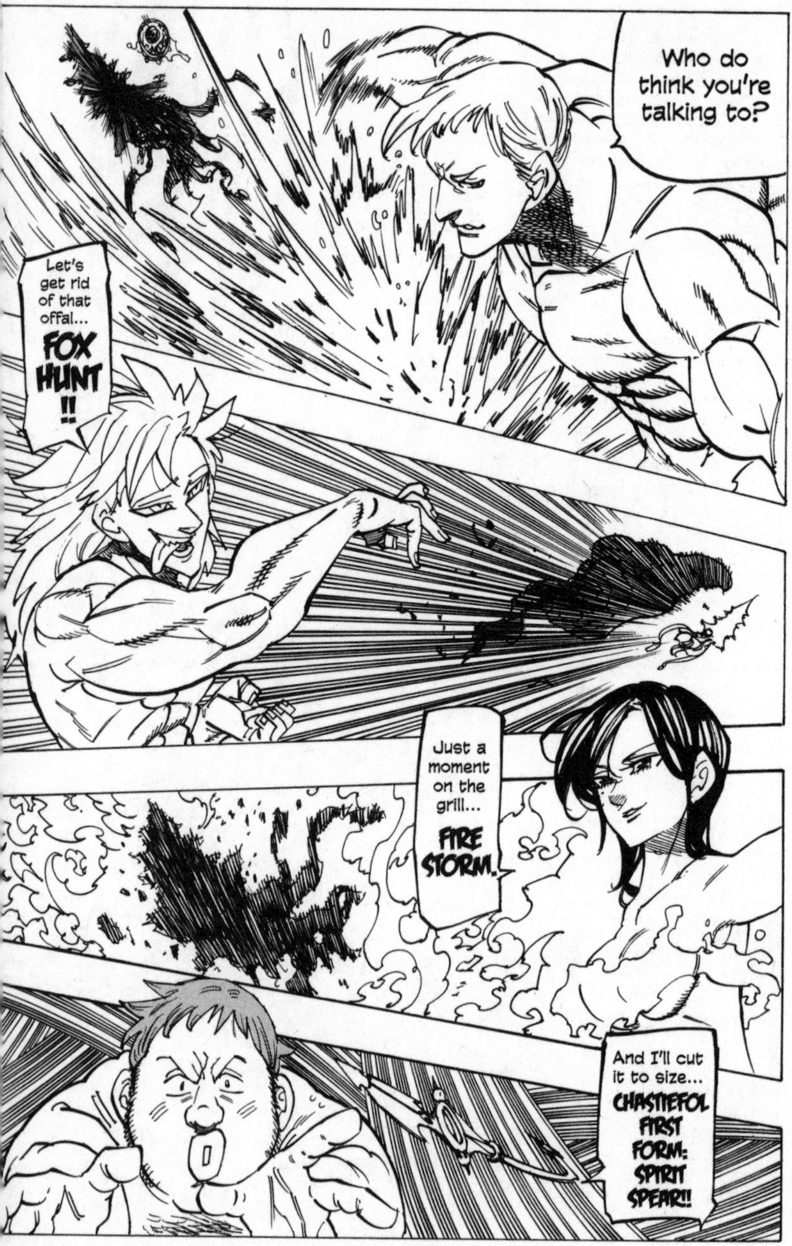
Who do think you're talking to?
Let's get rid of that offal... FOX HUNT!!
Just a moment on the grill... FIRE STORM.
And I'll cut it to size... CHASTIEFOL FIRST FORM: SPIRIT SPEAR!!

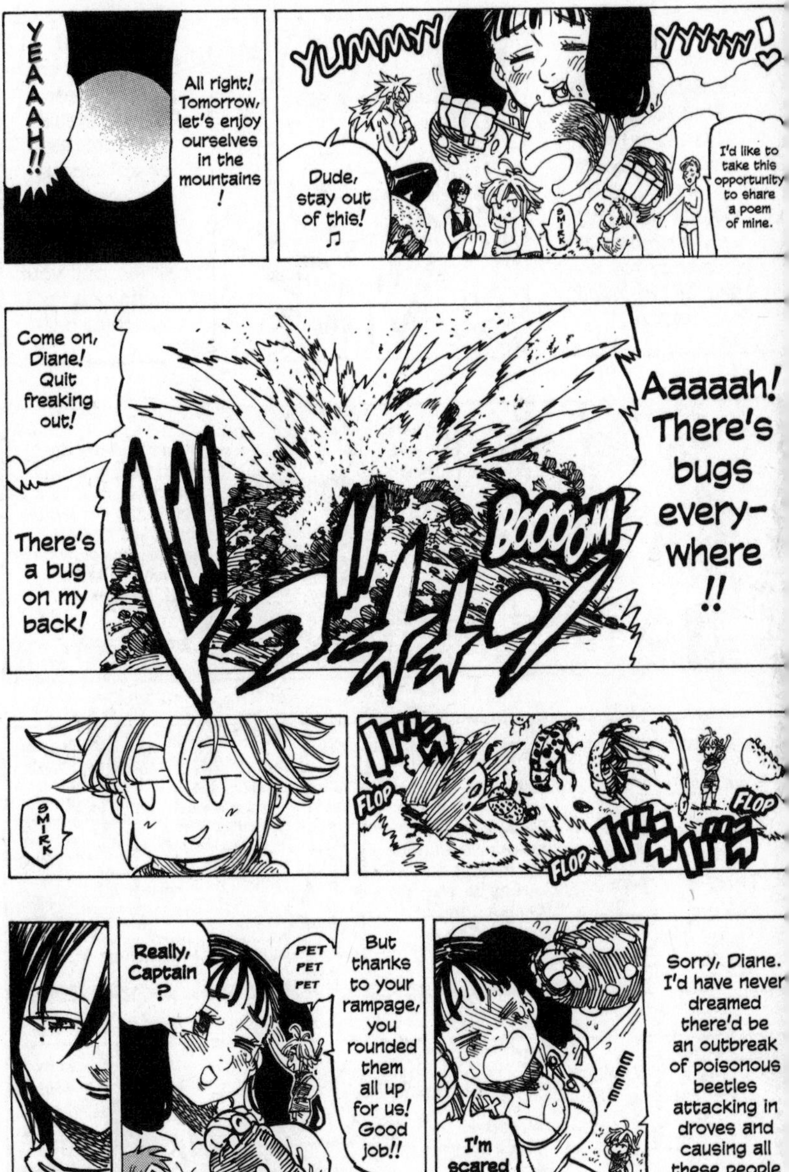

YUMMYYYYYYY!♡
I'd like to take this opportunity to share a poem of mine.
SMIRK
Dude, stay out of this! ♫
All right! Tomorrow, let's enjoy ourselves in the mountains!
YEAAAAH!!
Aaaaah! There's bugs every-where!!
BOOOOM
Come on, Diane! Quit freaking out!
There's a bug on my back!
FLOP
FLOP
FLOP
SMIRK
Sorry, Diane. I'd have never dreamed there'd be an outbreak of poisonous beetles attacking in droves and causing all these people trouble.
mmmm
I'm scared of bugs!!
But thanks to your rampage, you rounded them all up for us! Good job!!
PET PET PET
Really, Captain?

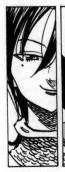

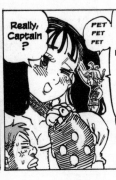

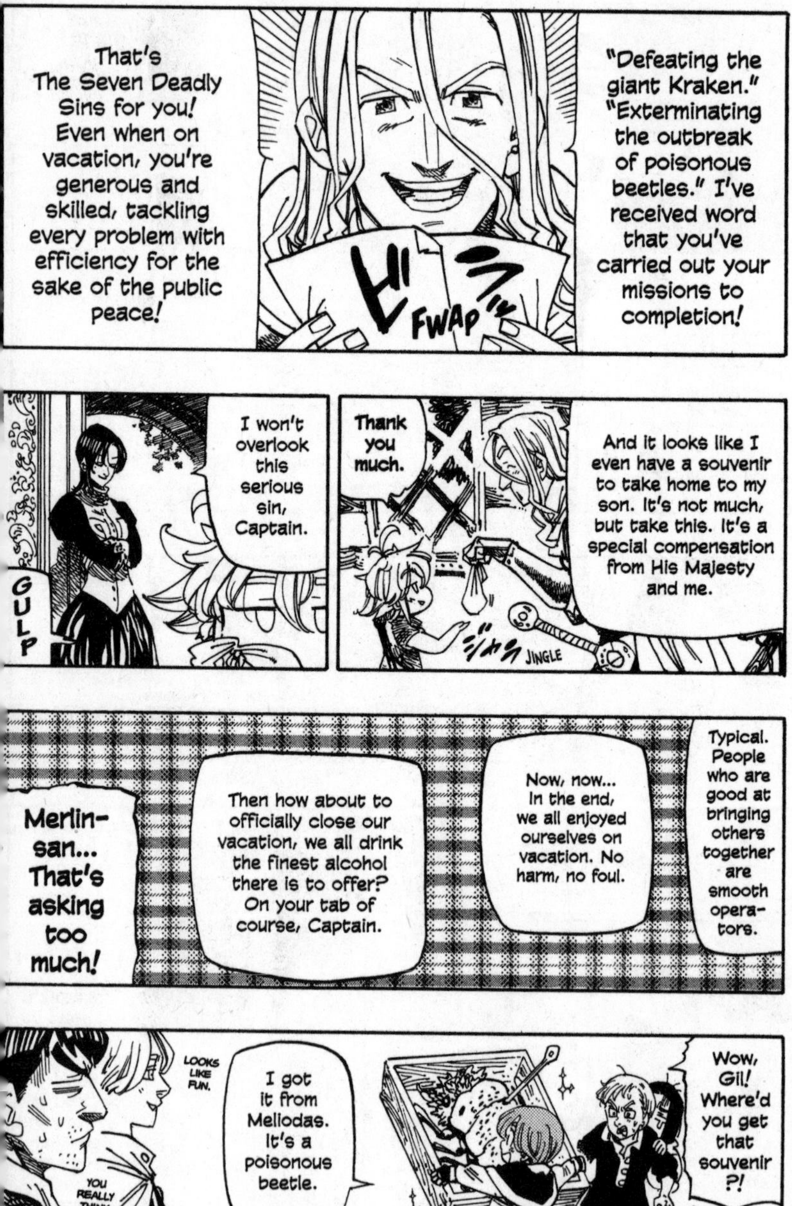
"Defeating the giant Kraken." "Exterminating the outbreak of poisonous beetles." I've received word that you've carried out your missions to completion!
FWAP
That's The Seven Deadly Sins for you! Even when on vacation, you're generous and skilled, tackling every problem with efficiency for the sake of the public peace!
And it looks like I even have a souvenir to take home to my son. It's not much, but take this. It's a special compensation from His Majesty and me.
Thank you much.
JINGLE
I won't overlook this serious sin, Captain.
GULP
Typical. People who are good at bringing others together are smooth opera-tors.
Now, now... In the end, we all enjoyed ourselves on vacation. No harm, no foul.
Then how about to officially close our vacation, we all drink the finest alcohol there is to offer? On your tab of course, Captain.
Merlin-san... That's asking too much!
Wow, Gil! Where'd you get that souvenir?!
I got it from Meliodas. It's a poisonous beetle.
LOOKS LIKE FUN.
YOU REALLY THINK SO?

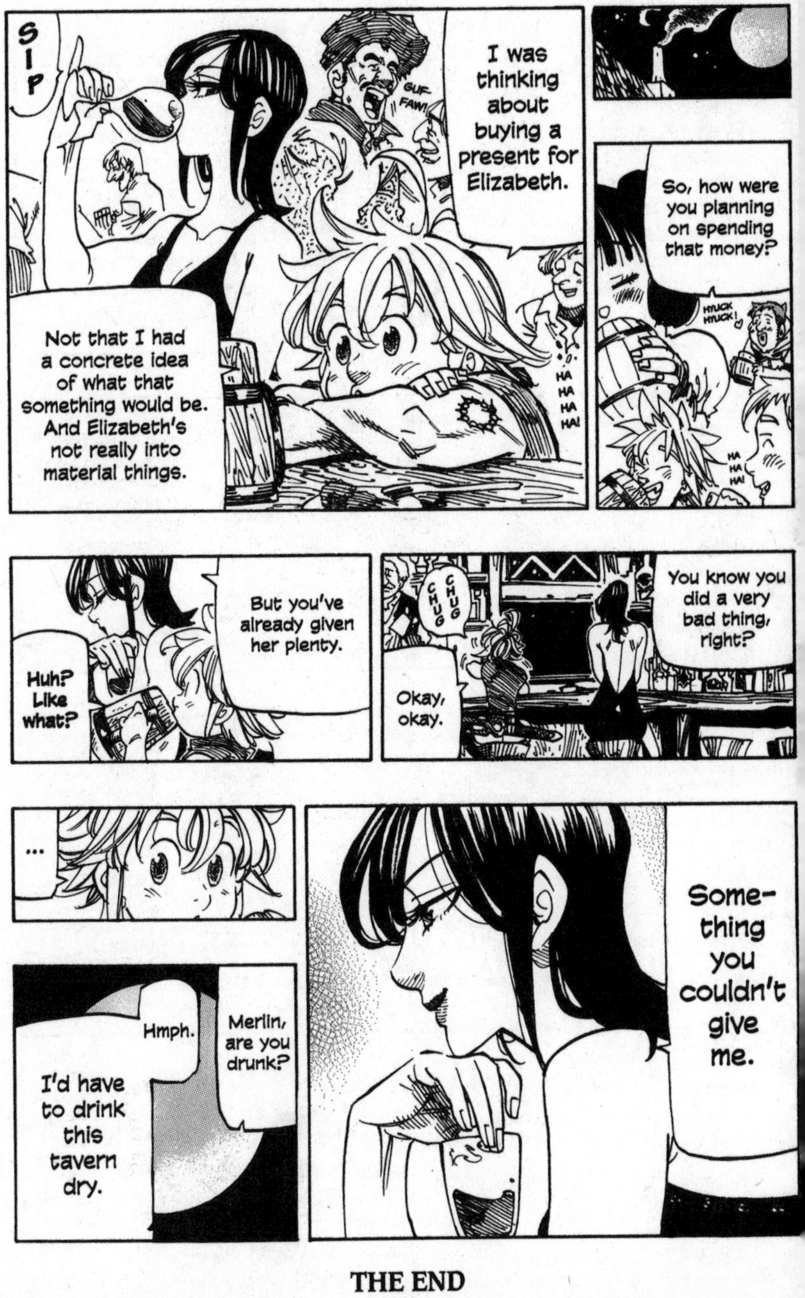
So, how were you planning on spending that money?
HYUCK HYUCK!
HA HA HA!
I was thinking about buying a present for Elizabeth.
GUF FAW!
HA HA HA HA!
SIP
Not that I had a concrete idea of what that something would be. And Elizabeth's not really into material things.
You know you did a very bad thing, right?
CHUG CHUG
Okay, okay.
But you've already given her plenty.
Huh? Like what?
Some-thing you couldn't give me.
...
Merlin, are you drunk?
Hmph.
I'd have to drink this tavern dry.

THE END

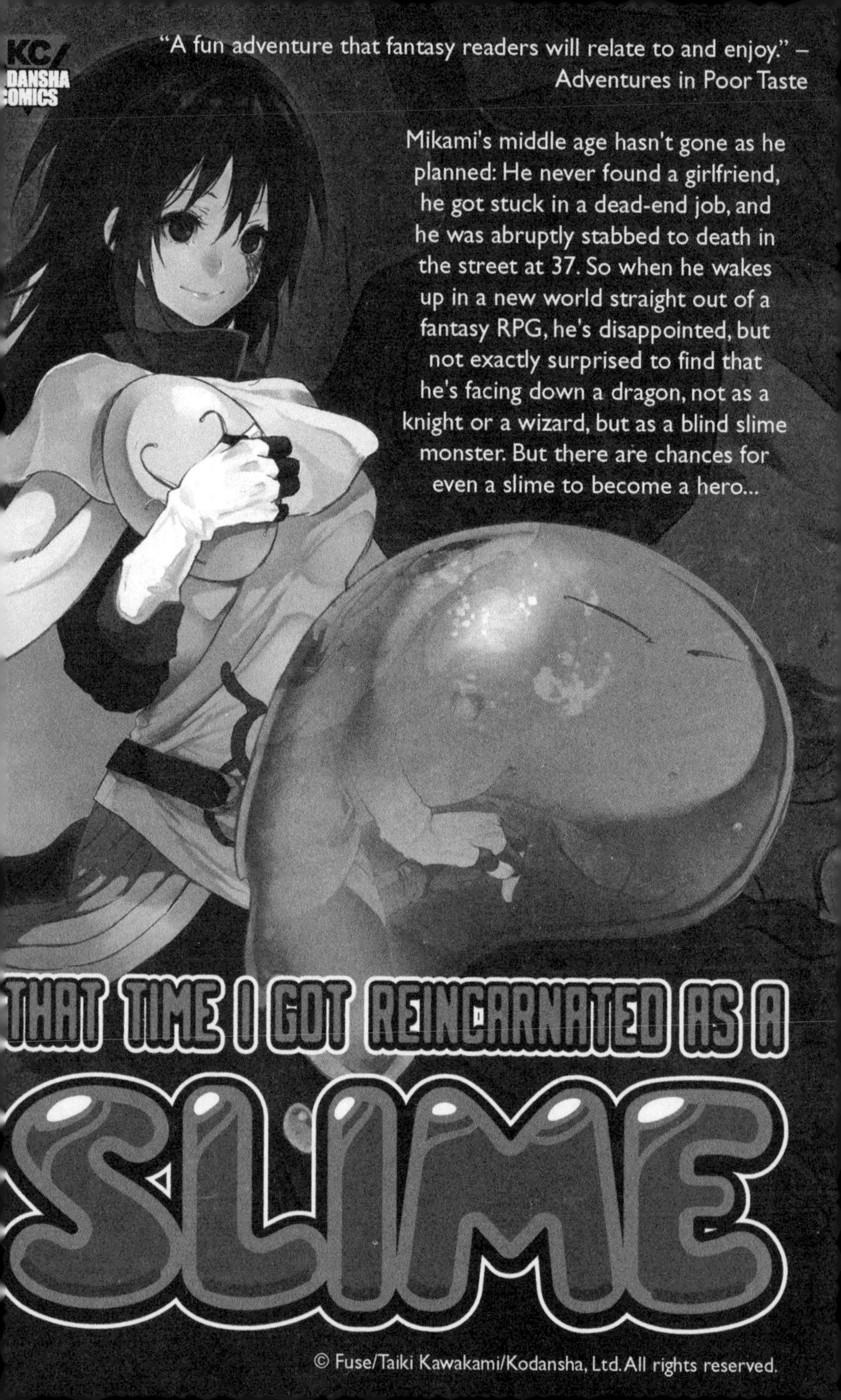

KC/ KODANSHA COMICS
“A fun adventure that fantasy readers will relate to and enjoy.” – Adventures in Poor Taste
Mikami's middle age hasn't gone as he planned: He never found a girlfriend, he got stuck in a dead-end job, and he was abruptly stabbed to death in the street at 37. So when he wakes up in a new world straight out of a fantasy RPG, he's disappointed, but not exactly surprised to find that he's facing down a dragon, not as a knight or a wizard, but as a blind slime monster. But there are chances for even a slime to become a hero...
THAT TIME I GOT REINCARNATED AS A
SLIME
© Fuse/Taiki Kawakami/Kodansha, Ltd. All rights reserved.

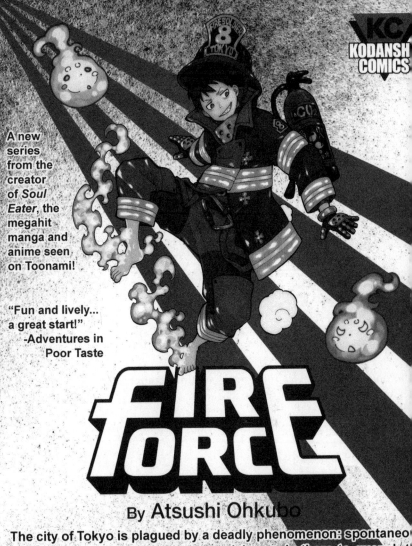

A new
series
from the
creator
of *Soul
Eater*, the
megahit
manga and
anime seen
on Toonami!

"Fun and lively...
a great start!"
-Adventures in
Poor Taste

FIRE FORCE

By Atsushi Ohkubo

The city of Tokyo is plagued by a deadly phenomenon: spontaneo
human combustion! Luckily, a special team is there to quench t
inferno: The Fire Force! The fire soldiers at Special Fire Cathedra
are about to get a unique addition. Enter Shinra, a boy who possess
the power to run at the speed of a rocket, leaving behind the famo
"devil's footprints" (and destroying his shoes in the proces
Can Shinra and his colleagues discover the source of this stran
epidemic before the city burns to ashes?

The Seven Deadly Sins volume 24 is a work of fiction. Names, characters, places, and incidents are the products of the author's imagination or are used fictitiously. Any resemblance to actual events, locales, or persons, living or dead, is entirely coincidental.

A Kodansha Comics Trade Paperback Original.

Published in the United States by Kodansha Comics, an imprint of Kodansha USA Publishing, LLC, New York.

Publication rights for this English edition arranged through Kodansha Ltd., Tokyo.

First published in Japan in 2016 by Kodansha Ltd., Tokyo.

ISBN 978-1-63236-566-8

Printed in the United States of America.

www.kodanshacomics.com

9 8 7 6 5 4 3 2 1

Translation: Christine Dashiell
Lettering: James Dashiell
Editing: Lauren Scanlan
Kodansha Comics edition cover design: Phil Balsman